The Last Apologist

The Last Apologist

A Commentary on Jude for Defenders of the Christian Faith

Rob Phillips

Table of Contents

Introduction

The General Epistle of Jude may be one of the most neglected of all New Testament books.[1] Perhaps this is because of its brevity - the entire epistle is only 25 verses. Or perhaps it's because Jude draws from two non-biblical sources, quoting from 1 Enoch and alluding to the Assumption of Moses. Or maybe it's because Jude is similar to the second chapter of 2 Peter and therefore is redundant - or worse, as some claim, uninspired. Or it could be because Jude is one of the lesser-known New Testament writers. In any case, many who read through the Bible may be tempted to skip over Jude on the way to Revelation, or to give the epistle little more than a glance.

This is unfortunate because this brief letter from a relatively obscure author speaks volumes about the urgency of defending the Christian faith. Whether exhorting fellow believers to contend for the faith delivered to the saints once for all (v. 3), or urging them to keep themselves in the love of God (v. 21), Jude addresses the issues of sound doctrine and false teachers with humility, boldness, and remarkable foresight.

When referring to Jude as "the last apologist," I don't mean that none has come after him, for God has raised up defenders of the Christian faith in every generation. Nor do I mean that Jude is the last, chronologically, of 27 New Testament books, for surely several were written after it. Nor am I implying that Jude is the final word on Christian apologetics, or the finest document ever written on defending the Christian faith, for truly all Scripture is God-breathed (2 Tim. 3:16-17).

By "the last apologist," I mean simply to express my hope that every Christian who reads this book would discover - or rediscover - the marvelous theological and practical insights of Jude. His divinely inspired words are a call to action for contenders of the Christian faith, and a final warning to those who reject it. This half-brother of Jesus, who humbly calls himself a slave of the Lord, speaks into a first-century church where false teachers have slipped in the side door and twisted the grace of God into a license to sin. It's a threat that has plagued the church in all succeeding ages. The evil one, who sows tares in Christ's wheat fields, hopes to choke the Word of God by making the church indistinguishable from the world.

Ultimately, false teachers are destined for an eternity apart from God. History is rife with examples of God's judgment of those who seek to overthrow His kingdom or undermine His rule. At the same time, believers confidently may look forward to the day when we are fully conformed to the image of Christ. Until then, we are to contend - to struggle earnestly and tirelessly - for the core doctrines of the Christian faith, recognizing that all glory, majesty, power, and authority belong to God our Savior through Jesus Christ our Lord (v. 25).

This commentary addresses basic questions that arise when reading Jude - questions about the sovereignty of God, the reliability of Scripture, the tactics of false teachers, and the promise of Jesus to set things right when He returns. In addition, each chapter of this study explores at least one key word or phrase, and poses challenging questions for personal or group study.

It is my hope that this short volume is especially helpful to those seeking to defend the Christian faith with gentleness and respect (1 Peter 3:15-16).

Rob Phillips
Jan. 31, 2017

1

Jude, a Slave:
The Attitude of Apologetics
Jude, a slave of Jesus Christ ... (Jude 1a)

My business card is standard fare. It identifies me and describes my role at my place of employment. It also offers several ways to get in touch with me. That's what most business cards do; they serve as practical, brief, and efficient introductions.

Some people, however, use business cards more creatively, with pop-up photos, odd shapes, and other features to grab your attention. And then there are truly unique characters who seek to leave a lasting impression another way: by making audacious claims.

Take Guangbiao Chen, for example. Chen is a Chinese tycoon and philanthropist. His business card details illustrious titles and heroic accomplishments. For example, his English business card describes him in the following ways:

- Most Influential Person of China
- Most Prominent Philanthropist of China
- China Moral Leader

- China Earthquake Rescue Hero
- Most Well-Loved and Beloved Chinese Role Model[1]

We're only halfway through Chen's list, but you get the idea. This may be one of the cheekiest business cards ever produced.

But how would you respond if someone handed you a business card that simply read, "Jude, a slave ..."? Let's see how Jude's profoundly humble self-introduction models the manner in which followers of Jesus should defend the faith.

Why does Jude call himself a slave?

The Greek word translated "slave" or "servant" is *doulos* and means "bond-slave," literally "one tied to another." The term speaks of one who is subject to the will of his or her master. While Jude rightly could have declared himself a half-brother of Jesus, he chooses to exalt his Master and express his absolute subjection to the Lord.

Jude calls himself a slave as a means of modeling Christian humility for all of us. In the New Testament, all believers are pictured as Jesus' bond-slaves because we are called to accept His Lordship (1 Peter 2:16; Rev. 1:1), and we have been "bought with a price" (1 Cor. 6:20; 7:22-23).

Equally important for Jude, he wants to set the proper tone for an epistle that otherwise might be seen as sharp-edged, confrontational, or even judgmental. Like a faithful bond-slave, he serves his Master without hesitation or compromise. In the short 25 verses of this oft-neglected letter, Jude acknowledges the Lordship of Christ as the impetus for engaging in Christian apologetics.

What is Christian apologetics?

Christian apologetics is the field of study concerned with the systematic defense of the Christian faith. Stated more simply, it is a reasonable defense of Christianity.

The term "apologetics" is derived from the Greek noun *apologia* and is used in a legal sense. The prosecution delivers the *kategoria*, or formal charges, and the defendant replies with an *apologia*, or a formal speech to counter the charges. The verb form, *apologeomai*, means "to make a defense." The Christian apologist is engaged in defending Christianity's claims to truth.

In Scripture, the apostle Paul uses the term *apologeomai* in his speech to Agrippa when he says, "I consider myself fortunate ... that today I am going *to make a defense* before you" (Acts 26:2 - emphasis added). Paul uses similar terms in his letter to the Philippians to describe his role as a defender of the gospel (Phil. 1:7, 16). The term is used in a negative sense in Rom. 1:20, where Paul says those who reject the revelation of God in creation are "without *excuse*" (emphasis added).

Peter encourages believers to be ready at all times to give a *defense* of their faith (1 Peter 3:15-16 - emphasis added). Then he adds this important caveat: *with gentleness and respect.* The apostle is well-known for his quick tongue and fast draw with a sword, but by the time he pens this epistle, he has matured and mellowed. We, too, should learn to tone down the rhetoric when taking a stand for biblical truth.

The ultimate goal of a conversation with Jehovah's Witnesses at our door, an atheist over the back fence, or a Muslim in the public square should not be to win an argument, speak more loudly than the other person, or get in the last word. Rather, it should be to share a winsome word of truth, leaving the results to the Holy Spirit.

In *Tactics: A Game Plan for Discussing Your Christian Convictions*, Gregory Koukl writes about his modest approach to apologetics: "All I want to do is put a stone in someone's shoe. I want to give him something worth thinking about, something he can't ignore because it continues to poke at him in a good way."[2]

Dallas Willard's posthumously published book, *The Allure of Gentleness: Defending the Faith in the Manner of Jesus,* reminds us that "The apologist for Christ is one characterized by 'humbleness of mind' (*tapeinophrosunen*; Col. 3:12; Acts 20:19; 1 Pet. 5:5) - a vital New Testament concept that cannot be captured by our word 'humility' alone." Peter's call to give an account, says Willard, is "first, not a call to beat unwilling people into intellectual submission, but to be the servant of those in need, often indeed the servant of those who are in the grip of their own intellectual self-righteousness and pride, usually reinforced by their social surroundings."[3]

Willard goes on to write, "What we are seeking to defend or explain is Jesus himself, who is a gentle, loving shepherd. If we are not gentle in how we present the good news, how will people encounter the gentle and loving Messiah we want to point to? ... Our apologetic happens in a context, and that context is strewn with enmity, hostility, abuse, and other opposition, which ultimately contradict the very things our message lifts up. That is why our apologetic has to embody the message and person we want to communicate. Only with 'gentleness and reverence' will people be able to see, verify, and be persuaded to respond to what we have to say."[4]

What can Jude teach us about being bond-slaves?

In the opening verses of his epistle, Jude reveals two essential qualities of Christian apologists.

First, we are bond-slaves of Jesus who obediently defend the Christian faith with gentleness and respect. The goal of the apologist should be to proclaim the kingdom as Jesus did - simply, clearly, repeatedly, and winsomely.

There are times for vigorous discussion, of course. Jesus doesn't pull any punches when tough love requires it; note the eight woes on the religious leaders in Matthew 23. Jude does not hold back, either, when exposing the dangers of false teachers in the church. But our primary goal when facing obstinacy is not to win a debate, or to send opponents away licking their wounds. It is to engage them lovingly with the truth, always keeping in mind they are slaves as well - slaves of sin, held captive by Satan - who desperately need the freedom only Jesus offers.

Second, Christian apologists like Jude are always ready to offer a defense. Jude tells his audience he intended to write about our common salvation - the marvelous and uplifting truths of the Christian faith. But something - more likely *someone*, the Holy Spirit - prompted him to set aside this joyful task, roll up his sleeves, and urge his fellow believers to earnestly contend for the faith.

To always be ready assumes: (1) that we know what we believe and why we believe it; (2) that we are burdened for others who don't know the truth or have rejected it; (3) that we are constantly alert to opportunities to share our faith; (4) that we acknowledge we don't have all the answers but serve the God who does; (5) that we may be opposed, or even rejected; (6) that the results are in God's hands; and (7) that our desire is to advance the kingdom of God rather than scorch the common ground we share with those who need to know Jesus.

It may help to keep in mind that Jude was not always a believer in Jesus. Evidently, growing up with the Son of God failed to convince him that Jesus was the Messiah. It took witnessing the death, burial, and resurrection of his half-brother - the essential facts of the gospel - to convince him that Jesus was God incarnate.

Jude identifies himself as a slave of Jesus. He also identifies himself as the author of the epistle and the brother of James - two important details we explore in the next chapter.

Key words

In this chapter, we learned two key terms. Test your knowledge by filling in the blanks.

Slave. The Greek word translated "slave" or "servant" is _____ and means "bond-slave," literally "one _____ to another." The term speaks of one who is subject to the _____ of his or her master.

Comparing English translations of *doulos*:

HCSB	KJV	NIV	NASB	ESV
Slave	Servant	Servant	Bond-servant	Servant (slave)

Apologetics. Christian apologetics is the field of study concerned with the _____ _____ of the Christian faith. Stated more simply, it is a _____ defense of Christianity. The term "apologetics" is derived from the Greek noun _____. The Christian apologist is engaged in _____ Christianity's claims to truth.

Comparing English translations of *apologia* (1 Peter 3:15):

HCSB	KJV	NIV	NASB	ESV
Defense	Answer	Answer	Defense (argument; explanation)	Defense

Application
Questions for personal or group study

Read 1 Peter 3:15-16 and ask:

1. What does it mean to "set apart the Messiah as Lord in your hearts"?

2. Why is this a prerequisite for successfully defending the Christian faith?

3. How are Peter's words similar to James' instruction to "submit to God" and then to "resist the Devil" (James 4:7)?

4. What are some situations you've faced that tested Peter's exhortation to "always be ready"?

5. How might you end a conversation about spiritual matters with an unbeliever who wants nothing more than to raise his or her voice, talk over you, and win an argument?

6. What should you do when you lose your cool - that is, you fail to defend the faith with humility and a genuine concern for others?

7. In verse 16, what does Peter say about the benefits of defending the faith with "gentleness and respect"?

8. How would you counsel a Christian friend who relishes a good argument with unbelievers, including name-calling, interrupting, and public humiliation? After all, he says, Jesus called Peter "Satan" (Matt. 16:23). And He referred to the scribes and Pharisees as "hypocrites," "blind guides," and "whitewashed tombs" (Matthew 23).

9. What's one step you could take this week to improve your preparedness as a defender of the Christian faith?

10. Who is one lost friend or acquaintance for whom you could start praying as you seek an opportunity to share your Christian faith?

15

We must scorn the earthly spoils of spiritual victories, for they do not originate in us, and like the miraculous manna hoarded in Israelite tents, they may putrefy over time if left to us alone.

2

Jude, Slave, Brother:
The Identity of Apologists

*Jude, a slave of Jesus Christ, and a brother
of James ... (Jude 1)*

In June 1989 a young man made headlines - and history - when he singlehandedly slowed the advance of tanks heading for China's Tiananmen Square. The Chinese government had begun cracking down on anti-communist demonstrations in Beijing. Feeling the crush of military muscle, most of the peacefully demonstrating Chinese dispersed, except for one man whose identity has never been positively confirmed.

Holding shopping bags, the man, dressed in dark pants and a white shirt, strode into the center of the broad street and, turning toward the approaching column of tanks, stood his ground. When the driver of the lead tank tried to maneuver around him, the bystander moved to his left and cut off the tank's advance. He then climbed onto the tank and tried to talk with the soldiers inside before two unidentified men whisked him away.

"Tiananmen Square Guy," as he came to be known, stands as a symbol of peaceful opposition to the oppression of totalitarian regimes. Conflicting claims about his name and whereabouts indicate that his true identity may never be discovered.

The names of other famous people in history may never be known, either, or at least positively confirmed - from the kissing sailor and nurse on VJ Day to the Zodiac Killer, and from "the babushka lady" in the Zapruder film of John F. Kennedy's assassination to Jack the Ripper.[1]

Sometimes famous people remain anonymous by design, and this is no less true of authors of New Testament books. For example, none of the Gospels is self-identified, although we're quite confident of the writers' identity. In contrast, the unnamed author of the book of Hebrews remains a mystery. Peter's authorship of 2 Peter is disputed.

But we face a different challenge with the book of Jude - namely, that Jude (Greek *Ioudas*, or Judas, Judah) is a common first-century name, and there happen to be eight such characters in the New Testament:

1. Judas Iscariot, one of the twelve apostles and the betrayer of Jesus (Matt. 10:4)

2. Judas the son of James, one of the twelve apostles (Luke 6:16; Acts 1:13)

3. Judas, Paul's host in Damascus (Acts 9:11)

4. Judas, called Barsabbas, a leading Christian in Jerusalem and a companion of Paul (Acts 15:22, 27, 32)

5. Judas, a revolutionary leader (Acts 5:37)

6. Judah, an otherwise unknown person in the genealogy of Jesus (Luke 3:30)

7. Judah, a son of Jacob in the genealogy of Jesus and an ancestor of an Israelite tribe (Matt. 1:2; Rev. 7:5)

8. Judas, a half-brother of Jesus and a brother of James (Matt. 13:55)[2]

Which Jude is our dude?

So which of these men is the author of the epistle that bears his name? Only two are associated with a person named James: Judas the *son* of James, and Judas the *brother* of James. Thanks to the author's three-fold identification (Jude, a slave of Jesus Christ, and a brother of James), we may conclude that our author is the one named along with James in Matt. 13:55: "Isn't this [Jesus] the carpenter's son? Isn't His mother called Mary, and His brothers James, Joseph, Simon, and Judas?"

But do we have the correct James? We address that question shortly. Meanwhile, we don't know a great deal about Jude. Of course, he and James are two of the four brothers of Jesus (Matt. 13:55; Mark 6:3). The evidence suggests that Jude does not believe in Jesus as Messiah prior to the crucifixion (Mark 3:21, 31; John 7:5). He likely becomes a believer after the resurrection, since Acts 1:14 says the Lord's brothers were part of the prayer meetings prior to Pentecost.

We learn from 1 Cor. 9:5 that the Lord's brothers are itinerant missionaries, and Jude probably is included here. "His missionary work would explain his writing to the church in an authoritative manner."[3]

By identifying himself simply as Jude, the author may have opened himself to charges of *pseudepigrapha* - falsely attributed writings named after prominent early followers of Jesus. However, it's highly unlikely that a forger would write a book impersonating a relatively unknown figure such as Jude; "pseudepigraphic works were attributed to well-known apostles, such as Peter or Paul. Nor would a forger pretending to be Jude have failed to identify himself as the Lord's brother."[4]

Why does Jude call himself a slave?

If the author of this epistle had identified himself only as Jude, we would be left to wonder which of the eight people named Jude in the New Testament is the true writer. But Jude further refers to himself as a "slave of Jesus Christ, and a brother of James." He is a half-brother of Jesus, but as we learned in the previous chapter, Jude embraces the humility of a true Christian apologist.

But there may be more to it. Coming from a Jewish background, where a sharp distinction is drawn between Jewish and Gentile slaves, Jude would have latched onto the proud tradition in which the Israelites thought of themselves as servants of Yahweh.[5] In ancient Israel, the idea emerges that it is a great privilege to be a servant (or slave) of God. Many Old Testament heroes are called servants. Consider just a few:

- Moses tells the Lord, "Remember that You swore to Your servants Abraham, Isaac, and Israel by Yourself and declared to them, 'I will make your offspring as numerous as the stars of the sky and will give your offspring all this land that I have promised, and they will inherit it forever'" (Ex. 32:13).

- "So Moses the servant of the Lord died there in the land of Moab, as the Lord had said" (Deut. 34:5).

- One night, the word of the Lord comes to Nathan, "Go to My servant David and say, 'This is what the Lord says ...'" (2 Sam. 7:5).

- "The Lord spoke through His servants the prophets ..." (2 Kings 21:10).

In addition, we should note the significance of the Servant Songs of Isa. 42:1-4; 49:1-6; 50:4-9; and 52:13-53:12, which originally refer to Israel but later are applied to Jesus, the Suffering Servant, and the Lamb of God who takes away the sin of the world (John 1:29).

Contrast this noble view of servanthood with the Greek concept of slaves, who are regarded as less than human, although depending on the country and culture, they may find themselves well treated.

Think also about the main sources of slavery in New Testament times. There are many: (a) being born to parents who are slaves; (b) the widespread practice of exposing unwanted children, who are available to anyone who cares to rear them; (c) the sale of one's own children into slavery; (d) voluntary slavery as a remedy for debt; (e) penal slavery; (f) kidnapping and piracy; and (g) spoils of war. "Slavery may have reached one-third of the population in Rome and the great metropolitan cities of the East."[6]

No matter how the institution of slavery works in the first century, the twelve apostles of Jesus apparently have no part in the system. We don't read of them as slaves of men or as slave owners. Slavery figures into the parables of Jesus, however. He uses common situations as the backdrop for lofty lessons about the kingdom of heaven (see Matt. 21:33-44; 22:1-14).

20

In addition, Jesus speaks of the relationship of the disciples to Himself as that of slaves (Matt. 10:24; John 13:16), yet He prefers to see His followers as emancipated men and women and, more important, as intimate friends (John 15:15). Jesus urges His followers to take up their crosses and follow Him, while, to their embarrassment, He washes the disciples' feet on the night of His betrayal (Matt. 16:24; John 13:1-17).

Modeling humility and self-denial, Jesus adopts a servant's role (Mark 10:45; John 13:4-5; Phil. 2:7), and indicates that His disciples should follow His example (Matt. 6:24; 10:24; 24:45-46; Luke 17:10; John 13:12-16).

Paul refers figuratively to the church as the household of God (Eph. 2:19), perhaps making reference to household slavery in which there are generally feelings of goodwill between master and servants.

As for Jude, he is not alone in carrying the moniker "slave." Paul, Timothy, James, Peter, and John also refer to themselves as slaves of Christ:

- Rom. 1:1 – "Paul, a slave of Christ Jesus ..."

- Phil. 1:1 – "Paul and Timothy, slaves of Christ Jesus ..."

- Titus 1:1 – "Paul, a slave of God, and an apostle of Jesus Christ ..."

- Philemon 1 – "Paul, a prisoner of Christ Jesus ..."

- James 1:1 – "James, a slave of God and of the Lord Jesus Christ ..."

- 2 Peter 1:1 – "Simeon Peter, a slave and an apostle of Jesus Christ ..."

- Rev. 1:1 – "The revelation of Jesus Christ that God gave Him to show His slaves what must quickly take place. He sent it and signified it through His angel to His slave John."

In a related term, the apostles are described as God's stewards, entrusted with the mysteries of God (1 Cor. 4:1). In addition, they make it clear that elders are God's stewards who must be above reproach (Titus 1:7). In fact, all believers are exhorted to use their spiritual gifts to serve one another, as good stewards of God's grace (1 Peter 4:10).

In all, the word "slave" appears 159 times in 144 New Testament verses (HCSB). While the context determines how the word is understood, in most cases slavery is not something to be desired, unless it is voluntary and joyful bond-servanthood to Christ. For Jude to call himself a slave of Jesus is to humble himself and to submit jubilantly to his Master.

One additional note: There are at least three other metaphorical uses of slavery in the New Testament: (1) A life of sin is spoken of as slavery to sin (John 8:34; Rom. 6:6, 16-20; Heb. 2:15); (2) legalism is a kind of slavery (Gal. 4:24-25; 5:1); however, (3) there is also a blessed slavery to righteousness (Rom. 6:16-22).[7]

When Christ frees us from the bondage of sin and death, we become bond-servants to Him, clothed in His righteousness and dwelling in His household. Christian apologists always should seek their identity, not in fame or prominence, but in Christ. Jude sets the bar as high as it gets for humility, and thus sets an appropriate platform for his defense.

Do we have the correct James?

Finally, Jude helps us positively identify him by calling himself not only "a slave of Jesus Christ" but "a brother of James" (v. 1). There are three men named James associated with Jesus. First, James the apostle. He is the son of Zebedee and a brother of John. He is martyred in A.D. 44 (see Acts 12:1-2). Jude's reference to James seems to indicate that his brother is still alive at the time of this writing, so this is not the James we seek.

Second, there is another apostle named James. He is the son of Alphaeus and is identified as James the less or James the younger (Mark 15:40). His mother's name is Mary, who is the wife of Clopas, or Cleophas, another name for Alphaeus (John 19:25). There is no reference to his being a brother of Jude. Probably not our James.

Finally, there is James, the half-brother of Jesus and brother of Jude. He is not an apostle. Likely, he is not a follower of Jesus during Christ's earthly ministry (John 7:3-5), but a post-resurrection appearance evidently convinces him that Jesus is the Messiah (Acts 1:14; 1 Cor. 15:7). Also known as James the Just, he becomes the influential leader of the Jerusalem church (Acts 1:14; 12:17; 15:13; 21:18; Gal. 2:9, 12).[8]

Commenting on Jude's reference to James, John MacArthur writes, "After the martyrdom of the apostle James there was no other James in the early church who could be referred to simply by name without further qualification. Thus Jude, like James, was one of the half-brothers of Jesus. Jude is the only New Testament writer who identifies himself by family relationship."[9]

So, by calling himself a brother of James as well as a slave of Jesus Christ, Jude makes clear his identity. Equally important, the manner in which he places his identity foremost in Christ is instructive to us as followers of Jesus.

We must resist the temptation to lead under our own name, or the name of our ministry, organization, or denomination. While these are helpful ways to communicate who we are and how we serve, they also may lead to sinful pride that puffs us up and unwittingly deceives others by causing them to look to us rather than to Jesus.

One final thought: The apostle Paul illustrates the difference between *imitation* and *identity*. He exhorts the Corinthians to "Be imitators of me, as I also am of Christ" (1 Cor. 11:1). To the Philippians he says, "Join in imitating me, brothers, and observe those who live according to the example you have in us" (Phil. 3:17). And to the Thessalonians he writes, "You know what kind of men we were among you for your benefit, and you became imitators of us and of the Lord when, in spite of severe persecution, you welcomed the message with the joy from the Holy Spirit. As a result, you became an example to all the believers in Macedonia and Achaia" (1 Thess. 1:5b-7).

Paul, like Jude and the other New Testament writers, understands the importance of modeling Christ-like behavior for the benefit of others. He imitates Christ so that others may be drawn to Jesus, and so that those who commit their lives to the Savior have an earthly example to follow.

Yet Paul refuses to be worshiped (Acts 14:11-18), and he is grieved to learn that the Corinthians are expressing their identity with Paul, Apollos, Peter, or Christ - as if somehow they are equally valid choices (1 Cor. 1:11-12). He addresses the divisions and quarrels this has caused: "Now I urge you, brothers, in the name of our Lord Jesus Christ, that you all say the same thing, that there be no divisions among you, and that you be united with the same understanding and the same conviction.... Is Christ divided? Was it Paul who was crucified for you?" (1 Cor. 1:10, 13a).

The identity of a Christian apologist - one who defends the faith with gentleness and respect - must be in Jesus Christ. Any degree of prominence, popularity, or earthly success a Christian receives must be subjected to the sovereign goodness of God and the glorification of His Son. Perhaps it is not too much to say that we must scorn the earthly spoils of spiritual victories, for they do not originate in us, and like the miraculous manna hoarded in Israelite tents, they may putrefy over time if left to us alone.

Always, we must beware of pride, especially the kind that hides itself in false humility and expresses itself in the fear of personal loss. The apostle John writes of Jewish believers in Jesus who, for fear of the Pharisees, would not confess Him openly because "they loved praise from men more than praise from God" (John 12:43).

May it not be so with us.

Key word

In this chapter, we learned the identity of the author of Jude. Test your knowledge by filling in the blanks.

Ioudas. There are _____ characters in the New Testament identified as Jude (or Judas, Judah), from _____ Iscariot to _____, a slave of _____ and a brother of James.

Only two New Testament characters named Jude are associated with a person named James: Judas the _____ of James, and Judas the _____ of James. Thanks to the author's three-fold identification (Jude, a slave of Jesus Christ, and a brother of James), we may conclude that our author is a _____ of James, who is named along with Jude in Matt. 13:55: "Isn't this [Jesus] the carpenter's son? Isn't His mother called Mary, and His brothers James, Joseph, Simon, and Judas?"

Comparing English translations of *Ioudas*:

HCSB	KJV	NIV	NASB	ESV
Jude	Jude	Jude	Jude (Judas)	Jude

Application
Questions for personal or group study

1. How do you identify yourself to others - in personal introductions, on your business card, your Facebook page, or other forums? What does this say about your character, your priorities in life, and your personal relationship with Christ? How does your self-introduction reflect on the reputation of Jesus?

2. In what ways does Jude's identity as "a slave of Jesus Christ, and a brother of James" express both his humility and his Jewish heritage?

3. With the historical baggage of the word "slave" in modern Western culture, do you think it's wise to identify yourself as a slave of Jesus Christ? Or is there another term that's more culturally sensitive yet biblically faithful?

4. How might you explain the positive aspects of being a bond-slave of Jesus Christ? This may require you to clarify the historical context in which Jude writes.

5. Look up the following passages and describe the metaphorical ways the terms "slave," "enslaved," and "slavery" are used:
    - John 8:34; Rom. 6:6; Heb. 2:14-15 (slavery to sin)
    - Gal. 4:21 – 5:1 (slavery to legalism)
    - Rom. 6:15-23 (slavery to righteousness and to God)

6. Why is it important for Christians to distinguish between *imitation* and *identity* when it comes to defending the faith? In what ways should we imitate Christ? And what are the dangers of identifying primarily with a Christian leader, ministry, organization, or denomination?

7. Read 1 Cor. 1:10-31. What is causing divisions in the church at Corinth? How does Paul seek to refocus his readers on their identity in Christ rather than in their human leaders? If Christians boast at all, who should they boast about? (See v. 31; Jer. 9:23-24.)

3

I Reckon So:

The Apologist's Standing in Christ

To those who are the called, loved by God the Father and kept by Jesus Christ. May mercy, peace, and love be multiplied to you (Jude 1b-2)

In *The Outlaw Josey Wales*, Clint Eastwood plays a Missouri farmer driven to revenge by the murder of his wife and son at the hands of pro-Union Jayhawkers during the Civil War. Having joined a band of pro-Confederate Bushwhackers, Wales refuses an offer of amnesty at the end of the war, only to watch as surrendering fighters are slaughtered in cold blood. He races to the scene, overpowers a Union soldier manning a Gatling gun, and turns it on the Kansas Redlegs.

Now an outlaw, Wales flees to Texas. Though preferring to travel alone, he crosses paths with a diverse cadre of companions, from a spry old Cherokee named Lone Watie, to a young Navajo woman he rescues from rape, to a crotchety Kansas grandmother whose family he frees from raiding Comancheros.

Throughout the story, Wales exhibits an uncanny ability to see the world as it is - cruel, unforgiving, yet capable of redemption - and often he acknowledges the truthful observations of others with a simple, "I reckon so."

Dogged by Redlegs and a Union officer known as Captain Fletcher, Wales helps his companions resettle a Texas homestead while negotiating peace with their Comanche neighbors. He then helps the settlers repel a Redlegs attack, finally avenging his family's murder by killing their leader.

Wounded, and knowing that his continued presence at the homestead only invites further attacks, he heads out on his own, but not before a final encounter with Captain Fletcher, who mercifully avoids revealing his identity to Texas Rangers by calling him "Mr. Wilson."

"I think I'll go down to Mexico and try to find him [Josey Wales]," says Fletcher.

"And then?" asks Wales.

"He's got the first move. I owe him that. I think I'll try to tell him the war is over. What do you say, Mr. Wilson?"

"I reckon so."

Wales gingerly mounts his horse and, listing badly, rides away. Fletcher turns away, leaving viewers convinced he and the outlaw have made their peace.

Like Josey Wales, some battle-hardened Christians have learned to see the world as it is without losing sight of who they really are. This comes to light in the opening verses of Jude's epistle. These believers are urged not to surrender to the false teachers among them, to continue the fight for sound doctrine, and to persevere to the very end.

And so, before going any further, Jude reminds these beloved apologists who they are in Christ. He tells them they are called, loved, and kept. This reality remains with them as a sovereign gift of God, despite the schemes of the evil one and the wiles of the false teachers who have set up shop in the church.

We can almost hear Jude saying, "God saves us and keeps us. Keep this in mind because, as you know, the evil one masquerades as an angel of light, and his ministers disguise themselves as ministers of righteousness. The church always has been the wheat field in which Satan sows his tares. So fight hard. Stand firm. God wins - and in the end, so do we."

I reckon so.

Who are "the called"?

Jude addresses his readers as "the called" (Greek *kletois*), which conveys the idea of being personally selected or chosen. A full inquiry into the doctrine of divine election is beyond the scope of this book. There are excellent treatments on the subject that offer a balanced approach.[1] However, we should take a few minutes to understand that Jude is writing to believers, all of whom he characterizes as "the called."

While Christians view divine election differently, we may find common ground by acknowledging that being called is but one link in an unbroken chain of God's work of redemption, stretching from eternity past to eternity future. The apostle Paul expresses this well in Rom. 8:29-30: "For those He foreknew He also predestined to be conformed to the image of His Son, so that He would be the firstborn among many brothers. And those He predestined, He also called; and those He called, He also justified; and those He justified, He also glorified."

There are at least five great stages of redemption outlined in this brief passage:

1. Foreknowledge. The Greek term *proginosko* simply means "to know beforehand." Scholars vigorously debate whether this word implies "choosing," "foreordaining," or "adopting" as opposed to simply foreknowing on God's part. Early church fathers such as Origen, Chrysostom, Augustine, and Jerome interpret the term as signifying foreknowledge rather than foreordination.

Frederick Godet's *Commentary on the Epistle to the Romans* devotes more than a page of fine print to this one word, summarizing, "Some have given to the word *foreknow* the meaning of *elect, choose, destine beforehand*.... Not only is this meaning arbitrary as being without example in the NT ... but what is still more decidedly opposed to this meaning is what follows: *He also did predestinate*."[2]

No matter how one understands the meaning of this word, it's clear that our omniscient God always has known believers and has reckoned them elected, chosen, and adopted from an eternal perspective. This encompasses the unsearchable depths of His divine sovereignty, and the certainty of a human response in faith to the gospel message.

2. Predestination. The Greek verb translated "predestinate" is *proorizo* and means "to mark off by boundaries." In other passages it is translated "foreordain." But in what way are foreknown believers predestined? We are predestined "to be conformed to the image of His Son." That is, God determines to complete the good work He begins in us until the day of Christ Jesus (Phil. 1:6).

Being conformed to Christ's image does not mean we become little gods, for deity is the exclusive domain of our transcendent Creator. He does not give His glory to another (Isa. 42:8). The word "image" is *eikon* and speaks of a derived likeness. Just as the imprint of a U.S. president on a coin is not the actual president, believers in Jesus are not scaled-down deities.

All people bear the image of God - the *Imago Dei* - and as such reflect His mental, social, and moral attributes. We do not, however, possess His divine qualities such as eternality, omnipotence, omniscience, omnipresence, and immutability. Nevertheless, God invites us to partake in the divine nature by grace through faith in Jesus Christ, who sends the Holy Spirit to defeat the sin nature in us, make us spiritually alive, take up permanent dwelling in our human spirit, and enable us to enjoy intimate fellowship with Him (John 3:3; 2 Cor. 5:17; Eph. 2:8-9; Titus 3:5; 2 Peter 1:3-4).

As a result of this miraculous work of God, we may look forward to the day when Christ's work of redemption is complete, and we stand before Him fully and finally purged of the last vestiges of our sin.

Jesus loses none of those belonging to Him - a joint effort with the Father expressed in John 6:39-40, "This is the will of Him who sent Me: that I should lose none of those He has given Me but should raise them up on the last day. For this is the will of My Father: that everyone who sees the Son and believes in Him may have eternal life, and I will raise him up on the last day."

God's foreknowledge leads naturally into His marking out boundaries on our lives so that we may live confidently, knowing that when Jesus appears, "we will be like Him, because we will see Him as He is" (1 John 3:2). Of further comfort is the knowledge that these boundaries not only keep us in His love; they keep out the evil one, who may never breach the walls God has built for our eternal security.

3. Calling. The Greek verb *kaleo* encompasses the outward invitation of preaching and the inward drawing of the Spirit of grace. "Because not all who are invited to believe are actually justified, the 'calling' here cannot refer to merely a general invitation but must refer to an effective call that creates the faith necessary for justification."[3]

John MacArthur writes, "Jude here is not speaking about God's general invitation to sinners.... Rather, he is speaking of God's special, internal call through which He awakens the human will and imparts spiritual life - enabling once-dead sinners to embrace the gospel by faith."[4]

God's effectual call to salvation is well explained in Jesus' words to His disciples in John 16:7-11, where He previews the work of the Holy Spirit in convicting the unbeliever of sin, righteousness, and judgment. The "Counselor" convinces lost people that their sin of unbelief keeps them out of the kingdom; that their human righteousness is but filthy rags in the eyes of God and is grossly insufficient to repay a sin debt owed to an eternally offended Sovereign; and that if they persist in rejecting God's provision for sin - the finished work of Christ - they choose the same judgment that falls upon Satan, namely, eternity in outer darkness.

The same Spirit that convincingly condemns the hardened unbeliever also has the power to remove a heart of stone and impart a heart of flesh (Ezek. 36:26), resulting in regeneration, which leads to justification.

4. Justification. The noun *dikaiosis*, or justification, describes the act of God declaring sinners righteous on the basis of the finished work of Christ. Believing sinners are acquitted - freed of all guilt - as their sins are transferred to the account of Christ and exchanged for Christ's righteousness.

Justification is grounded in Christ's death, burial, and resurrection. The apostle Paul puts it succinctly, "He was delivered up for our trespasses and raised for our justification" (Rom. 4:25). Paul further writes, "So then, as through one trespass [Adam's] there is condemnation for everyone, so also through one righteous act [Christ's] there is life-giving justification for everyone. For just as through one man's disobedience the many were made sinners, so also through the one man's obedience the many will be made righteous" (Rom. 5:18-19).

"Christ's one act of righteousness (i.e., his death and resurrection, considered as one event) leads to our justification as an antidote to the one trespass of Adam that brought humankind into the bondage of sin and death."[5]

Justification comes only through faith, apart from human effort (Rom. 5:1; Gal. 3:24). It is a one-time, instantaneous, non-repeatable act of God, placing us in right standing before His holy bench, and ensuring that we are never subject to double jeopardy. To add works to justification, such as returning to Old Covenant practices that served as types and shadows of greater things to come, is to trample on the Son of God and regard as profane the blood of the New Covenant (Heb. 10:29).

Justification is not to be confused with sanctification, which is the work of God setting believers apart and engaging in a lifelong process by which we become more Christ-like (1 Cor. 1:18; 1 Thess. 5:23). Justification and sanctification may be distinguished but not separated; both are divine elements of God's redemption.

5. Glorification. The verb translated "glorified" is *edoxase*. All those who are justified will be glorified; that is, they will receive resurrected bodies and be fully and finally conformed to the image of Christ. In Rom. 8:29-30, Paul speaks of glorification in the past tense. "In the divine foreknowledge our glorification is already seen as an event accomplished."[6]

This is a marvelous revelation that places an exclamation point on God's sovereign work of grace. What cannot be said to have a beginning, since it is eternal (God's foreknowledge of us), climaxes at a point in time and continues on without end (God's glorification of us).

So, when does glorification take place? At the resurrection of the just, which Jesus describes in John 5:28-29, and Paul details in 1 Corinthians 15. Specifically, the apostle tells us that our corrupted earthly bodies are raised incorruptible. Sown in dishonor, they are raised in glory. Sown in weakness, they are raised in power. Sown as natural bodies - or bodies subject to the sinful flesh - they are raised as spiritual bodies powered by the Holy Spirit.

Paul writes, "Listen! I am telling you a mystery: We will not all fall asleep [experience physical death], but we will all be changed, in a moment, in the twinkling of an eye, at the last trumpet. For the trumpet will sound, and the dead will be raised incorruptible, and we will be changed. Because this corruptible must be clothed with incorruptibility, and this mortal must be clothed with immortality. Now when this corruptible is clothed with incorruptibility, and this mortal is clothed with immortality, then the saying that is written will take place: Death has been swallowed up in victory. O Death, where is your victory? O Death, where is your sting? Now the sting of death is sin, and the power of sin is the law. But thanks be to God, who gives us the victory through our Lord Jesus Christ!" (1 Cor. 15:51-57).

Though we do not know the time of the Lord's return for His saints, we know what is to happen: "Since we believe that Jesus died and rose again, in the same way God will bring with Him those who have fallen asleep through Jesus. For we say this to you by a revelation from the Lord: We who are still alive at the Lord's coming will certainly have no advantage over those who have fallen asleep. For the Lord Himself will descend from heaven with a shout, with the archangel's voice, and with the trumpet of God, and the dead in Christ will rise first. Then we who are still alive will be caught up together with them in the clouds to meet the Lord in the air; and so we will always be with the Lord" (1 Thess. 4:14-17).

According to Phil. 3:20-21, our citizenship is in heaven, and when the Lord Jesus returns, "He will transform the body of our humble condition into the likeness of His glorious body, by the power that enables Him to subject everything to Himself."

Foreknowledge. Predestination. Calling. Justification. Glorification. Five acts of God in redemption. These do not express the full range of God's work in salvation. Paul could have listed regeneration, baptism by the Holy Spirit, sanctification, adoption, and others. But by placing "calling" in the middle, he grounds our salvation in time, and tethers it to the redemptive work of God stretching from eternity past to eternity future.

While salvation is of the Lord, we do well not to consider it fatalistically, sloughing off our responsibility to respond to Christ in repentance and belief. Regarding Paul's listing of five redemptive acts of God, William Sanday and A.C. Headlam write, "There can be no question that St. Paul fully recognized the freedom of the human will. The large part which exhortation plays in his letters is conclusive proof of this. But whatever the extent of human freedom there must be behind it the Divine Sovereignty. It is the practice of St. Paul to state alternately the one and the other without attempting an exact delineation between them."[7]

Paul's words in Romans 8 provide a natural link to the opening verses of Jude's epistle. By referring to Christians as "the called," Jude assures us of God's election unto salvation. He also exhorts us to remember that God's call is not merely to salvation but to bond-servanthood. Salvation is not a ticket to be obtained in life and cashed in at death, but an everlasting relationship that spurs us to walk the path of good works God, who called us, laid out for us in eternity past (Eph. 2:10).

How are Christians "loved"?

The word translated "loved" is a form of the Greek *agape*, which refers to the highest level of love expressed by God toward His people.[8] It illustrates the intimate relationship between God the Father and Jude's readers. It also shows that God has set His special love on us for salvation. God placed His love on believers in eternity past (Eph. 1:4-6), with results that continue into the present and future.

It is a costly love that spurs the Father to sacrifice His Son on a Roman cross, an audacious act of tender mercy for the good of His enemies, and in their place. The prophet Isaiah depicts it in dramatic terms 700 years in advance: "But He was pierced because of our transgressions, crushed because of our iniquities; punishment for our peace was on Him, and we are healed by His wounds. We all went astray like sheep; we all have turned to our own way; and the Lord has punished Him for the iniquity of us all" (Isa. 53:5-6).

Jesus expresses His mission with divine purpose and human grit when He tells His bickering disciples, "For even the Son of Man did not come to be served, but to serve, and to give His life - a ransom for many" (Mark 10:45). He understands fully the will of His Father in securing redemption for us, as well as His voluntary role as the Lamb of God. "This is why the Father loves Me," He says, "because I am laying down My life so I may take it up again. No one takes it from Me, but I lay it down on My own. I have the right to lay it down, and I have the right to take it up again. I have received this command from My Father" (John 10:17-18).

The Father's love is seen not only in the fragrant life of the Lord Jesus, but in the work of the Holy Spirit, convicting unbelievers of their sin, drawing them to saving faith, and imparting new life into their once-dead human spirits (John 3:3-8; 16:7-11; Titus 3:5-7). Even more, expressing the Father's love, the Spirit secures and protects God's children, ensuring them a relationship with Him that endures for time and eternity (Eph. 1:13-14; 4:30; 1 Peter 1:3-5).

We did nothing to merit the Father's love. In fact, we did everything to invite His wrath. Yet He loved us unconditionally from eternity past - a love that swept into time and space and climaxed in the death, burial, and resurrection of Jesus and carries out into eternity future.

This type of love cannot be broken, as Paul reminds us in Rom. 8:38-39: "For I am persuaded that neither death nor life, nor angels nor rulers, nor things present, nor things to come, nor powers, nor height, nor depth, nor any other created thing will have the power to separate us from the love of God that is in Christ Jesus our Lord!"

How are we "kept" by Jesus Christ?

"Kept by" comes from the Greek *teteremenois*. The verb *tereo* means "to observe, pay attention to, keep under guard, maintain." Jesus promises to keep believers secure for all eternity (John 6:35-40; 10:27-30). This security rests in the efficacy of His sacrifice (1 Peter 3:18), the unshakeable power of the Father (1 Peter 1:5), and the sealing of the Holy Spirit (Eph. 4:30).

As the ESV Study Bible notes, "At the outset of his letter to Christians who are threatened by false teachers, Jude reminds them that they will be kept and preserved by God's power from falling away."[9]

Being kept by Jesus Christ secures the full range of His redemption. Think about that for a moment. If the finished work of Christ can be unraveled at any point, His sinless life, sacrificial and substitutionary death, burial, and physical resurrection from the dead somehow failed to accomplish the eternal plan of the triune Godhead.

If we can lose a salvation that we never earned to begin with, what does that say about our Savior? And what, exactly, do we lose? Our election? Predestination? Calling? Justification? Glorification? The apostle Paul reckons all of these as accomplished facts by referring to them in the past tense (Rom. 8:29-30).

To be sure, disobedient Christians may lose rewards at the judgment seat of Christ (Rom. 14:10-11; 1 Cor. 3:11-15; 2 Cor. 5:9-10; 1 John 2:28; Rev. 3:11-12). Meanwhile, the Lord may chasten us as disobedient children, even to the point of taking us out of this world (1 Cor. 11: 27-32; Heb. 12:3-12). But our position in Christ as justified saints ensures our place in His kingdom.

As we walk the earth, His persevering power enables us to endure hardship and navigate the wreckage of living in a sinful and fallen world. Ultimately, this guarantees our victory over Satan, sin, and death. Even when we suffer hardship or persecution for the sake of Christ, "we are more than victorious through Him who loved us" (Rom. 8:37).

In Christ's letters to the seven churches of Asia Minor, we see the Lord's loving reward for those who, by His power, persevere in times of persecution. The hope of this reward links the promises of Jesus in the opening pages of Revelation to their fulfillment at His return. Note that in each of the seven letters to the churches of Asia Minor, Jesus offers a word of encouragement to the overcomer:

To Ephesus: "I will give the victor the right to eat from the tree of life, which is in the paradise of God" (Rev. 2:7b).

To Smyrna: "The victor will never be harmed by the second death" (Rev. 2:11b).

To Pergamum: "I will give the victor some of the hidden manna. I will also give him a white stone, and on the stone a new name is inscribed that no one knows except the one who receives it" (Rev. 2:17b).

To Thyatira: "The victor and the one who keeps My works to the end: I will give him authority over the nations - and He will shepherd them with an iron scepter; He will shatter them like pottery - just as I have received [this] from My Father. I will also give him the morning star" (Rev. 2:26-28).

To Sardis: "In the same way, the victor will be dressed in white clothes, and I will never erase his name from the book of life, but will acknowledge his name before My Father and before His angels" (Rev. 3:5).

To Philadelphia: "The victor: I will make him a pillar in the sanctuary of My God, and he will never go out again. I will write on him the name of My God, and the name of the city of My God - the new Jerusalem, which comes down out of heaven from My God - and My new name" (Rev. 3:12).

And to Laodicea: "The victor: I will give him the right to sit with Me on my throne, just as I also won the victory and sat down with My Father on His throne" (Rev. 3:21).

The comforting words of Jesus to His disciples should warm our hearts as well: "Because I live, you will live too" (John 14:19b). Our lives are bound inextricably to the life of Christ. He promises to prepare a place for us in heaven and to come for us one day (John 14:2-3). Meanwhile, He asks the Father to send the Holy Spirit as another Comforter to be with us and in us (John 14:16-17). We are assured that He will never leave us or forsake us (Heb. 13:5b; Deut. 31:6), and His faithfulness continues steadfast for He remains the same yesterday, today, and forever (Heb. 13:8).

And one day, when He returns to earth as King of kings and Lord of lords, we return with Him in our glorified bodies and serve Him in the new heavens and the new earth - a place where there is no sanctuary because the Lord God Almighty and the Lamb are its sanctuary; a place where there is no need of sun or moon because God's glory illuminates it, and its lamp is the Lamb; and a place so thoroughly purged of sin that the Lord gently wipes away the last tears we will ever shed (Rev. 21:4, 22-23).

What's the significance of "mercy, peace, and love"?

The phrase "mercy and peace" is a common Jewish greeting. Paul employs it in his letters to Timothy, and John includes it early in his second epistle. But Jude adds to this common greeting the word "love," creating a three-fold blessing that occurs only here in the New Testament.

Jude has just sought to strengthen his readers by reminding them of their standing with God; they are called, loved, and kept. Now, he rounds out the greeting by listing some of the key benefits of their position in Christ, and by wishing these benefits would multiply - not just in their own hearts, but in the hearts of others as they stand firm in the faith.

Mercy (*eleos*) carries with it the idea of compassion, kindness, and pity. It is closely related to grace (*charis*) and in some respects cannot be separated from it. In terms of our salvation, it is impossible to conceive of one without the other. From God's perspective, we might think of His mercy as preceding grace, although we know both are eternal qualities of our Sovereign Lord.

Even so, God loved the world in an extreme way; that is, He pitied us in our lost and desperate state, giving us His only begotten Son and thus shedding His grace on us (John 3:16). From a human perspective, grace comes first. The kindness of God, Paul writes, leads us to repentance (Rom. 2:4). Experiencing the goodness of God in a general sense and then experiencing His grace in an effectual call, we are able to comprehend the good news of Christ's sinless life, sacrificial death, and resurrection that paves a path of return to our offended God.

Mercy is more than God's extension of divine patience toward sinners; it is an everyday reality in the lives of believers. We are recipients of His mercy, having been saved by it (Eph. 2:4-5; Titus 3:5-7). Even more, God's mercies are new every morning - and as redeemed people still subject to fleshly desires, we desperately need His willingness to cut us some slack.

When we confess our sins, He remains faithful to His covenant promises and mercifully forgives us and cleanses us (1 John 1:9). When we approach His throne of grace, we receive mercy (Heb. 4:16).

Paul reminds the Roman believers that God manifests the riches of His glory upon "objects of mercy that He prepared beforehand for glory" (Rom. 9:23b).

Next, there is peace (*eirene*). The verb form is *eiro*, to join. Thus, making peace is bringing together that which has been separated. Christ brought justifying peace through His shed blood, enabling sinful people to be declared in right standing before a holy God. But Jude here seems to be writing about sanctifying peace, the tranquility in which we, as redeemed people, stand. This includes knowing our sins are forgiven - that we are no longer enemies of God, under His wrath, and bound for an eternity in outer darkness.

But it's even more. There is peace in knowing that we are His adopted children; that He walks with us through every trial; that He enables us to be ambassadors of peace in a hostile world; and that ultimately when the King returns, He will establish His peace throughout a restored creation, so that even in the animal kingdom, predator and prey lie down together like a kindle of kittens.

It is a peace that cannot be explained fully in human terms; a peace that passes all understanding. And it is a peace that abides deeply in our spirits, even when all around us is chaos. "Peace I leave with you," Jesus tells His followers. "My peace I give to you. I do not give to you as the world gives. Your heart must not be troubled or fearful" (John 14:27).

Last, Jude writes, there is love (*agape*), the divine love that God directs toward us and is meant to be shared as we partake in the divine nature (2 Peter 1:4). The more we become like Christ, the purer becomes our love for Him and for others.

Jude has just assured us that we are loved by God - a divine, unfathomable reality that burned deeply in the heart of God before creation, continues now, and extends into the limitless future. It is a blazing torch whose light cannot be diminished by time, and whose warmth cannot be vanquished by the icy gales of a sinful and fallen world. The agent of this love is the Holy Spirit. Paul writes in Rom. 5:5, "God's love has been poured out in our hearts through the Holy Spirit who was given to us."

We do well to remember that the Lord's *agape* must be distinguished from brotherly love (*philia*), love of family (*storge*), and erotic passions (*eros*). While these have their proper places, God's love surpasses them all and serves as the north star by which all other affections are properly aligned.

Peter seems to grasp this in a rare moment when Jesus asks three times about his love of the Lord (John 21:15-17). The first two times, Jesus uses the word *agapao*, asking, "do you love Me?" That is, does Peter possess the highest form of love - the love Jesus has for him? Peter responds, "Yes Lord ... You know that I love You," but both times he employs the word *phileo*. In other words, Peter does not confess to owning the same depth of divine love Jesus has for him.

The third time, Jesus asks, "Simon, son of John, do you love (*phileo*) Me?" To which Peter replies, "Lord, You know everything! You know that I love (*phileo*) You." The apostle who only days earlier boasts he will never deny Jesus - and then promptly does so on the night of Jesus' arrest - now thinks more sensibly of himself and responds with sincere humility.

Finally, we should avoid the temptation to see God's love as a mere emotional response to His fallen creatures: a Jesus who never gets angry or raises His voice; a Savior who never sends anyone to hell; a benevolent Judge who eschews guilty verdicts in favor of universal pardons. Even a casual reading of the New Testament shows that *agape* rests securely and undiminished in company with holiness, purity, and divine wrath.

The real Jesus of Scripture condemns scribes and Pharisees to hell (Matt. 23:15, 33); overturns the tables of money changers at the Temple (Matt. 21:12-13; John 2:13-17); speaks truth to power, thus inviting His own death (Matt. 26:62-64); and will come one day with a sword and a bloody robe to set things right (Rev. 19:11-21). Our loving Master is no Milquetoast.

The blessings of God - among them mercy, peace, and love - are unending and irrevocable. The deeper our understanding of them, the greater the sense of responsibility to walk the path of good works God laid out for us in eternity past. This includes defending the Christian faith against those who attack it from without and sully it from within. To this duty Jude now turns his attention.

Key words

In this chapter, we learned several key terms relating to God's redemption. Review the text and then fill in the blanks to test your knowledge.

Foreknowledge. The Greek term *proginosko* simply means "to know _____." Scholars vigorously debate whether this word implies "choosing," "foreordaining," or "adopting" as opposed to simply _____ on God's part.

Predestination. The Greek verb translated "predestinate" is *proorizo* and means "to mark off by _____." In other passages it is translated "_____." Believers are predestined to be conformed to the image of _____.

Calling. The Greek verb *kaleo* encompasses the _____ invitation of preaching and the _____ drawing of the Spirit of grace.

Justification. The noun *dikaiosis*, or justification, describes the act of God declaring sinners _____ on the basis of the finished work of Christ. Believing sinners are _____, or freed of all guilt, as their sins are transferred to the _____ of Christ and exchanged for Christ's righteousness.

Glorification. The verb translated "glorified" is *edoxase*. All those who are _____ will be glorified; that is, they will receive resurrected bodies and be fully and finally _____ to the image of Christ.

Application

Questions for personal or group study

1. Jude is about to exhort his readers to contend for the Christian faith. But first, he assures them of their standing in Christ. For example, he tells them they are "the called," a clear reference to God's effective call to salvation. This raises questions that often divide those who hold to Reformed theology[10] from those who partially or fully reject it. So, consider the following questions:

   - How might you try to reconcile the sovereignty of God with the divinely given ability of all people to make choices for which God holds them accountable?

   - Why do you think the doctrine of divine election is so divisive in the church today?

   - Is there common ground on which Christians can stand together, even when holding different views of divine election?

   - Does it seem to you that some really important doctrines - like the Trinity, the virgin birth of Jesus, Christ's full deity and full humanity, and the exact order of events surrounding the second coming - all seem shrouded in mystery? Why do you think that's the case?

   - How should you approach a study of these deeper and more difficult doctrines?

2. Do you think God loves Christians more - or at least differently - than He loves non-Christians? Does His love change in kind, or degree, when a lost person comes to faith in Christ? If so, does that make God's love conditional?

3. Jude comforts us by saying we are kept by Jesus; that is, we are secure in His sovereign hand. That being the case, consider:

   - How can this knowledge comfort us if and when we fall into grievous sin?

- How might we take unwarranted advantage of this security?

- Do you think God wants believers to live in the tension between security and doubt? Why or why not?

- Do you think the false teachers in Jude's epistle, who he makes clear do not have the Spirit (v. 19), know they are lost? Is it possible they think they are doing the Lord's work, only to discover in the judgment that they are mistaken (see Matt. 7:21-23)? Or, might they be so far gone in their rebellion that there is no turning back (see Rom. 1:24-32)?

4. How would you respond biblically to the following scenarios:

- You have struggled all your life with a particularly nasty habit - perhaps violent anger, arrogance, or unwanted sexual desires. God saved you in dramatic fashion and, for a time, you were free of these sins. But lately the old habits have returned with a vengeance, and now you wonder if you've ever been saved.

- A good friend, who calls herself a Christian, and who is active in her local church, likes to party on Saturday nights. It's okay, she tells you. She just claims 1 John 1:9 on Sunday mornings. "I'm under grace," she boasts, "not under the law."

- Your small group leader is taking you through a study of "perseverance of the saints." He confesses that he believes it's true except in the case of apostasy - a deliberate walking away from the faith. He further states that someone who rejects the faith in such a manner can never be saved again, citing Heb. 6:4-6.

- A friend has been studying the doctrine of election and has come to the conclusion that Muslims may be closer to the truth than Christians. Allah fatalistically determines everything - good and evil alike. He creates us as objects of love or hate and then, like chess pieces, moves us around the board in the game of life. "Isn't that what Romans 9-11 really teaches?" he asks.

- A family member comes to you, expressing doubts about her salvation. She says the Bible is so confusing that she'll never be able to know if she's saved or lost. Some days she feels saved, and some days she feels she has lost her salvation. Is it possible, she asks, to be saved and lost several times, or is a fall from grace "one strike and you're out"?

5. Read ahead to Jude 24-25. *Who* (not what) keeps the elect from stumbling, even in the midst of persecution? Though we address this later in our study, what do you think Jude means by "stumbling"?

4

Copycats?
The Apologist's Challenge Concerning Jude and 2 Peter 2

History is rife with famous plagiarists. Primatologist Jane Goodall "borrowed" from sources ranging from Wikipedia to astrology websites to produce a 2013 book, *Seeds of Hope: Wonder and Wisdom from the World of Plants*.

Alex Haley's epic *Roots* is now considered a mixture of facts, fiction, and thievery.

Joe Biden scuttled his own run for president in 1987 by stealing lines - and even whole pages - from other people's speeches, from the British Labor Party's Neil Kinnock to American President John F. Kennedy.

And that's not all. Martin Luther King Jr., rocker Led Zeppelin, and composer John Williams all stand accused in varying degrees of taking other people's creative work and calling it their own.[1]

So, how do we deal with the reality that portions of Jude and Peter's second epistle are uncannily similar? Are we dealing with one or more plagiarists claiming divine inspiration?

A question of canon

Take a look at the nearby table comparing passages from Jude and 2 Peter 2-3. The similarities may tempt us to question the divine inspiration of one text or the other - or even to doubt their place in the canon of Scripture. However, there is no good reason to write off either of these epistles.

Commentators generally offer three explanations for the parallels between Jude and the second chapter of 2 Peter:

1. Peter borrows from Jude.

2. Jude borrows from Peter.

3. Both Peter and Jude draw from a common written or oral source, or a combination of written and oral sources.

Since both epistles are written at about the same time - likely the mid-60s A.D. - it's not possible to say with certainty that one predates the other.[2]

According to Thomas R. Schreiner, most scholars now believe that 2 Peter depends on Jude.[3] After all, why would Jude have written his letter in the first place if he were merely restating much of what Peter had already written? And why the urgency to abandon writing about "our common salvation" in order to exhort readers to "contend for the faith" (v. 3) if Peter already has addressed the issue?

However, a significant number of scholars argue that Jude draws from 2 Peter, smoothing out the language and improving Peter's writing. In addition, a distinct motive for Jude still exists because his main purpose in writing, and the crucial part of his letter, is verses 20-23, which is not found in 2 Peter 2.[4]

Further, Peter uses the future tense a number of times in the first few verses of 2 Peter 2 - for example, "there *will be* false teachers among you" (v. 1 - emphasis added) - while Jude uses the present tense throughout his epistle to describe the damage these false teachers already have inflicted.

Finally, Jude's reference to "the words foretold by the apostles of our Lord Jesus Christ" (v. 17) leads in the next verse to an approximate quote from 2 Peter 3:3 - "In the end time there will be scoffers walking according to their own ungodly desires" (v. 18). If in fact Jude is quoting from 2 Peter in this verse, then perhaps he draws much of his epistle from Peter's.

The common-source view should not be ruled out, although it's a more complex hypothesis than the others. Perhaps there is an oral or written tradition from which both men glean common themes. Or, it's possible they both use portions of an apologetic message that has been preached throughout the churches.

A fourth possibility exists, as noted by Arno Gaebelein, a prominent 19th and 20th century Methodist speaker and commentator. While there are unmistakable similarities between the two texts, they rarely agree in the exact words used, and each author expresses his thoughts differently. Therefore, "Jude may have known Peter's Epistle, but that does not mean that he used Peter's Epistle." Rather, the Holy Spirit may have given both men similar inspired testimonies.[5]

The doctrine of divine inspiration does not rule out any of these explanations. There is overlapping detail in many Old Testament books, as any chronological Bible attests. Further, the synoptic Gospels at the very least share a common oral tradition.[6] Even the quoting of pagan writers and pseudepigraphical works does not disqualify a text from divine inspiration (Acts 17:28; 1 Cor. 15:33; Titus 1:12; Jude 9, 14-15).

The bottom line is that we do not know for certain why Jude and 2 Peter 2 have so much in common. We may conclude, however, that the two texts are complementary rather than contradictory. They address the common theme of false teachers in the church. And originally, they may have reached different audiences at different times under different circumstances. To charge Peter or Jude with plagiarism is to deny the Holy Spirit - the divine Author of Scripture - the right to repeat Himself.

Similarities Between Jude and 2 Peter 2-3

Jude (HCSB)	2 Peter (HCSB)
Jude 4 For certain men, who were designated for this judgment long ago, have come in by stealth; they are ungodly, turning the grace of our God into promiscuity and denying our only Master and Lord, Jesus Christ.	**2 Peter 2:1-3** But there were also false prophets among the people, just as there will be false teachers among you. They will secretly bring in destructive heresies, even denying the Master who bought them, and will bring swift destruction on themselves. Many will follow their unrestrained ways, and because of them the way of truth will be blasphemed. In their greed they will exploit you with deceptive words. Their condemnation, pronounced long ago, is not idle, and their destruction does not sleep.
Jude 6-7 … and He has kept, with eternal chains in darkness for the judgment of the great day, angels who did not keep their own position but deserted their proper dwelling. In the same way, Sodom and Gomorrah and the cities around them committed sexual immorality and practiced perversions, just as they did, and serve as an example by undergoing the punishment of eternal fire.	**2 Pet. 2:4, 6** For if God didn't spare the angels who sinned, but threw them down into Tartarus and delivered them to be kept in chains of darkness until judgment … and if He reduced the cities of Sodom and Gomorrah to ashes and condemned them to ruin, making them an example to those who were going to be ungodly …
Jude 8-9 Nevertheless, these dreamers likewise defile their flesh, despise authority, and blaspheme glorious beings. Yet Michael the archangel, when he was disputing with the Devil in a debate about Moses' body, did not dare bring an abusive condemnation against him, but said, "The Lord rebuke you!"	**2 Pet. 2:10-11** … especially those who follow the polluting desires of the flesh and despise authority. Bold, arrogant people! They do not tremble when they blaspheme the glorious ones; however, angels, who are greater in might and power, do not bring a slanderous charge against them before the Lord.

Jude (HCSB)	2 Peter (HCSB)
Jude 10 But these people blaspheme anything they don't understand, and what they know by instinct, like unreasoning animals - they destroy themselves with these things.	**2 Pet. 2:12** But these people, like irrational animals - creatures of instinct born to be caught and destroyed - speak blasphemies about things they don't understand, and in their destruction they too will be destroyed ...
Jude 11-13 Woe to them! For they have traveled in the way of Cain, have abandoned themselves to the error of Balaam for profit, and have perished in Korah's rebellion. These are the ones who are like dangerous reefs at your love feasts. They feast with you, nurturing only themselves without fear. They are waterless clouds carried along by winds; trees in late autumn - fruitless, twice dead, pulled out by the roots; wild waves of the sea, foaming up their shameful deeds; wandering stars for whom is reserved the blackness of darkness forever!	**2 Pet. 2:13b-15, 17a** They consider it a pleasure to carouse in the daytime. They are blots and blemishes, delighting in their deceptions as they feast with you, having eyes full of adultery and always looking for sin, seducing unstable people, and with hearts trained in greed. Accursed children! By abandoning the straight path, they have gone astray and have followed the path of Balaam, the son of Bosor, who loved the wages of unrighteousness ... These people are springs without water, mists driven by a whirlwind ...
Jude 16 These people are discontented grumblers, walking according to their desires; their mouths utter arrogant words, flattering people for their own advantage.	**2 Peter 2:18** For uttering bombastic, empty words, they seduce, by fleshly desires and debauchery, people who have barely escaped from those who live in error.
Jude 18 ... they told you, "In the end time there will be scoffers walking according to their own ungodly desires."	**2 Peter 3:3** First, be aware of this: scoffers will come in the last days to scoff, following their own lusts ...

Key words

With respect to the reliability of Scripture, here are some key terms to keep in mind, and their definitions:

Inspired. The apostle Paul writes in 2 Tim. 3:16, "All Scripture is inspired by God ..." The phrase "inspired by God" comes from the Greek *theopneustos*. It means "God-breathed" and conveys the idea that Scripture is the product of a holy exhalation. God did not breathe *into* the Scriptures, thus inspiring them; He breathed *out* His Word. The Bible's origin is God Himself.

Inerrant. The inerrancy of Scripture means the Bible is fully truthful in all of its teachings. The Chicago Statement of Biblical Inerrancy puts it this way: Scripture in its entirety is "free from all falsehood, fraud, or deceit."[7] Inerrancy is tied to inspiration in that the Holy Spirit superintended the Bible's human authors so that using their own personalities, experiences, and writing styles, they recorded His revelation without error. Equally important, inerrancy refers to the original "autographs" that were breathed out by God and recorded by human authors over a period of 1,500 years. Subsequent manuscript copies may not claim inerrancy, although we have a treasure trove of manuscripts that give us confidence the Scriptures have been faithfully preserved and carefully copied.

Infallible. By infallibility, we mean the original manuscripts are incapable of error. This is because the Bible is inspired, or God-breathed, resulting in "autographs" that are inerrant and infallible. If the Holy Spirit is the Author of Scripture, and His breathed-out words are exactly what He wants to communicate to us, then we can rightly say these autographs are incapable of error because God is wholly dependable. He does not lie, make mistakes, or lead us astray. Infallibility may be distinguished from inerrancy but not separated from it. Inerrancy essentially refers to the original documents, while infallibility leans heavily on the character of their divine Author.

Sufficient. "The sufficiency of Scripture means that Scripture contained all the words of God he intended his people to have at each stage of redemptive history, and that it now contains all the words of God we need for salvation, for trusting him perfectly, and for obeying him perfectly," writes Wayne Grudem.[8] By sufficient, we mean the

Bible is the supreme authority in all matters of doctrine and practice. It's what the Reformers called *sola scriptura* - by Scripture alone. In practical terms, this means the Bible answers life's most important questions, such as: Is there a God? What's wrong with the world? And what happens when I die? Not that Scripture is an exhaustive catalogue of everything God knows, for omniscience cannot be confined to a single set of divinely inspired writings. Equally important, sufficiency does not prevent God from speaking to us today through Spirit-filled leaders, dreams and visions, or even an audible voice if He so chooses, although these forms of communication are better classified as *illumination*, not revelation, and they must conform to Scripture.

Application
Questions for personal or group study

1. Read 2 Tim. 3:16-17 and consider the following questions:
    - When Paul writes, "All Scripture is inspired by God," to what, specifically, is he referring?
    - Since the New Testament canon is not complete at the time Paul writes this letter, how can we be assured the 27 books of the New Testament are inspired? The following passages may prove helpful: John 14:26; 16:13; 1 Timothy 5:18 (Luke 10:7); 2 Peter 3:15-16.
    - In what ways is Scripture "profitable" for us, according to Paul?
    - What is the goal of our study of Scripture (v. 17)?
    - Since Paul wrote many of the New Testament books, how might we respond to the argument that Paul uses circular reasoning to call his own writings Scripture?

2. Read 2 Peter 1:20-21 and consider the following questions:
    - Where does "prophecy of Scripture" originate?
    - How might you respond to the following statements about Scripture:
        a. "I believe the Bible is true because, well, I just believe it."
        b. "The Bible is true because it's the best-selling book of all time."

c. "The Bible is true because it changed my life."

d. "The Bible is true because it has stood the test of time."

e. "I believe the Bible is true because credible eyewitnesses accurately recorded the acts of God throughout human history, under divine direction, free of personal agendas and in the presence of hostile witnesses who often made them pay for their testimonies with their lives."

- Why is it important that the Bible's 40 human authors are credible eyewitnesses of the acts of God in human history?

- How do the Scriptures support the claim that its human authors are free of personal agendas? The following passages may prove helpful: Luke 1:3-4; Acts 3:12-16; 8:9-25; 14:8-18.

- According to Scripture, church history, and tradition, it appears that all of the apostles, except John, may have died martyrs' deaths. How does this reflect on their claims to be telling the truth about the person and work of Jesus Christ?

3. What do you think is the best explanation for the similarities between Jude's epistle and the second chapter of 2 Peter?

5

I Found It Necessary:
Going from Good to Better
in Defense of the Faith

Dear friends, although I was eager to write you about our common salvation, I found it necessary to write and exhort you to contend for the faith that was delivered to the saints once for all. (Jude 3)

It's Christmas night 1776, and General George Washington's Continental Army could use some rest. Tired, cold, and harried, the soldiers would welcome a blazing fire, a warm meal, and a good night's sleep as a holiday respite from their travails.

But instead, Washington leads 2,400 troops across the icy Delaware River, where they stun German Hessian mercenaries garrisoned at Trenton, New Jersey. The Patriot forces catch the British-sponsored enemy completely off guard. "The lasting effect was that the success raised rebel morale and proved that the most professional army in the West could be beaten."[1]

Some 17 centuries earlier, Jude ponders a good thing for the harried believers besieged by false teachers. Evidently, he has given much thought to writing about their common salvation, but the Holy Spirit prompts him to take a more aggressive tack and spur his fellow believers to engage in a doctrinal battle that influences the course of the early church.

Jude demonstrates a sensitivity to the Holy Spirit, and a willingness to turn from something good to something better in defense of the Christian faith.

Our common salvation

Jude's original intent is to fashion a letter that celebrates the "common salvation" of all believers. By this, no doubt, Jude means the redemptive work of Christ that reaches across geographical boundaries, language barriers, and cultural divides. As one who came to faith only after witnessing Christ's resurrection, Jude knows first-hand the grace and mercy of God; the sin debt paid through the sacrificial and substitutionary death of His sinless half-brother; the authority over Satan, sin, and death secured through Jesus' bodily resurrection; and the security of everlasting life by grace alone, through faith alone, in Christ alone.

Perhaps Jude had resolved to summarize the core doctrines of the Christian faith in order to encourage fellow believers to endure persecution. Or maybe he wanted to remind them that the finished work of Christ ensured the coming of the Holy Spirit, who now lives in them and is working patiently and persistently to conform them to the image of their Savior. Or, it's possible he wanted them to persevere in their faith, live in the light of eternity, and look forward to the return of the Messiah, who had dramatically ascended from the Mount of Olives a few decades ago.

In any case, he has devoted considerable thought to writing about the beliefs Christians share in common. The Greek word translated "common" in verse 3 is *koinos*, the verbal form being *koinoneo*, "to become a sharer, a partner." Thus, the idea of a "common salvation" refers to those cherished truths possessed in common with others.

Before we move on in our study of Jude, it may be good for us to think about the non-negotiable doctrines that bind us together as the Body of Christ. With an estimated 2.2 billion Christians in the world, worshiping in more than 41,000 denominations,[2] one may legitimately wonder how we can possibly fulfill the prayer of Jesus that we all be as one (John 17:22). Indeed, the fact that Christians worship in so many different ways offers up all the proof some cults[3] need to declare that their leader alone has the truth, and that their organization is the only genuine form of Christianity.

But diversity does not necessarily mean division. The differences among the world's Christian denominations generally have more to do with location, culture, worship styles, missionary efforts, and forms of church government than they do with major doctrinal differences. Even so, it's good to ask: What are the core doctrines of the Christian faith? Can we come to full agreement on every shade of belief and practice? And if not, which doctrines are worthy of a vigorous defense?

How do we identify the non-negotiables?

Albert Mohler, president of The Southern Baptist Theological Seminary, refers to the process of discerning biblical truth as "theological triage."[4] The word "triage" comes from the French word *trier*, which means to sort. In emergency rooms, on the battlefield, and elsewhere, triage is the process by which medical personnel evaluate and prioritize the urgency of patient needs. A scraped knee can wait; a severed artery cannot.

Mohler suggests that a similar method be used in our churches to determine a scale of theological urgency. Other Christian leaders have offered similar suggestions, and church history seems to show that a similar system was used in the past, largely through church councils.

So, let's set some standards for theological triage in our churches. Mohler and others suggest three different levels of theological urgency - what some call primary, secondary, and tertiary issues.

Primary issues

Primary theological issues, sometimes called first-order doctrines, focus on beliefs most essential to preserving the Christian faith. These doctrines include, but are not limited to, the Trinity; the full deity and full humanity of Jesus; justification by faith; and the authority of Scripture. Here are brief summaries of these great doctrines, along with false teachings that at times have challenged the church throughout its history:

The Trinity. The doctrine of the Trinity states that there is one living and true God, who exists and reveals Himself to us as Father, Son, and Holy Spirit, with distinct personal attributes, but without division of nature, essence, or being.

False teachings about this doctrine include:

- Tritheism - a belief in three separate gods who share the same substance.

- Modalism (also called Sabellianism) - which explains the Father, Son, and Holy Spirit as different modes of God's self-revelation; in other words, God exists as Father, Son, and Spirit in different eras, but never as triune.

- Partialism - which teaches that Father, Son, and Holy Spirit are components of God; each person is part God, becoming fully God only when the three come together.

The full deity and full humanity of Jesus. Scripture reveals Jesus as the eternal Son of God, co-equal and co-eternal with the Father and the Holy Spirit. Some 2,000 years ago He set aside His privileged position in heaven and came to earth, adding to His deity sinless humanity via the miracle of the virgin birth. Thus, Jesus rightly may be described as the God-Man, fully divine and fully human.

This so-called "hypostatic union" describes how God the Son took on human nature yet remained fully God. Jesus sometimes operated within the limitations of His humanity (John 4:6; 19:28), and other times in the power of His deity (Matt. 14:13-21; John 11:43-44). In both, He remained one person with two natures, thus living a sinless life by which He secured the redemption of people through His sacrificial and substitutionary death on the cross.

False teachings about this doctrine include:

- Arianism - the belief that the preexistent Christ is the first and greatest of God's creatures but not fully divine.

- Docetism - a belief that Jesus is a purely divine being who only had the appearance of a man.

- Adoptionism - which posits that Jesus is born totally human, only to be "adopted" by God in a special way either at His baptism or at His resurrection.

Justification by faith. Justification is God's gracious and full acquittal of all sinners who repent and believe in Jesus. It is based on the finished work of Christ on the cross and is received by grace alone, through faith alone, in Him alone. To be justified is to be declared righteous before God and thus to be freed from the penalty of sin. God ensures that all those who are justified by faith are glorified one day - that is, given resurrected bodies free of the curse of sin - as the completion of God's redemptive work (Rom. 8:29-30).

False teachings about this doctrine include:

- Antinomianism - a view that Christians are freed by grace from obligations to any moral law; in essence, it twists the doctrine of justification by faith into a license to sin.

- Legalism - the polar opposite of antinomianism; it is the notion that obedience to a code of religious law - such as the Mosaic Law - is necessary for salvation.

- Pelagianism - a belief that original sin did not taint human nature and that mortal will is capable of choosing good or evil without the aid of God.

Authority of Scripture. As we learned in the last chapter, the Bible is the inspired, inerrant, infallible, and sufficient Word of God. When we speak of its authority, we mean that Scripture is the sole and final authority for Christians in all matters of faith and practice. The Bible is authoritative because it is God's Word, which He breathed out through human authors, and by whom He reveals His sovereignty over all things.

Scripture "reveals the principles by which God judges us, and therefore is, and will remain to the end of the world, the true center of Christian union, and the supreme standard by which all human conduct, creeds, and religious opinions should be tried."[5]

False teachings about this doctrine, particularly with respect to divine inspiration, include:

- Neo-orthodox - the view that God is so different from us that the only way to know Him is through direct revelation. Thus, the words in the Bible are not God's words but mere human concepts. The Bible is only "inspired" in that God can sometimes use these words to speak to individuals.

- Dictation - a theory of inspiration that acknowledges God as the Author of Scripture but limits man to the role of merely taking dictation rather than engaging his mind and experiences under the divine direction of the Holy Spirit.

- Limited inspiration - the opposite of the dictation theory; limited inspiration sees Scripture as primarily man's work. God guided the human authors but allowed them the freedom to express themselves in their work, even to the point of committing factual and historical errors.

In the earliest centuries of the church age, heretics directed their most dangerous attacks on the church's understanding of who Jesus is, and in what sense He is the Son of God. Docetists, for example, upheld the deity of Christ but denied His humanity, arguing that He only "appeared" human. The term "Docetism" is derived from the Greek *dokein*, "to seem."

The apostle John faces this attack head-on in his first epistle: "This is how you know the Spirit of God: Every spirit [person claiming divine gifting for service] who confesses that Jesus Christ has come in the flesh is from God. But every spirit who does not confess Jesus [that is, that He has come in the flesh] is not from God. This is the spirit of the antichrist; you have heard that he is coming, and he is already in the world now" (1 John 4:2-3).

In the fourth century, an Alexandrian priest named Arius convinced many of his followers to accept his view that Jesus is the first and greatest of God's creatures, but is not divine. The Nicene Creed[6] addressed the Arian controversy in plain language. It begins:

> We believe in one God,
> the Father almighty,

maker of heaven and earth,
of all things visible and invisible.
And in one Lord Jesus Christ,
the only Son of God,
begotten from the Father before all ages,
God from God,
Light from Light,
true God from true God,
begotten, not made;
of the same essence as the Father.
Through him all things were made.
For us and for our salvation
he came down from heaven;
he became incarnate by the Holy Spirit and the virgin Mary,
and was made human.
He was crucified for us under Pontius Pilate;
he suffered and was buried.
The third day he rose again, according to the Scriptures.
He ascended to heaven
and is seated at the right hand of the Father.
He will come again with glory
to judge the living and the dead.
His kingdom will never end.[7]

The deity and humanity of Jesus are essential to the Christian faith. If Jesus is not divine, He cannot be the Messiah; His claims and proofs of divinity are bold deceptions. At the same time, if Jesus is not fully human, He cannot be our Savior, for then His death, burial, and resurrection are illusions, and we must yet await a perfect human substitute to take away our sins. As the apostle Paul writes concerning the bodily resurrection of Christ, which presupposes His bodily crucifixion and burial, "And if Christ has not been raised, your faith is worthless; you are still in your sins" (1 Cor. 15:17).

The earliest creeds and councils of the church - Nicaea, Constantinople, and Chalcedon - were, in essence, emergency measures to protect the core doctrines of the faith. As doctrinal lines in the sand, they separated orthodoxy from heresy. From that point on, the church has affirmed the essential truths of the Incarnation, including Jesus' virgin birth, full deity and full humanity, sinless life, sacrificial and substitutionary death on the cross, physical resurrection, ascension to the Father's right hand, and imminent return. Those who deny these essential truths are, by definition, not Christians.

The same is true of the Trinity, the doctrine of justification by faith, and the belief in the inspiration, inerrancy, infallibility, and sufficiency of Scripture. These are non-negotiable doctrines for any believer and any church that truly claims to be Christian.

Secondary issues

Next are secondary, or so-called second-order, doctrines. These are important issues, but they may be distinguished from primary issues in that Christians may disagree on secondary issues without accusing one another of heresy. Nevertheless, disagreement on second-order doctrines leads to significant boundaries between believers.

When Christians organize themselves into local congregations, and these congregations form into denominations, conventions, associations, or networks, the boundaries become clear. One example of secondary issues is the meaning and mode of baptism.

Baptists and Presbyterians disagree over the most basic understanding of Christian baptism. Baptists reject infant baptism (paedobaptism), while Presbyterians trace infant baptism to their most basic understanding of the covenant.

Baptists and Presbyterians stand united on primary theological issues. They recognize each other as brothers and sisters in Christ. Yet their doctrinal convictions concerning paedobaptism prevent them from fellowship within the same congregation or denomination.

Other second-order issues include, but are not limited to:

- The role of women as pastors and/or deacons in the church
- The understanding of baptism in the Holy Spirit and its impact on devotional life and corporate worship
- Elder-led vs. elder-ruled forms of church government
- And the doctrine of divine election

As Mohler points out, "First-order issues determine Christian identity and integrity. Second-order issues determine ecclesiology."[8]

Tertiary issues

Tertiary, or third-order, doctrines are beliefs over which Christians may disagree while remaining in close fellowship, even within local congregations. Unfortunately, third-order issues can and do split churches, but they shouldn't.

Examples of tertiary issues include:

- Eschatology. Pre-, post-, and amillennialists may understand the Day of the Lord differently with respect to the order of events, or to the meaning of apocalyptic symbols. However, they should agree on first-order doctrines pertaining to the second coming: Christ's imminent, glorious, physical return; the resurrection and final judgment of all people; the separation of the righteous from the unrighteous; and the creation of new heavens and a new earth.

- Types of worship formats - contemporary, traditional, blended, etc.

- Days and hours of worship services and other local-church activities

- Frequency of observing the Lord's Supper / Communion

- How the local church engages its community

- Discipleship strategies - for example, Sunday school vs. small groups, age-graded ministries, curriculum choices, etc.

- How missions are supported financially

Mohler cautions that there are two extremes to avoid. The first is theological liberalism. The dumbing down of first-order doctrines, over which believers have sacrificed their lives, cheapens the redemptive work of Christ and pollutes His bride. True liberalism often is marked by its denial that primary theological issues even exist.

First-order doctrines are demoted to secondary or tertiary issues. Thus they are relegated to the status of issues no greater or less important than the color of the carpet, or which church member's three-bean salad is the tastiest.

The second extreme to be avoided is theological fundamentalism. The error here is in the opposite direction. Rather than minimizing the theological weight of primary issues, fundamentalism raises most or all theological issues to the rank of first-order doctrines. The result is contention in the local church, division among believers, and serious wrongful harm to individual Christians.[9]

In Jude's day, there already is great diversity in the church, as we see by reading through the Book of Acts and the epistles. There also are the tell-tale cracks of division as the next generation of church leaders following the apostles are, in some cases, teaching another Jesus, a different Spirit, and a different gospel (2 Cor. 11:4). Jude's desire to write about our "common salvation" may have been a longing to affirm the core doctrines of the Christian faith, while urging his fellow believers not to fight over secondary and tertiary issues.

However, there *are* doctrinal issues worthy of vigorous defense. Thus, prompted by the Holy Spirit, Jude changes his approach - mid-sentence - from a message of remembrance to a message of exhortation.

Why is contending for the faith necessary?

Jude expresses great concern with these words: "I found it necessary to write and exhort you to contend for the faith that was delivered to the saints once for all" (v. 3b). He places on hold his plans to write about the common salvation grounded in the person and work of Christ in order to address an urgent matter. "Circumstances had arisen that demanded immediate action, thus presenting an emergency situation. Jude addressed himself to a recognized problem, and exhorted the believers to respond with positive determination."[10]

The Greek word translated "necessary" is *anagke* and means by constraint, compulsion, distress, or hardship. In other New Testament passages, the term is used to describe the influence of other persons, circumstances, or a sense of obligation or duty.

For example, in urging the Corinthians to share their financial resources, Paul writes, "Each person should do as he has decided in his heart - not out of regret or out of *necessity*, for God loves a cheerful giver" (2 Cor. 9:7 - emphasis added). In his appeal to Philemon to welcome back a runaway slave, Paul remarks, "But I didn't want to do anything without your consent, so that your good deed might not be out of *obligation*, but of your own free will" (Philemon 14 - emphasis added).

The writer of Hebrews addresses his audience with an appeal to consider the superiority of the new covenant ministry in Christ. About the law's requirements for the shedding of blood, he writes, "Therefore it was *necessary* for the copies of the things in the heavens to be purified with these sacrifices, but the heavenly things themselves to be purified with better sacrifices than these" (Heb. 9:23 - emphasis added).

And in regard to a Christian's duties to the state, Paul remarks, "Therefore, *you must* submit, not only because of wrath, but also because of your conscience" (Rom. 13:5 - emphasis added).

For Jude, the necessity to write an urgent exhortation comes not from peer pressure or an obligation to fleshly authority. Rather, it appears the Holy Spirit has stirred Jude's heart and caused him to grieve over the manner in which his beloved friends are allowing false teachings to seep into the church. They must not sit idly by while interlopers undermine the first-order doctrines established by the eyewitnesses of the life of Christ.

Warren Wiersbe comments, "I must confess that I sympathize with Jude. In my own ministry, I would much rather encourage the saints than declare war on the apostates. But when the enemy is in the field, the watchmen dare not go to sleep. The Christian life is a battleground, not a playground."[11]

Exhort and contend

Like Paul, who writes that "an obligation is placed on me" to preach the gospel (1 Cor. 9:16), Jude senses a heavy burden that compels him to address false teachers in the church. He and his readers are not able to share a common salvation if they lose the doctrinal truths that define it. Therefore, Jude exhorts them to contend for the faith.

The Greek word *parakaleo* (exhort) conveys the idea of encouraging, urging, or appealing. By exhorting his readers, Jude is not scolding them; he saves his scathing rebuke for the false teachers that have infiltrated the church. Rather, he is gently, but firmly, counseling them to stop being observers and start being defenders. They have witnessed the influx of false teachers into their congregation, but evidently have not taken action to confront them. If they don't do something soon, the first-order doctrines are likely to be lost.

But what, exactly, is Jude exhorting his readers to do? Contend. This is a strong word that translates the Greek compound verb *epagonizomai*, found only here in the New Testament and translated "earnestly contend" in some translations. The simple verb *agonizomai* first meant to compete in an athletic contest, and then, more generally, to fight, struggle, or strive.[12] It's where we get the English transliteration "agonize."

Reading through the New Testament, we see that the apostles invest themselves heavily in teaching sound doctrine to followers of Jesus and preparing church leaders to defend their congregations against "savage wolves." In his tearful farewell to the Ephesian elders, Paul urges them, "Be on guard for yourselves and for all the flock, among whom the Holy Spirit has appointed you as overseers, to shepherd the church of God, which He purchased with His own blood. I know that after my departure savage wolves will come in among you, not sparing the flock. And men from among yourselves will rise up with deviant doctrines to lure the disciples into following them. Therefore be on the alert, remembering that night and day for three years I did not stop warning each of you with tears" (Acts 20:28-31).

Even though they must contend with Jewish lawyers, Roman rulers, Greek philosophers, and miracle-working sorcerers, the apostles engage in their fiercest battles *inside* the seemingly safe confines of the confessing church. That's where the greatest challenges to Christianity lie. The church has withstood - and even flourished under - persecution, but it threatens to bleed out from the self-inflicted wounds of false doctrine. Jude senses this and urges his readers to "agonize" in defense of the faith.

He does not suggest a violent response to false teachers, and neither do the apostles. Peter encourages us with his balanced plan of attack, urging us to "set apart the Messiah as Lord in your hearts, and always be ready to give a defense to anyone who asks you for a reason for the hope that is in you. However, do this with gentleness and respect, keeping your conscience clear, so that when you are accused, those who denounce your Christian life will be put to shame" (1 Peter 3:15-16).

Finally, by earnestly contending for "the faith," Jude is not referring to saving faith or trust in God's promises, although he would heartily agree they are important aspects of our rest in the sufficiency of Christ. Rather, Jude is writing about the body of doctrine that defines Christianity - principally the first-order issues that pertain to our common salvation.

Luke writes about this in Acts 2:42, as first-century believers continually devote themselves to the apostles' teaching, fellowship, breaking bread, and prayer. Further, Paul instructs Timothy to protect the faith - the sound words the young pastor has heard from Paul. He is to guard the treasure entrusted to him through the indwelling Holy Spirit (2 Tim. 1:13-14).

Jude further wants his readers to know that "the faith" is firmly established and unchanging. The work of Christ is finished. He is seated at the Father's right hand as our Mediator and Intercessor. He has sent the Holy Spirit to convict the world about sin, righteousness, and judgment, as well as to regenerate, baptize, indwell, seal, fill, comfort, and lead His own. He is preparing a place for us in His kingdom. And He is coming one day in power and great glory to fulfill all things. The gospel of the kingdom is written in the blood of Jesus and confirmed in the empty tomb. It is "delivered to the saints once for all" (Jude 3b).

The Greek word *hapax*, rendered "once for all," means something completed one time, with lasting results. John MacArthur writes, "Through the Holy Spirit, God revealed the Christian faith to the apostles and their associates in the first century. Their New Testament writings, in conjunction with the Old Testament Scriptures, make up the 'true knowledge' of Jesus Christ, and are all that believers need for life and godliness."[13]

So, who are the people with whom Jude's readers must contend? In the next chapter of our study, Jude offers a graphic introduction.

Key words

In this chapter, we learned several key terms. Test your knowledge by filling in the blanks.

Common salvation. The idea of a "common salvation" refers to those cherished _____ possessed in common with others.

Necessary. The Greek word translated "necessary" is *anagke* and means by constraint, _____, distress, or hardship. In other New Testament passages, the term is used to describe the _____ of other persons, circumstances, or a sense of _____ or duty.

Comparing English translations of *anagke*:

HCSB	KJV	NIV	NASB	ESV
Necessary	Needful	Compelled	The necessity	Necessary

Contend. Jude exhorts his readers to contend for the faith. "Contend" is a strong word that translates the Greek compound verb *epagonizomai*, found only here in the _____ _____ and translated "earnestly contend" in some translations. The simple verb *agonizomai* first meant to _____ in an athletic contest, and then, more generally, to fight, _____, or strive. It's where we get the English transliteration "_____."

Comparing English translations of *epagonizomai*:

HCSB	KJV	NIV	NASB	ESV
Contend	Earnestly contend	Contend	Contend earnestly	Contend

Application
Questions for personal or group study

1. How would you classify the following issues with respect to their importance in the life of the local church? Are they: P = Primary; S = Secondary; or T = Tertiary? Be prepared to answer why you classified them in this way.

   _____ Modes of baptism (immersion; sprinkling; pouring)

   _____ Baptism in the Holy Spirit

   _____ The role of women as pastors and/or deacons in the local church

   _____ Granite, quartz, concrete, or laminate countertops in the church kitchen?

   _____ The deity of Christ

   _____ Justification by faith alone

   _____ Elder-led vs. elder-ruled form of church government

   _____ Canceling Sunday evening services for the Super Bowl

   _____ The Trinity

   _____ The inerrancy of Scripture

   _____ Affiliation with a Christian denomination or network

   _____ Financial support of state, national, and international missions

2. Joseph Smith, founder of the Church of Jesus Christ of Latter-day Saints, claimed God revealed to him that Christianity had fallen into complete apostasy after the death of the apostles, and that he was chosen to restore the one true church. What does the Bible say about the church that exposes Smith's claim as false?

3. What's the toughest issue with which your local church has dealt? Would you classify that issue as primary, secondary, or tertiary? How did your congregation deal with it?

4. Christians are called to defend the faith with gentleness and respect (1 Peter 3:15-16). Yet, as we see in the next chapters of our study, Jude has harsh words for false teachers in the church. Peter and other New Testament writers don't mince their words, either. And Jesus was exceptionally pointed in pronouncing eight woes on the religious leaders of His day (see Matthew 23). So how do you balance the command to be gentle and respectful with the exhortation to boldly confront false teachers?

5. How would you respond to the following:
   - A pastor claims "revelations" from God, and exposes private details about people in the church - all without going privately to these people first (see Matt. 18:15-20).

   - A new church member volunteers to fill a teaching vacancy in a Sunday school class. The pastor quickly agrees, only to discover the new member is teaching a form of hyper-Calvinism that denies common grace and insists that God cares only for the elect, with nothing but hatred for the non-elect.

   - An elderly couple - and your church's most generous financial supporter - threatens to leave the church because young people are bringing sodas and bottled water into the worship center.

   - A lesbian couple visits your church and wants to know how they will be treated.

   - A deacon is cheating on his wife and makes no secret of it.

   - Your church is split down the middle about whether to replace the brown carpet in the worship center with mauve- or ocean mist-colored floor covering.

6. Look up the words "important" and "urgent." How do they compare? What situations in your local church are important but not necessarily urgent? Urgent but not necessarily important? Would you say the situation about which Jude writes is important, urgent, or both?

6

Who Are Those Guys?

How Apologists Identify False Teachers

For certain men, who were designated for this judgment long ago, have come in by stealth; they are ungodly, turning the grace of our God into promiscuity and denying our only Master and Lord, Jesus Christ. (Jude 4)

In the 1969 film *Butch Cassidy and the Sundance Kid*, a relentless posse interrupts the legendary duo's run of train robberies. Fleeing across rivers, plains, and rocky outcroppings, Butch and Sundance engage in playful, but increasingly annoyed, banter about the skilled men tracking them. At one point, Butch tries to assure Sundance that their escape tactics are working. Sundance is not convinced and keeps looking back over his shoulder.

"Ah, you're wasting your time," says Butch. "They can't track us over rocks."

"Tell *them* that," Sundance replies, nodding toward the horizon.

Butch looks for himself and sees that the trackers indeed are still hot on their trail. "They're beginning to get on my nerves," he says. "Who *are* those guys?"

Who indeed. "Who *are* those guys?" becomes a running gag line throughout the film.

Butch and Sundance eventually discover their pursuers' names, as well as the identity of the railroad executive bankrolling the posse. The news forces them to flee to South America, where they revive their nefarious careers before meeting a bloody end.[1]

Like Butch and Sundance, Jude can't seem to shake the posse on his trail. Rather than pistol-packing bounty hunters, however, these are false teachers doggedly determined to bring down the infant church. Jude avoids calling them by name, choosing instead to describe them as "certain/some men" (HCSB, NIV, KJV), "certain people" (ESV), or "certain persons" (NASB). In a parallel passage, Peter simply refers to them as "false teachers" (2 Peter 2:1).

Why doesn't Jude name these false teachers?

But who, exactly, are these false teachers? And why doesn't Jude call them out? After all, other New Testament writers have no hesitation naming names:

- Luke records an encounter between Peter and John, and a sorcerer by the name of Simon, who professes faith in Christ and then seeks to purchase the gift of conferring the Holy Spirit on people (Acts 8:9-24).

- Paul writes to Timothy about Hymenaeus and Alexander, who have "suffered the shipwreck of their faith" and whom Paul delivers to Satan (1 Tim. 1:19-20).

- Paul again lists Hymenaeus, this time with Philetus, two men engaged in "irreverent, empty speech" that produces godlessness; these men have "deviated from the truth, saying that the resurrection has already taken place" (2 Tim. 2:16-18).

- Paul mentions Alexander the coppersmith, who "did great harm to me" and whom "The Lord will repay ... according to his works." He is one who "strongly opposed our words" (2 Tim. 4:14-15).

- The apostle John warns about Diotrephes, "who loves to have first place" among believers, and who engages in "slandering us with malicious words," refusing to welcome the brothers, and stopping those who want to do so by expelling them from the church (3 John 9-10).

Other examples could be cited, but the point is that Jude delivers serious warnings about the religious scoundrels who have infiltrated the church - without naming them.

Perhaps this is because there are far too many to name - an indication of how widespread the movement has become. Or maybe it's because no single person is so well known as to have a heretical movement named after him; no Arius or Nestorius has yet emerged. Perhaps it's because Jude's readers know full well who is being discussed, as Paul's readers in Corinth do when he identifies "super apostles" who are, in fact, "false apostles" proclaiming another Jesus, a different Spirit, and a different gospel (see 2 Corinthians 11-12).

Or perhaps Jude neglects to name the false teachers because he is writing, not only to the church in his day, but to believers throughout the church age. It's even possible he resists the temptation to call them out personally because he is determined not to grant them a taste of the credibility they so ravenously desire.

In any case, we may be able to find clues about the false teachers' identity and their first-century aberrant doctrines. Jude recognizes that a battle is brewing, "a conflict that marked Satan's newest campaign in his long war against the truth. And that is why Jude writes this letter: to alert his readers to the doctrinal dangers they faced from Satan's covert agents."[2]

It's clear these false teachers are *in* the church, for Jude says they have "come in by stealth." This makes them especially dangerous. Many false prophets outside the church have spawned lies about Jesus while conducting anti-Christian campaigns. For example, Muhammad's insistence that Jesus is merely a prophet - not the divine Son of God - has led to 14 centuries of bloody Muslim conquest resulting in the deaths of 270 million people, many of them Christians.[3]

But an even greater threat resides *within* the church. "[T]he counterfeit pastors, elders, deacons, and teachers within the church are usually far more dangerous [than those outside Christianity]. Attacks from outside the church often unite God's people, but attacks from inside - coming from false teachers - usually divide and confuse the flock."[4]

Consider just a few of the many apostolic warnings about interlopers in the body of Christ:

- Acts 20:28-31. Paul urges the Ephesian elders to be on guard, because after his departure "savage wolves will come in among you, not sparing the flock." Further, "men from among yourselves will rise up with deviant doctrines and lure the disciples into following them."

- 2 Cor. 11:12-15. Paul writes to the Corinthians about "false apostles, deceitful workers" who disguise themselves as apostles of Christ. He even refers to them, tongue-in-cheek, as "super apostles" (11:5; 12:11). And he urges believers not to be surprised that these intruders disguise themselves as "servants of righteousness" because Satan masquerades as an angel of light.

- Gal. 1:6-9. Paul expresses amazement that the Galatians have fallen so quickly under the spell of "some who are troubling you and want to change the gospel of Christ." He singles out the Judaizers, who add traditional Jewish requirements such as circumcision, food laws, and Sabbath-keeping to Christ's finished work on the cross (3:1-3).

- Col. 2:8, 18-19. Paul cautions the Colossians not to be taken captive through "philosophy and empty deceit based on human tradition." Further, he warns about one who could cheat believers of their prize by "insisting on ascetic practices and the worship of angels, claiming access to a visionary realm and inflated without cause by his fleshly mind."

- 1 John 2:18-23. John reminds his readers that "Antichrist is coming." Meanwhile, "many antichrists have come." They are known by their denial of Jesus as Messiah, and their denial of the Father and the Son, a clear reference to a skewed Christology.

- 1 John 4:1-6. John further addresses the Docetists, who deny the full humanity of Jesus. "Every spirit [person claiming divine gifting for service] who confesses that Jesus Christ has come in the flesh is from God. But every spirit who does not confess Jesus is not from God. This is the spirit of the antichrist." (See also 2 John 7-11.)

Many of these first-century false teachers are itinerant "evangelists" who settle in communities that welcome and support them. John is adamant about such people: "[D]o not receive him into your home, and don't say, 'Welcome,' to him; for the one who says, 'Welcome,' to him shares in his evil works" (2 John 10b-11).

Modern travel and technology have changed the tactics, but not the stripes, of 21st century false teachers. They hold services in cavernous venues originally designed for sports. They produce self-help books that ride atop the best-seller lists in Christian bookstores. They peddle everything from anointing oil to survival kits on Christian television stations that are barely distinguishable from satellite shopping networks. They glean followers on Twitter and friends on Facebook, and parlay them into a frenzied army of loyal soldiers. All the while they fleece the flock rather than feed it (see 1 Peter 5:1-4). Satan always sows tares among the wheat and never fails to produce an odious bumper crop.

John MacArthur writes, "Although Jude's description of the apostates as *certain persons* is vague, their specific historical identity is not essential to his main point - namely, that any and all spiritual pretenders pose a clear and present danger to the church, whatever their error."[5]

Who might these false teachers be?

Still, the question persists: Who might these "certain persons" be? A few possibilities:

Gnostics. Although Gnosticism did not blossom fully until the second century, these interlopers may have fired "the opening shots in the fateful struggle between the Church and Gnosticism," according to J.N.D. Kelly, who sees "Gnostic colouring" in their libertinism and suspects they embraced Christological heresy.[6]

"Gnosticism was perhaps the most dangerous heresy that threatened the early church during the first three centuries," according to the popular Christian website gotquestions.org. Influenced by such philosophers as Plato, Gnosticism is based on two false premises:

1. A dualism of spirit (good) and matter (evil); therefore, anything done in the body, even the grossest sin, bears no true consequences because real life exists in the spirit realm only.

2. An elevated knowledge, a "higher truth" known only to select individuals. "Gnostics see themselves as a privileged class elevated above everybody else by their higher, deeper knowledge."[7]

No doubt this "secret knowledge" denies either the deity of Jesus or His full humanity, undermining His finished work on the cross and changing the gospel message.

Jude's reference to dreaming (v. 8) perhaps suggests that the false teachers claim to receive Gnostic dreams and visions. By reviling angelic powers, they demonstrate their rejection of the material world created by the Demiurge (a lesser god often seen as malevolent) since, in Gnostic thinking, angelic powers helped created the physical world.

Finally, Jude's mention of Cain (v. 11) may indicate the false teachers are part of the Gnostic Cainite sect that lived immorally.

Libertines. These sexually immoral people bow to no authority and recognize no moral absolutes. Jude exposes them as ungodly, promiscuous, doctrinally unstable, dreamers, defilers of the flesh, despisers of authority, blasphemers, brute beasts, and the list goes on. These false teachers, while offering little evidence of Gnostic Christology, nevertheless deny Christ's Lordship by the way they live. It's likely they revile angels, not because they feel superior to them, but because angels, as mediators of the law, uphold moral standards that confront their antinomian lifestyles.

They are, in some respects, the life of the church party. They show kindness to gain an edge, flatter to reduce opposition, and ply false humility to marshal support. They are all smoke and mirrors, writing checks no one may cash. Jude calls them waterless clouds, fruitless trees, wild waves of the sea, and wandering stars. When some discerning folk catch wind of their game, they quickly turn into discontented grumblers. Like the enemies of the cross Paul describes to the Philippians, "their god is their stomach; their glory is in their shame. They are focused on earthly things ..." (Phil. 3:19).

Pneumatics. These ecstatic seers claim to receive heavenly visions, thus they despise angels because they fancy themselves above them as spiritual elites. Just as the angels who sinned (v.6) breached their created boundaries to inhabit earth, the pneumatics, through ecstatic visions, try to transcend their created sphere of the physical realm to participate in the heavenly world. With a strong emphasis on grace and the Holy Spirit - but little spiritual maturity to match - they see themselves as exalted above angelic beings.

Judaizers. The term "Judaizer" is used in a theological sense to describe the opponents of Paul and Barnabus at the Jerusalem Council (Acts 15), as well as "false brothers smuggled in" to preach "another gospel" in the churches of Galatia (see Gal. 2:4, 12; 6:12). In this sense, the term refers to Jewish Christians who seek to induce Gentiles to observe Jewish religious customs, limiting the admission of Gentiles into the covenant people of God through circumcision and keeping the ceremonial law. Insisting that "Unless you are circumcised ... you cannot be saved!" (Acts 15:1), these professing believers, who belong to the party of the Pharisees (Acts 15:5), pose a serious threat to the gospel of grace and the universality of the Christian mission.

As R. David Rightmire explains, "Paul's Galatian epistle portrays the Judaizers as having come from the Jerusalem church to his churches in Galatia, stressing the need for Gentiles to be circumcised and keep the law, both for full acceptance by God (legalism) and as the basis for Christian living (nomism). They understood keeping the law not only as the means by which the blessings of the Abrahamic covenant could be appropriated, but also as the regulative guide for Christian life within that covenant relationship."[8]

Nicolaitans. Very little is known of this group apart from what we read in Rev. 2:6, 15. Jesus affirms the believers at Ephesus because they "hate the deeds of the Nicolaitans," which He also hates (*miseo* - to abhor or find utterly repulsive), although no further details are given. Meanwhile, Christ calls the church at Pergamum to repentance because some "hold fast to the teaching of the Nicolaitans." Here, an association with Balaam (Rev. 2:14) seems to connect the Nicolaitans with those who eat food sacrificed to idols and practice sexual immorality. These same behaviors reflect Jezebel's false teachings, described later in the letter to Thyatira (Rev. 2:20).

There are two main views concerning the Nicolaitans. The first view holds that they are an early Christian cult that either follows or perverts the teachings of Nicolas, one of the seven men chosen as deacons by the congregation in Acts 6:5. The second view understands the designation "Nicolaitan" as denoting the error of creating an unnatural distinction between the clergy and the laity. Those who hold the second view point out that the name "Nicolaitans" is derived from the Greek word *nikolaos*, a compound word that means "one who conquers and subdues the people."[9]

In any case, evidence from Scripture and early-church leaders indicates that the Nicolaitans teach a doctrine of compromise; that is, total separation between Christianity and paganism is not essential. "It is significant that the 'deeds' and 'doctrines' of the Nicolaitans are only mentioned in connection with the churches in these two occultic and pagan cities [Ephesus and Pergamum]. It seems that the 'doctrine' of the Nicolaitans was that it was alright to have one foot in both worlds and that one needn't be so strict about separation from the world in order to be a Christian. This, in fact, was the 'doctrine' of the Nicolaitans that Jesus 'hated.' It led to a weak version of Christianity that was without power and without conviction - a defeated, worldly type of Christianity."[10]

Wandering prophets or teachers. Jude describes the false teachers as having come in by stealth, implying they have hidden their true character and motives. It also indicates they are outsiders, perhaps wandering prophets or teachers. "They are surreptitious and crafty, pretending to be godly members of the Christian church. Paul, similarly, criticized the Judaizers who had infiltrated the ranks of the church to spy out and destroy the liberty of those committed to the gospel (Gal. 2:3-5)."[11]

We may never know with certainty which of these errant groups - Gnostics, libertines, pneumatics, Judaizers, Nicolaitans, or wandering prophets - Jude is describing. But the text gives us a clear picture of their attitudes, demeanors, lifestyles, and tactics. They are ungodly, sneaky, promiscuous, dismissive of authority, blasphemers, profiteers, self-centered, grumblers, arrogant, flatterers - and clearly unbelievers (v. 19).

This harks back to the words of Jesus in the Sermon on the Mount as He warns of false prophets, whom He describes as wolves in sheep's clothing. They may fool people for a while, but ultimately are known by their fruit - their doctrines and lifestyles. "Are grapes gathered from thornbushes or figs from thistles?" He asks. "In the same way, every good tree produces good fruit, but a bad tree produces bad fruit. A good tree can't produce bad fruit; neither can a bad tree produce good fruit. Every tree that doesn't produce good fruit is cut down and thrown into the fire. So you'll recognize them by their fruit" (Matt. 7:16-20).

Jude and his divine half-brother

A doctrinal gem often overlooked in Jude is a reference to the deity of Christ. In verse 4, Jude describes "certain men" who are guilty of "denying our Master and Lord, Jesus Christ." Immediately after this warning, he offers examples from Jewish history, beginning with the rebellion of the Israelites in the wilderness: "Now I want to remind you, though you know all these things: the Lord, having first of all saved a people out of Egypt, later destroyed those who did not believe" (v. 5).

Note that Jude calls Jesus "Lord" in verse 4, and then he refers to the "Lord" of the Israelites in the very next verse. The Lord who delivered the Israelites out of Egypt and then destroyed the apostates can be none other than the Lord Jesus.

In fact, many of the earliest manuscripts of Jude actually say "Jesus" instead of "the Lord" in verse 5, and this is most likely the original meaning. Several modern translations, including the New Living Translation (NLT), English Standard Version (ESV), and the NET Bible all refer to "Jesus" rather than "the Lord" in this passage.

Robert M. Bowman Jr. and J. Ed Komoszewski, in *Putting Jesus in His Place: The Case for the Deity of Christ*, write that three principles of textual criticism, when considered together, point to that conclusion.

First, all other things being equal, the earlier and more widely attested reading is to be preferred. In this case both "Lord" and "Jesus" are found in the earliest writings, but "Jesus" is more widely attested, especially among early translations of the New Testament into other languages such as Coptic, Ethiopic, and Latin.

Second, all other things being equal, the harder or more difficult reading - "the one that sounds the strangest, to put it crudely" - is more likely to be original. That's because a copyist is more likely to change a text from something that sounds strange to something that doesn't, rather than the other way around. This gives "Jesus" a decided edge over "the Lord," since it's strange to picture Jesus in the wilderness with the ancient Israelites.

Third, whatever reading is more likely to have given rise to the others as alterations is probably the original reading. Thus, "Jesus" is probably original because it's more likely that copyists would change "Jesus" (the more difficult reading) to "the Lord," but not the other way around.

Bowman and Komoszewski write, "According to Jude, the Lord Jesus not only existed during the time of the Exodus but was the one who both delivered Israel from Egypt and then destroyed the unbelieving Israelites in the wilderness."[12]

What are false teachers like?

Lastly, we should take note of how Jude summarizes the character traits of the false teachers who plague his beloved readers. In verse 4, he lists five such attributes.

First, they were designated for judgment long ago. The word "designated" in the Greek is *prographo* and means "to write beforehand" or "ordain," a reference no doubt to Enoch's prophecy (see vv. 14-15). This does not mean God fatalistically selects these false teachers and forces them to oppose the early church. Rather, in His sovereign foreknowledge, He writes out their death sentences in eternity past. He is fully aware that their determination to oppose His Son and His Son's Bride will not prevail. Further, He sets a day of reckoning for them before the great white throne, at which He confirms their desire to live independently of Him, and from which He sends them into the lake of fire (see Rev. 20:11-15).

While God has every right to create vessels of honor and of dishonor - and does so (Rom. 9:21) - this does not mean He crafts robot-like creatures to be wound up and set loose for pre-programmed good or evil. It seems more biblically faithful to see God creating us with a certain capacity for making choices for which He holds us responsible. The false teachers Jude writes about have so abandoned the wooing of God in creation, conscience, canon, and Christ that they have passed a point of no return. Thus, their future in outer darkness is fixed - not by God's lack of mercy or grace but by their continuous, willful rejection of His call to salvation.

Another way to look at it is that the false teachers themselves were predicted long ago, and thus their everlasting punishment was fixed by divine decree. Kenneth Wuest's translation of Jude renders this part of verse 4, "For certain men ... were of old predicted with reference to this judgment."[13]

Second, the false teachers have come in by stealth. Put another way, they have slipped in through an unlocked side door, feigning brotherhood, flattering God's people, eager to gain a hearing. But they are not in the church to become disciples of Christ; they are here to gain a foothold, an advantage. Their teachings are not so contrary to that of the apostles that they are rejected out of hand, but in tiny increments they twist the Scriptures so that their listeners are more comfortable with easy believism, sexual immorality, and the mingling of pagan practices until it's nearly impossible to separate truth from falsehood.

In a parallel passage, Peter says these false teachers "secretly bring in destructive heresies" (2 Peter 2:1). Paul writes that these interlopers - following Satan's lead - disguise themselves as ministers of righteousness (2 Cor. 11:13-15). The Greek *metaschematizo*, rendered "disguise" in the HCSB and "be transformed" in the KJV, "refers to the act of an individual changing his outward expression by assuming an expression put on from the outside, an expression that does not come from nor is it representative of what he is in his inner character."[14]

Third, the false teachers are ungodly. The Greek word is *asebes* and means "destitute of reverential awe of God." A careful examination of their lifestyles and teachings demonstrates that they are tares in God's wheat field (Matt. 13:24-30, 36-43), bad fish in the kingdom's dragnet (Matt. 13:47-50). Despite their apparent eloquence, persuasiveness, and attractiveness, they are whitewashed tombs, filled with vile doctrines and destructive lifestyles. The early church fathers use the term *asebes* to refer to atheists and heretics. In preparing his readers for "difficult times" to come, Paul warns of those who hold to the form of religion but deny its power (2 Tim. 3:1-5).

Fourth, they turn the grace of God into promiscuity. Also rendered "lasciviousness" (KJV), the Greek word *aselgeia* describes a person who "acknowledges no restraints, who dares whatever his caprice and wanton petulance may suggest."[15]

God's *charis* - His unmerited favor - offers us great freedom. We are no longer bound to the law, which only served as a school teacher to show us our depraved condition and need of a Savior. But these false teachers have twisted grace into a license to live immorally. They celebrate the words of Paul - "where sin multiplied, grace multiplied even more" - and thus advance the notion that deep sin helps plumb the depths of God's unfathomable grace, without heeding the apostle's follow up: "What should we say then? Should we continue in sin in order that grace may multiply? Absolutely not! How can we who died to sin still live in it?" (Rom. 5:20; 6:1-2). Nevertheless, the false teachers are well pleased to indulge their fleshly desires under "the tyranny of their unredeemed passions."[16]

Finally, these false teachers deny our only Master and Lord, Jesus Christ. By this, Jude probably does not mean these people are teaching "another Jesus" (2 Cor. 11:4) - that is, denying His deity or His full humanity, doubting the efficacy of His work on the cross, or redefining the meaning of His resurrection. More likely, Jude is describing the manner in which they throw off the authority of Christ over every facet of their lives.

Just as Jude describes himself as a "slave" of Jesus (v. 1), Christians likewise must recognize the Lordship of Christ - His authority not only as our Mediator and Intercessor at the Father's right hand, but His right to define an appropriate response to His grace, and His power to correct our bad behavior. The false teachers have decided

80

that Christians, being under grace, are free to call the shots in their lives, including the right to mingle sexual immorality and pagan practices with the disciple's daily walk.

The word for "Master" in this text is *despotes*, which speaks of one who is an absolute owner, wielding uncontrolled power over another. It is nearly always used of God the Father in the Greek New Testament, but here Jude applies *despotes* to Jesus, perhaps to underscore the fact that He is co-equal with the Father, and that all authority in heaven and on earth has been given to Him (Matt. 28:18; John 10:30).

John MacArthur writes of the false teachers, "Thus they deny Christ His rightful position as God (John 5:23), as King (Matt. 25:34; John 1:49-51; 12:13; 18:37), and as Messiah (Matt. 2:4-6; Mark 8:27-29; Luke 2:25-35; John 4:25-26). In so doing, they confirm that they are counterfeits; 'they profess to know God, but by their deeds they deny Him, being detestable and disobedient and worthless for any good deed' (Titus 1:16)."[17]

Jude's urgent wake-up call to his beloved readers is designed to signal the impending threat of slick, smooth-talking false teachers who by nature are crafty, ungodly, promiscuous, and unrepentant. Many in the church may be clueless, but the exalted Christ is fully aware of their devilish schemes. They won't get away with it, as Jude makes clear in the verses to come, reminding us of God's sovereign reach over human affairs and into the unseen realm.

Key words

In this chapter, we learned several key terms. Test your knowledge by filling in the blanks.

Gnostics. Gnosticism did not fully blossom until the second century, but false teachers in Jude's day may have fired the first Gnostic shots across the church's bow. Gnosticism is based on two false premises: (1) a dualism of _____ (good) and _____ (evil); and (2) an elevated _____, a "higher truth" known only to select individuals.

Libertines. These sexually immoral people bow to no _____ and recognize no moral _____.

Judaizers. The term refers to Jewish Christians who seek to induce Gentiles to observe Jewish _____ customs, limiting the admission of Gentiles into the covenant people of God through _____ and keeping the _____ law.

Promiscuity. Rendered "lasciviousness" in the KJV, the Greek word *aselgeia* describes a person who acknowledges no _____, an apt description of the false teachers of whom Jude writes.

Comparing English translations of *aselgeia*:

HCSB	KJV	NIV	NASB	ESV
Promiscuity	Lasciviousness	License for immorality	Licentiousness	Sensuality

Application
Questions for personal or group study

1. How might you respond to the following views:
   - The natural world is all there is; the idea of gods, angelic beings, and the human soul is nothing more than a byproduct of the brain's chemical and electrical processes.
   - Men may attain deity, in part, by participating in secret temple rituals.
   - There is a difference between sinning in my spirit and sinning in my flesh.
   - Under grace, I can pretty much do whatever I want; if I cross the line, I just claim 1 John 1:9.
   - God is not finished speaking to us; every so often, He sends anointed prophets to reveal new truth that is added to the ever-expanding Scriptures.
   - My religion's leader is accountable only to God; when he speaks, God speaks.

2. A friend insists that she has acquired a secret knowledge of God, enabling her to discern whether people are saved, called to Christian service, possessed by demons, or guilty of crimes. She is causing quite a stir in your church as she confronts individuals with "messages from God." What should you do?

3. Read Rom. 5:18 - 6:23. How does the apostle Paul build a case for salvation by grace without making it a license to sin?

4. What are some warning signs that a popular television evangelist might be a modern-day Nicolaitan - someone comfortable mixing the wisdom of the world with the doctrines of Scripture?

5. Over coffee with a friend, you criticize a best-selling Christian author for teaching that people can't go to heaven unless they believe Jesus suffered for them in hell. Your friend whips out his iPhone, punches up the Bible app, and reads out loud

Matt. 7:1, "Do not judge, so that you won't be judged." He then stares at you, waiting for your response. What do you say?

6. How might you discuss Jude's statement that "certain men ... were designated for this judgment long ago" (v. 4)? What are some ways to explore the tension that exists in Scripture between the sovereignty of God and the free will of people?

7. From the pulpit, your pastor calls out a nationally televised Christian speaker who promotes the prosperity gospel. After the service, you overhear a church member say to the pastor, "You didn't follow the Matthew 18 model. You should have gone to this Christian speaker privately, and then with two or three others, before making your views public." Do you agree with this person? Why or why not?

7

The Lessons of History:
Remembering the Past
to Defend the Faith

Now I want to remind you, though you know all these things: the Lord, having first of all saved a people out of Egypt, later destroyed those who did not believe; and He has kept, with eternal chains in darkness for the judgment of the great day, angels who did not keep their own position but deserted their proper dwelling. In the same way, Sodom and Gomorrah and the cities around them committed sexual immorality and practiced perversions, just as they did, and serve as an example by undergoing the punishment of eternal fire. (Jude 5-7)

In *The Life of Reason, Vol. 1* (1905-06), George Santayana famously wrote, "Those who cannot remember the past are condemned to repeat it."[1] Many others have fashioned their own versions of this quip to make the point that our past does not have to determine our future - as long as we're careful to learn the lessons of history.

Not everyone agrees. Author Kurt Vonnegut once offered this pithy response, "I've got news for Mr. Santayana: we're doomed to repeat the past no matter what. That's what it is to be alive."[2]

Both men have a point. Santayana implores us to learn from past mistakes, while Vonnegut reminds us that the depths of human depravity virtually guarantee that, if given the chance, we'll repeat the same bad choices.

The Bible speaks to both sides of the issue. God and His servants often instruct us in Scripture to remember. Moses tells the Israelites to remember their slavery in Egypt, and God's mighty deliverance with a strong hand and an outstretched arm (Deut. 5:15). Jesus instructs the apostles to observe the Lord's Supper - particularly the symbolism of the bread and cup - in remembrance of Him (Luke 22:19). And in visiting the church at Ephesus - a hard-working congregation whose members have cooled in their passion for Christ - Jesus urges them to remember how far they have fallen (Rev. 2:5).

Other passages could be cited, but the point remains that remembering the goodness of God, and rehearsing the acts of obedience He has given us to honor Him, lead to blessings, while neglecting the things of God invariably results in a downward spiral of sinful patterns.

Having introduced himself, and having stated the reason for his urgent letter, Jude offers three lessons from history to remind his readers that wickedness leads inescapably to God's wrath. Jude selects examples involving Jews, Gentiles, and the angelic host. In a similar passage, Peter refers to fallen angels, Noah, and Lot, laying out the stories of their encounters with God's justice in historical order (2 Peter 2:4-10).

Jude's version is not chronological, perhaps because he seeks to establish a pattern of descending ungodliness. He begins with an example of unbelief, then disobedience, and finally depravity. In some ways, it's similar to Paul's message in Romans 1, where the rejection of God's self-revelation is followed by the exaltation of substitute objects of worship, and ultimately ends in a complete loss of moral convictions.

In this chapter, we examine the examples Jude offers from ancient Israel and Sodom and Gomorrah. In the next chapter, we take a closer look at the story of rebellious angels.

Why does God save some people only to destroy them?

Jude begins with the words, "Now I want to remind you," and follows with, "though you know all these things." This suggests that Jude's initial readers are Jews. At the very least, they are well acquainted with God's dealings with Israel stretching back to the days of Abraham.

Jude begins with a history lesson from the desert. After watching His people endure more than four centuries of slavery, God delivers the Israelites out of bondage, convincing pharaoh, through Moses, to let His people go free after mighty displays of divine power. The Lord then parts the Red Sea after pharaoh - who decides it's not such a good idea after all to send cheap migrant labor away - pursues the escaping Israelites. God manifests His presence as a pillar of cloud by day and a pillar of fire by night, providing a wall of separation between His people and pharaoh's army. He provides food and water in the wilderness, makes sure the people's shoes don't wear out, and commissions twelve spies to scope out the Promised Land.

When the spies return and confirm that Canaan is a land flowing with milk and honey, but also is populated by strong adversaries, the people lose heart. Siding with the ten spies who bring a fearful report, they refuse to enter the land, forgetting so quickly God's miraculous provision, and doubting that the God who defeated the gods of Egypt can now deliver them from mortal men. "This was apostasy, sinning with eyes wide open, and could only be dealt with by the infliction of the death penalty. That generation died a physical death in the wilderness."[3]

The apostle Paul shares a similar message in his first letter to Corinth: "Now I want you to know, brothers, that our fathers were all under the cloud, all passed through the sea, and all were baptized into Moses in the cloud and in the sea. They all ate the same spiritual food, and all drank the same spiritual drink. For they drank from a spiritual rock that followed them, and that rock was Christ. But God was not pleased with most of them, for they were struck down in the desert. Now these things became examples for us, so that we will not desire evil as they did" (1 Cor. 10:1-6).

Interestingly, Paul follows these words with exhortations that match Jude's warnings about the influence of false teachers:

- "Let us not commit sexual immorality ..." (1 Cor. 10:8). Compare this with Jude's warnings about those who practice "promiscuity" (v. 4), "defile their flesh" (v. 8), perform "shameful deeds" (v. 13), and walk "according to their desires" (v. 16).

- "Let us not tempt Christ ..." (1 Cor. 10:9). Compare this with Jude's description of false teachers who deny "our only Master and Lord, Jesus Christ" (v. 4), "despise authority, and blaspheme glorious beings" (v. 8).

- "Nor should we complain ..." (1 Cor. 10:10). Consider this alongside Jude's depiction of the interlopers as "discontented grumblers" (v. 16).

The writer of Hebrews also uses the experiences of ancient Israel to warn his Jewish audience against the perils of unbelief. Consider his words in light of Jude's call to remembrance: "Watch out, brothers, so that there won't be in any of you an evil, unbelieving heart that departs from the living God. But encourage each other daily, while it is still called today, so that none of you is hardened by sin's deception.... For who heard and rebelled? Wasn't it really all who came out of Egypt under Moses? And with whom was He 'provoked for 40 years'? Was it not with those who sinned, whose bodies fell in the desert? And to whom did He 'swear that they would not enter His rest,' if not those who disobeyed? So we see that they were unable to enter because of unbelief" (Heb. 3:12-13, 16-19).

Jude is well aware that his readers know this story, and he seeks to connect the apostates in the desert with the false teachers in the church. Hanging out with God's people doesn't make you a citizen of His kingdom any more than swimming in the Amazon River makes you a pink dolphin. Those who fell in the desert are Israelites by lineage, but not by faith, just as the apostle Paul declares, "For not all who are descended from Israel are Israel" (Rom. 9:6).

In Numbers 14, the Lord speaks to Moses and Aaron, asking how long He should endure this wicked generation of grumblers. He has heard the complaints of His people and has measured their hard-hearted response to His miraculous provision. So, several times He declares that the corpses of unbelievers 20 years and older will fall in the wilderness, and after 40 years of wandering, the younger generation, along with the older faithful, will enter the Promised Land. God declares a penalty of 40 years, one year for each day that the spies are in the Promised Land. Of the twelve spies, only Joshua and Caleb, who bring good reports, are spared.

Like the ancient Israelites, the church is the recipient of God's grace. Many in the first-century church have heard first-hand the apostles' eyewitness accounts of the crucified and risen Christ. Many have witnessed the apostles' miracles and experienced their authoritative teaching. And yet, like the unbelieving spies who accompanied Joshua and Caleb into the land of milk and honey, they follow only their own selfish desires, fall prey to their fears borne of unbelief, and reject the truth.

Surely, the false teachers of Jude's day realize that God will not tolerate their wickedness. Though He always saves a remnant, He destroys those who seek to poison the well with their unrestrained ways and corrupt doctrines. The grumbling, unbelieving Israelites fall in the wilderness, their corpses a reminder of the severity of their sin. In like manner, Jude wants his readers to know that God will judge the false teachers who worm their way into the hearts of the first-century faithful.

Warren Wiersbe shares a word of keen insight: "Keep in mind that Jude was using a historical event as an illustration, and we must not press every detail. The entire nation was delivered from Egypt, but that does not mean that each individual was personally saved through faith in the Lord. The main point of the account is that privileges bring responsibilities, and God cannot lightly pass over the sins of His people. If any of Jude's readers dared to follow the false teachers, they too would face the discipline of God."[4]

Next, Jude focuses on "angels who did not keep their own position but deserted their proper dwelling" (v. 6b). We are saving our inquiry into this curious group of wicked spirits for the next chapter. For now, let's travel to Sodom.

What is the sin of Sodom?

Jude writes that "Sodom and Gomorrah and the cities around them committed sexual immorality and practiced perversions ... and serve as an example by undergoing the punishment of eternal fire" (v. 7). In this, the third lesson from history, Jude completes the illustration of the progressive nature of sin: unbelief leads to rebellion, which ultimately gives way to depravity. Perhaps no place in history is more readily identified with debauched behavior than Sodom (not to neglect its nasty neighbor, Gomorrah, or the surrounding communities[5]). From the red-light district of De Wallen in Amsterdam to the Strip in Las Vegas, no modern-day place on earth holds a candle to the ancient flesh pot on the plains of Canaan.

Before the destruction of these cities, Moses favorably describes the area as fertile - a good place to raise crops and animals (Gen. 13:10). But God's wrath against the sinful inhabitants is so severe that the cities are reduced to ashes. In fact, God's judgment is so complete that the ruins remain undiscovered, and the cities' precise location is yet in doubt. It's possible, but not proven, that the ruins lie beneath what is now the mineral-dense water in the southern portion of the Dead Sea.[6]

The Lord's judgment not only buries the bodies of the wicked beneath the ashes; it plunges their souls into everlasting punishment - in part, as a dire warning to future generations that unrepentant depravity leads to an unmitigated divine response. Jude wishes to remind his readers that the false teachers who have infiltrated the church possess the same depraved nature as the Sodomites and will share the same fate - everlasting punishment in hell.

But what, exactly, is the sin of Sodom and Gomorrah? Jude seems quite clear that they engage in sexual immorality and practice perversions - particularly homosexuality. Yet some recent commentators argue that the Sodomites, though a salty bunch, are falsely accused and badly misunderstood.

Admittedly, sexual sin is not their only sin. Ezekiel says they also are punished for pride and a lack of concern for the poor (Ezek. 16:49). The Apocryphal books of Sirach and 3 Maccabees mention their arrogance and injustice (Sir. 16:8; 3 Macc. 2:5). And Josephus criticizes Sodom for its pride and hatred of foreigners (*Antiquities of the Jews* 1.194).

But Jude focuses on Sodom's "sexual immorality" and "perversions" (*sarkos heteras*, v. 7). The Greek literally says they "went after other flesh," which "refers to a desire for those of the same sex; they desired flesh other than that of women."[7]

Let's take a closer look at the story, which is found in Genesis 13-19. Here, we find that God destroys Sodom and Gomorrah because of the people's wickedness, expressed most egregiously in their homosexual behavior. Jews and Christians traditionally have understood the story of Sodom and Gomorrah to speak directly to the issue of homosexuality - revisionist explanations of this passage notwithstanding.

Gen. 13:13 tells us, "Now the men of Sodom were evil, sinning greatly against the Lord." When two angels and the Lord Himself visit Abram, the Lord says, "The outcry against Sodom and Gomorrah is immense, and their sin is extremely serious" (Gen. 18:20). Their sin clearly is homosexual behavior, for they surround Lot's house and demand that his guests be given to them so they may "have sex with them!" (Gen. 19:5). Lot implores the men, "Don't do this evil, my brothers" (v. 7), and he takes the extraordinary step of offering his two virgin daughters to them, if they only abandon their intent for the three guests under his roof.

Other references to these two cities cast them in the light of grievous, unrepentant sin. In a parallel passage to Jude 7, for example, Peter describes "the unrestrained behavior of the immoral" (2 Peter 2:7). The depiction of the "men" of Sodom surrounding Lot's house shows that the entire populace is corrupt. The "whole population" - young and old, and from every quarter - is engaged in this immoral practice (Gen. 19:4). For this sin, the Lord destroys the cities in an act of divine judgment.

Not so fast, say some commentators, who wish to defend the citizens of Sodom against what they perceive as false charges. The most common objection to the plain reading of the text is the interpretation that the sin of Sodom is primarily inhospitality, not same-sex behavior. Proponents of this view often cite Ezek. 16:48-49 to say that the sin of the Sodomites is their refusal to take in needy travelers.

No doubt the men of Sodom are unsociable rascals, but reading the next verse changes the perspective: "They were haughty and did detestable things before Me, so I removed them when I saw this" (Ezek. 16:50). The word "detestable" - or "abomination" in other translations - brings us back to Leviticus, specifically Lev. 18:22 and Lev. 20:13, where homosexual conduct is in view.

Another challenge is that the use of the word *yada* - translated "know" in the KJV and ESV - does not necessarily refer to homosexual conduct. It's true that the word *yada* appears numerous times in the Bible and normally refers to knowing factual information, but at times *yada* plainly means to know someone intimately in a sexual fashion.

For example, in Gen. 4:1 Adam "knew Eve his wife; and she conceived ..." (KJV). Further, a look at Judges 19:22-25 offers a close parallel to the story of Lot in Sodom. Certain "perverted men of the city" surround the home where two guests have been taken in, demanding, "Bring out the man who came to your house so we can have sex (*yada*) with him!" (v. 22). The homeowner describes their intent as "evil" and "horrible" (v. 23), and he offers his virgin daughter and the guest's concubine in exchange. The men take the concubine, rape (*yada*) her and abuse her all night (v. 25). The context determines the correct understanding of the word *yada*.

A third challenge is that Jesus mentions Sodom and Gomorrah but does not connect the cities with homosexuality. It's true that in Matt. 10:14-15, as Jesus commissions the twelve disciples, He does not specifically refer to any sin for which the residents of the cities are guilty. His exact words are, "If anyone will not welcome you or listen to your words, shake the dust off your feet when you leave that house or town. I assure you: It will be more tolerable on the day of judgment for the land of Sodom and Gomorrah than for that town."

As James White and Jeffrey Niell explain, "Sodom's judgment had become axiomatic for the fullest outpouring of God's wrath throughout the Old Testament.... The issue is that these cities will be held accountable to God for their grievous sins. And the comparison is that it will be more tolerable for Sodom and Gomorrah in that day than for those cities that had experienced the visitation of the very apostles of the incarnate Lord, but refused their message of repentance and faith."[8]

92

A final challenge is that the story of Sodom and Gomorrah is not germane to the same-sex debate because it does not address loving, monogamous relationships. It only rails against homosexual gang rape and violence. Even if that were the case, it begs the question of what the Bible says, if anything, about loving, monogamous same-sex relationships. Again, White and Niell are helpful: "To call a relationship 'loving' in a Biblical sense means it is in accordance with God's will and is fulfilling His purpose, resulting in His glory."[9] The Bible speaks positively of loving, monogamous, lifelong relationships between a man and a woman, but never of two women or two men.

So, the sin of Sodom and Gomorrah and the cities around them clearly is that of unrepentant same-sex behavior, which leads to "the punishment of eternal fire" (Jude 7b). Jude tells us not only that these cities are destroyed and their inhabitants killed, but that the punishment of the wicked is everlasting, not temporal. Further, he writes, this story serves as an example to us of the consequences of grievous sin.

Seven biblical truths about same-sex attraction

Does that mean homosexuality is an unpardonable sin? Do all people who engage in same-sex behavior inevitably find themselves in hell? We should consider several biblical truths that help us formulate a response to our friends struggling with same-sex attraction.[10]

First, the Bible condemns all forms of sexual behavior outside the bonds of heterosexual, monogamous, life-long marriage. Homosexuality is not a special class of sin that makes it any more or less an act of rebellion against God than premarital sex, adultery, polygamy, polyandry, pornography, or other sexual sins. We do injustice to God's Word, and to those struggling with same-sex attraction, when we make homosexual conduct a special class of sin.

Second, God has spoken clearly. The Bible never speaks of homosexuality in a positive - or even a neutral - light. Sexual relations between members of the same gender are always depicted as sinful in Scripture. The Bible describes such conduct as "an abomination," "degrading," "unnatural," "shameless," and a "perversion." Those who commit same-sex acts, refuse to acknowledge them as sinful, and reject the call to repentance, are outside the kingdom of God.

Third, God's creative intent for sexual relations is good. God created us male and female, and He designed a unique, complementary sexual union between us in the bonds of heterosexual, monogamous, life-long marriage. Summarizing the 2,000-year-old Christian narrative on sexuality and marriage, Pascal-Emmanuel Gobry writes, "The sexual act is meant to reflect God's love by fostering a union at once bodily and spiritual - and creates new life.... The fruitfulness of the marriage act reflects that God is a creator and has charged man to be an agent of his ongoing work of creation. And, finally, if God's love means total self-giving unto death on a Cross, then man and wife must give themselves to each other totally - no pettiness, no adultery, no polygamy, no divorce, and no nonmarital sexual acts."[11]

Genesis 1-2 establishes at least seven norms for marriage: Marriage is covenantal, sexual, procreative, heterosexual, monogamous, non-incestuous, and symbolic of the gospel, according to Denny Burk in *What is the Meaning of Sex?*[12]

Fourth, Jesus affirms Old Testament teachings about sexuality and marriage. Matt. 19:1-12 is instructive. The Pharisees confront Jesus after He crosses over the Jordan into Judea, and they ask, "Is it lawful for a man to divorce his wife on any grounds?"

Rather than debate the lawfulness of failed marriages, Jesus takes the religious leaders back to the Garden of Eden. "Haven't you read," He replies, "that He who created them in the beginning made them male and female ... For this reason a man will leave his father and mother and be joined to his wife, and the two will become one flesh? So they are no longer two, but one flesh. Therefore what God has joined together, man must not separate."

The Pharisees respond, "Why then did Moses command us to give divorce papers and to send her away?" Jesus tells them, "Moses permitted [not commanded] you to divorce your wives because of the hardness of your hearts. But it was not like that from the beginning."

Clearly, the Lord has not changed His reasons for creating men and women, nor has His divine accommodation (allowing divorce under terms of the Mosaic Law) lowered His standards for sexual purity and marriage. There is no divine accommodation for homosexual conduct.

Fifth, Christians share with our homosexual friends a struggle against sinful desires. Everyone is born with "original sin" - a natural tendency to live independently of God. When we act upon fleshly desires, we violate God's holy standards and are in need of His saving grace. The apostle Paul, quoting from the Psalms, reminds us, "There is no one righteous, not even one; there is no one who understands, there is no one who seeks God. All have turned away, together they have become useless; there is no one who does good, there is not even one" (Rom. 3:10-12).

Paul further reminds us in Rom. 3:23, "For all have sinned and fall short of the glory of God." He then points out both the consequences of our sin and the remedy, "For the wages of sin is death, but the gift of God is eternal life in Christ Jesus our Lord" (Rom. 6:23). Paul even calls himself chief among sinners (1 Tim. 1:15 KJV).

Christians are far from perfect. We struggle with sins like lust, anger, lying, selfishness, arrogance, and all other ways people rebel against their Creator. Remembering our sinful tendencies helps us see the sins of other people in a more accurate and gracious light. Yes, Christians have the Holy Spirit who dwells within us and gives us power over sin. But we often give in to our fleshly desires - and even make such excuses as, "I can't help it," or, "I've always had this weakness." Perhaps the reminder of the beams in our own eyes helps us deal more gently with those suffering from a speck of dust in theirs. This commonality with our gay and lesbian friends makes us vulnerable, but also more genuine and compassionate.

Sixth, people can change. Paul makes this clear in 1 Cor. 6:9-11. He begins with a negative: "Do you not know that the unjust will not inherit God's kingdom? Do not be deceived: no sexually immoral people, idolaters, adulterers, male prostitutes, homosexuals, thieves, greedy people, drunkards, revilers, or swindlers will inherit God's kingdom." Then, he reminds his fellow believers, "Some of you were like this; but you were washed, you were sanctified, you were justified in the name of the Lord Jesus Christ and by the Spirit of our God."

The evidence indicates that same-sex attraction typically is discovered early in life and involves a combination of biological, psychological, and environmental factors, and that it tends to stay with people for a lifetime.[13] In other words, an individual with same-sex attraction likely will struggle with that throughout his or her lifetime. The difference is that the One who resides in followers of Jesus - that is, the Holy Spirit - is greater than the one who is in the world.

God gives His own the ability to overcome even the strongest sinful urges. Numerous testimonies by formerly gay individuals, and by Christians who acknowledge same-sex attraction but remain celibate, serve as a witness to the transforming power of Christ. How do we challenge self-defined "gay Christians" to reshape their identity with the gospel? Despite our culture's view, sexual gratification is not a sacrament, and celibacy is not a fate worse than death. Sexual abstinence can promote a life "devoted to the Lord without distraction" (1 Cor. 7:35).

Seventh, we should welcome into our churches those struggling with same-sex attraction. This does not mean that those living unrepentant, openly gay lifestyles should be received as members, or should play any role in the leadership of the church. But it does mean that the church should be a safe place for anyone struggling with same-sex attraction to have a candid, caring conversation.

We should not deny church membership to those who confess same-sex attraction, and who agree that same-sex lust and conduct are sinful, and who seek to overcome these sinful desires and behaviors by the power of God and the accountability of a community of fellow believers. Would we not afford the same consideration to those struggling with heterosexual lust, gossip, pride, or gluttony?

At the same time, we need to be consistent in our stand on biblical conduct and church discipline. For two people living together outside of marriage, or engaged in adultery, or any other activity the Bible clearly condemns, we need to follow the pattern of church discipline Jesus lays out in Matthew 18 and we see exemplified in other passages of Scripture.

As we seek to minister to our gay and lesbian friends, it's important to draw a distinction between the *temptation* known as unwanted same-sex attraction, which is not a sin, and same-sex lusts and behaviors, which the Bible always characterizes as sinful. Every human being struggles with what the apostle Paul calls the flesh - the tarnished image of God warring against God's Word and, for the believer, against God's indwelling Spirit.

We should explore what God has to say about sex and marriage; they're both good, by the way. We should rejoice in God's creative design, earnestly pursue personal holiness, vigorously contend for the faith, and love those who experience same-sex attractions, whether they celebrate these attractions or acknowledge them as foreign to the will of God.

Serving as an example

As we close this chapter, it's important to remember that Jude's reference to ancient Israelites, fallen angels, and Sodomites is to "serve as an example" (v. 7b). The false teachers who have wormed their way into the church are not necessarily guilty of exactly the same sins, particularly with respect to homosexuality. But they most certainly demonstrate the same depravity as their predecessors: unbelief, violating the boundaries God established for angels and humans, and engaging in licentious behavior. Jude's reminder of the past points to what God will do to the unrepentant wicked in the future.

As Thomas R. Schreiner cautions, "We must also be aware of overinterpreting the examples Jude presented of judgment in the past. Surely Jude was not implying that the opponents [false teachers] had sexual intercourse with angelic beings (v. 6). Nor was he necessarily implying that they engaged in homosexual activity. His purpose was to emphasize that those who sin are judged, not to say that the opponents had committed the same sins as their predecessors. It is likely, however, that the intruders were guilty of sexual sin, as we will see in subsequent verses."[14]

Key words

In this chapter, we learned several key terms. Test your knowledge by filling in the blanks.

In the same way. Jude wants his readers to remember that God does not tolerate wickedness indefinitely, so he offers three historical examples of the limits of God's patience: (1) Jewish unbelievers who fell in the _____ after God delivered them from Egypt; (2) angels who did not keep their own position but deserted their proper _____; and (3) the citizens of Sodom and Gomorrah, who committed sexual immorality and practiced _____.

Know. The Hebrew word *yada* appears numerous times in the Bible and normally refers to knowing _____ information, but at times *yada* plainly means to know someone intimately in a _____ fashion. The _____ determines the correct understanding of the word *yada*.

Comparing English translations of *yada* in Gen. 19:5:

HCSB	KJV	NIV	NASB	ESV
have sex	know	have sex	have relations	know

Serve as an example. Jude's reference to ancient _____, fallen angels, and Sodomites is to "serve as an example" (v. 7b). The false teachers who have wormed their way into the church are not necessarily _____ of exactly the same sins, but they most certainly demonstrate the same _____ as their predecessors: unbelief, violating the _____ God established for angels and humans, and engaging in _____ behavior. Jude's reminder of the past points to what God will do to the unrepentant _____ in the future.

98

Comparing English translations of *sarkos heteras* in Jude 7:

HCSB	KJV	NIV	NASB	ESV
Perversions	Strange flesh	Perversion	Strange (or other) flesh	Unnatural desire

Application
Questions for personal or group study

1. Jude reminds us that God deals decisively with wicked men and fallen angels. But He does it on His time schedule. Read Num. 14:26-38. Why do you think God lets the wicked die in the wilderness over a period of 40 years? Why doesn't He just strike them dead on the spot as He does the firstborn in Egypt (Ex. 12:29-30); 185,000 Assyrians encamped against Jerusalem (2 Kings 19:35); and Ananias and Sapphira in the early church (Acts 5:5, 10)?

2. In what ways are Jude's lessons from history meant both to warn us and to assure us?

3. How are false teachers in the church similar to the unbelieving Israelites who fell in the desert? The citizens of Sodom and Gomorrah?

4. What would you say to the person who argues that the sin of Sodom was inhospitality, not homosexuality? How would you counter the claim that Jesus never addressed the issue of same-sex behavior? Why is it false to state that the Bible condemns only violent or promiscuous same-sex behavior, not loving, monogamous homosexual and lesbian relationships?

5. Your pastor receives a phone call from a person claiming to be a "gay Christian," who plans to attend worship services this Sunday at your church. What questions would you advise the pastor to ask the visitor in order to offer discerning counsel to the "gay Christian" and to your church?

6. Do you think the false teachers about whom Jude writes are engaged in homosexual behavior? If not, why might Jude compare them to the wicked men of Sodom?

7. Think back over the last 200 years of church history (or even the last 20). Can you recall some prominent church leaders whose lifestyles match that of the ancient Israelites or the citizens of Sodom? How do their actions - and the consequences of their actions - serve as a reminder to us today?

8

Kept, with Eternal Chains:
When Angels Desert

... and He has kept, with eternal chains in darkness for the judgment of the great day, angels who did not keep their own position but deserted their proper dwelling.
(Jude 6)

In a scene from the 1971 film *Fiddler on the Roof*, a Jewish peasant named Tevye, living in prerevolutionary Russia, mulls over the prospect of his daughter, Tzeitel, marrying an impoverished tailor, Motel. He watches the starry-eyed young couple from a distance, alternately scratches his neck and strokes his beard, and says to himself:

"He is beginning to talk like a man. On the other hand, what kind of a match would that be, with a poor tailor? On the other hand, he's an honest, hard worker. But on the other hand, he has absolutely nothing. On the other hand, things could never get worse for him; they could only be better."[1]

"On the other hand" is Tevye's way of expressing his uncertainty about the outcome of his daughter's romance. Verbally, he weighs the evidence for and against his beloved Tzeitel's happiness.

As we explore Jude 6, we may need a little of Tevye's humble uncertainty about what lies before us, because the author's reference to a particular class of angels has left biblical scholars scratching their necks (or more likely their heads) and stroking their beards for centuries. At the same time, Jude's story of fallen angels offers an opportunity to hone our apologist's skills in dealing with difficult passages of Scripture.

Who are these angels?

The identity of the "angels who did not keep their own position but deserted their proper dwelling" is a matter of much debate. While many views have emerged over the centuries, two seem to be most popular - and both views are tied, at least in part, to Gen. 6:1-4, and to a lesser extent the apocryphal Book of Enoch.[2]

It should be noted that Jude is calling his readers to remember what they already have learned: lessons from the past with respect to God's judgment on the Israelites, the citizens of Sodom and Gomorrah, and certain fallen angels (vv. 5-7). So, Jude offers few details, but we may rest assured that his audience is familiar with the texts from the Torah and, perhaps, the Apocrypha.

Let's begin with the text in Genesis 6: "When mankind began to multiply on the earth and daughters were born to them, the sons of God saw that the daughters of man were beautiful, and they took any they chose as wives for themselves. And the Lord said, 'My Spirit will not remain with mankind forever, because they are corrupt. Their days will be 120 years.' The Nephilim [perhaps 'fallen ones' or 'giants;' the meaning here is uncertain] were on the earth both in those days and afterwards, when the sons of God came to the daughters of man, who bore children to them. They were the powerful men of old, the famous men" (vv. 1-4).

Cohabitating angels

One popular interpretation of Jude's reference to angels ties directly to Gen. 6:1-4, where the "sons of God" are identified as rebellious angels who cohabitate with the "daughters of man," producing a race of giants God destroys in the great flood. Proponents of this view generally note the following:

1. Jewish tradition links together the sin of angels in Gen. 6:1-4, the judgment of Sodom and Gomorrah, and the judgment of the wilderness generation. For example, the Testament of Naphtali 3:4-5 designates the angels of Genesis 6 as "Watchers" who have "departed nature's order" and thus are cursed with the flood. Jubilees teaches that the Watchers sinned sexually with the daughters of men (Jub. 4:22). And the Book of Enoch offers an extensive depiction of these evil angels fornicating with women (1 Enoch 10:11).[3]

2. Based on Jude 14-15, where the author references a prophecy of Enoch, we may conclude that Jude is familiar with 1 Enoch and is influenced by it. The book details the angels' sexual sin and punishment. For example, the angel Raphael is ordered to "'Bind Azaz'el hand and foot (and) throw him into the darkness!' And he made a hole in the desert which was in Duda'el and cast him there; he threw on top of him rugged and sharp rocks. And he covered his face in order that he may not see light; and in order that he may be sent into the fire on the great day of judgment."[4]

3. Jude draws a parallel between the sin of Sodom and Gomorrah and the rebellion of deserting angels. Verse 7 begins, "*In the same way*, Sodom and Gomorrah … committed sexual immorality and practiced perversions" (emphasis added). Therefore, it seems clear that sexual sin is prominent in both instances.

Angels breaking rank

Proponents of the second popular view contend that the angels' sin is one of breaking rank, not cohabitating with women. Instead of being content with the dignity assigned them under their Creator (Jesus), they aspire to higher ranks and thus rebel, meddling directly in human affairs. Supporters of this position posit the following:

1. If Jude is referring to Gen. 6:1-4, he is not accusing angels of sexual sin. In fact, he may not have this passage in mind at all. Warren Wiersbe summarizes, "The simplest explanation of Genesis 6 is that the godly line of Seth ('the sons of God') began to mingle with the ungodly line of Cain, and this broke down the walls of separation, resulting in compromise and eventually degrading sin."[5]

2. Angels are a different class of creature than human beings. They are greater in power and intelligence, but they lack physical bodies. In the Old Testament, angels sometimes appear in human form (see Genesis 18-19), but there is no evidence they actually take on flesh and blood.[6]

3. Angels do not have sexual intercourse. Jesus makes this clear in His rebuttal of the Sadducees' arguments against the resurrection (Matt. 22:30). While angels appear anatomically as men on the earth, and even partake of food, there is no biblical evidence that God created them with the ability to reproduce.

4. God sent the flood because of *man's* wickedness, not angelic mischief. "My Spirit will not remain with mankind forever … When the Lord saw that man's wickedness was widespread on the earth and that every scheme his mind thought of was nothing but evil all the time, the Lord regretted that He had made man on the earth, and He was grieved in His heart" (Gen. 6:3, 5-6).

5. The phrase, "In the same way, Sodom and Gomorrah …" (Jude 7), does not necessarily mean the angels sinned *in the same way* (sexually) as the citizens of Lot's city. Another way to understand this phrase is that God's judgment of rebellious angels is the same sort of judgment He brings to bear on Sodom and Gomorrah.

6. Therefore, it makes more sense to conclude that the angels to which Jude refers are guilty of leaving their heavenly dwelling, despising the limits of their assigned authority, and engaging in wicked, but non-sexual, activities with humans created in the image of God. For breaking rank, they are kept with eternal chains in darkness.

There you have it: two sides of the debate over the identity of the angels who "deserted their proper dwelling" (v. 6). Which of these two positions better matches the biblical narrative? When we get to the Application at the end of the chapter, we'll explore some ways to approach this debate.

Another alternative?

But before moving on, let's go back to Gen. 6:1-4. Let's assume that Jude is referring to this passage from the Torah (it seems a more familiar reference to his readers than 1 Enoch but doesn't rule it out). And let's consider the possibility that the "sons of God" are neither angels engaging directly in sexual relations with women, nor the godly line of Seth.

A third option has much to commend it. What if, by "sons of God," Moses is referring to demons who possess powerful earthly rulers determined to engage in widespread mischief? Wouldn't this fit well with Jude's lessons from history - the unbelieving Israelites, and the wicked men of Sodom and Gomorrah - not to mention the context of Genesis 6?

Perhaps Jude is describing angels who violate their assigned sphere of authority and thus incur divine punishment, just as the false teachers in Jude's day are attracting divine retribution. In other words, what if Jude is not suggesting that the sin of these fallen angels is fornicating with women (although 1 Enoch reports such behavior)? Rather, what if the angels are determined to transcend their lofty rank as angelic beings, thus rejecting their created position in much the same way the Sodomites rejected the natural distinctions between men and women?

Allen Ross, in his commentary on Genesis, describes the sons of God in Gen. 6:1-4 "probably ... [as] powerful rulers who were controlled (indwelt) by fallen angels. It may be that fallen angels left their habitation and inhabited bodies of human despot warriors, the mighty ones of the earth."[7] After all, the phrase "sons of God" almost without exception in the Old Testament refers to angelic beings, not people. It's not until we get to the New Testament that followers of Jesus are depicted as adopted children of God - a term denoting relationship, not deity.

Ross goes on to point out that great kings of the earth have "princes" ruling behind them, and these princes are demons (Ezek. 28:11-19; Dan. 10:13). It is no surprise, then, to find in the literature of surrounding nations that kings often are described as divine, half-divine, or demigods. Pagans revered these great leaders, and many mythological traditions describe them as the offspring of gods themselves. Writes Ross, "Thus for the pagans, gods had their origin in copulation between gods and humans. Any superhuman individual in a myth or other mythological or actual giant would suggest divine origin to the pagans."[8]

So, this passage, rather than confirming sexual relations between fallen angels and humans, refutes these pagan beliefs with divine truth. The "sons of God" are demons who indwell and control mighty men of earth. These demon-possessed men marry as many women as they please to satisfy their baser instincts, perhaps introducing the practice of harems. But in the end, these "powerful men of old ... famous men" are flesh, and they die as all men do. "When God judges the world - as He was about to - no giant, no deity, no human has any power against Him. God simply allots one's days and brings his end."[9]

In the final analysis, Gen. 6:1-4 and Jude may be common references to the first recorded instance of demon possession, resulting in a special place of punishment for the angels who "deserted their proper dwelling."

Gen. 6:1-4 and Jude 6 are difficult passages of Scripture. Godly men and women wrestle with their meaning and come to different conclusions. It's wise to approach these verses with humility, thus averting dogmatism. Even better, let's make sure we grasp Jude's primary point in sharing this story: God judges not only wicked people, but rebellious angels as well.

Principles of biblical interpretation

As we wrestle with the identity of Jude's angels, it may help to consider some basic principles for interpreting Scripture. Biblical hermeneutics is "the science and art of understanding, translating, and explaining the meaning of the Scripture text," according to Wayne McDill, author of *12 Essential Skills for Great Preaching*.[10] In 2 Tim. 2:15, Paul commands Timothy to engage in hermeneutics: "Be diligent to present yourself approved to God, a worker who doesn't need to be ashamed, correctly teaching the word of truth."

McDill offers seven principles for "rightly dividing" (KJV) the Word of God:

1. Identify the kind of literature your text is for insight into its meaning. Bible scholars call this the genre of the text. Is the text

106

law, history, wisdom, poetry, narrative, epistles, prophecy, apocalyptic, or something else? All genres are not created equal when it comes to conveying divine revelation. Carefully discerning the genre of a passage, or an entire book, is key to understanding. The genre of Jude is that of an epistle - a letter written to a general or specific audience conveying greetings and instruction.

2. Consider the context of the passage for a better understanding of its meaning. What is the historical setting of the passage? Who is the intended audience? What are the social, political, and religious situations that the Holy Spirit and the human author seek to address? Jude likely is written in the mid 60s A.D., when Israel is about to experience God's wrath at the hands of the Romans, and when the early church is on the cusp of great dangers from false teachers.

3. Read the text for its plain and obvious meaning. "A common and persistent myth about the Bible is that its real meaning is hidden behind the surface message," writes McDill. "Even though the Bible uses symbolic or figurative language, most of it is clear to the reader. Even when you do not know about the people, places, and events in question, you can grasp the point of the text."[11] While Jude alludes to apocryphal books and employs graphic images to describe the lifestyles of false teachers, his message is plain to the reader: Now is the time to take a stand for the Christian faith.

4. Try to discern the writer's intentions when he wrote the text. Luke, for example, tells us he has "carefully investigated everything from the very first, to write to you in orderly sequence, most honorable Theophilus, so that you may know the certainty of the things about which you have been instructed" (Luke 1:3-4). In the case of Jude, the author makes it clear that he intends to warn his readers about false teachers who have infiltrated the church, and to spur them to earnestly contend for the faith.

5. Look carefully at the language of the text for what it reveals about its meaning. The words of the text are all we have of the writer's thoughts, says McDill. If he hadn't written it down, we wouldn't know what he was thinking. So we should carefully examine the author's words and phrases, and how he constructs his message. Jude uses strong language to characterize false teachers. It may help if we study these terms in the original language using lexicons and word-study books. In addition, Jude often organizes his thoughts in groups of three. For example, in calling his readers to remember how God judges the wicked, he lists three lessons from history: unbelieving Israelites, fallen angels, and the citizens of Sodom and Gomorrah.

6. Notice the various theological themes in the text. Though a text generally has one intended meaning, it can have a number of significant theological themes - and a variety of applications. When Jude writes about false teachers denying their only Master and Lord, Jesus Christ (v. 4), we might draw from this the urgency of knowing sound doctrine concerning the person and work of the Messiah.

7. Always take a God-centered perspective for interpreting your text. The "theological interpretation" arises from the assumption that the Bible is really God's means of making Himself known to us, notes McGill. What it says about Him always is central to every text. "The Bible was not given by God to tell us about ancient religious people and how we should all try to be like them," he writes. "It was given to tell us about the faithful God whom they either served or denied. Their response is not the central message; God's will and his involvement with his creation are. Even texts that give instructions as to how we should behave reveal something about God."[12] Jude's epistle, while warning of false teachers and calling believers to contend for the faith, ultimately points to a sovereign God who is holy, loving, faithful, and just.

What does Jude mean by "eternal chains in darkness"?

Whoever these particularly nasty angels are, God is keeping them under wraps until the day they are cast into the lake of fire. The word "kept" in Jude 6 is from the same root word Jude uses in verse 1 to describe believers, who are "kept" by Jesus Christ. Some translations render it "reserved" rather than "kept." In a parallel passage, Peter writes that these fallen angels are "delivered ... to be *kept* in chains" (2 Peter 2:4 - emphasis added).

The questions, then, are *where* these demons are imprisoned, and *how*. Certainly, if they are spiritual beings, physical chains cannot hold them. The Greek actually describes them as being confined, without hope of escape. While Jude does not name this place (or state) of confinement, Peter, in the parallel passage just referenced, calls it *Tartarus*.

Many translations render this word, found only in 2 Peter 2:4, as "hell," including the King James Version and the New American Standard Bible, while others, like the English Standard Version and the New International Version, provide footnotes linking the English word "hell" to the Greek name *Tartarus*.

The Holman Christian Standard Bible simply transliterates the Greek word in this passage, which reads: "For if God did not spare the angels who sinned, but threw them down into *Tartarus* and delivered them to be kept in chains of darkness until judgment ..." A footnote in the HCSB reads, "*Tartarus* is a Greek name for a subterranean place of divine punishment lower than Hades."[13]

In the apocryphal Book of Enoch (20:2), *Tartarus* is used as a place where fallen angels are punished, an interpretation Peter affirms.

So, *Tartarus* seems to be a place separate from *Sheol*, the Hebrew term for the abode of the dead; *Hades*, roughly the Greek equivalent of *Sheol*; and *Gehenna*, the lake of fire created for the Devil and his angels (Matt.25:41), where wicked people also spend eternity (Rev. 20:15). Ancient Greeks regarded *Tartarus* as a place where rebellious gods and other wicked ones are punished.

Pits of darkness

Peter reminds us that while Satan's ultimate destiny is hell, currently he is free, roaming the earth like a lion, looking for anyone he can devour (1 Peter 5:8). In a similar fashion, many of his demons are free - tempting, tormenting, and even possessing individuals. At the same time, some angels are incarcerated and experience conscious torment as they await the Day of Judgment.

Note first of all in 2 Peter 2:4 that God has cast some angels into *Tartarus*, committing them to "pits of darkness" or, as some translations render it, "chains of darkness." This Jewish apocalyptic phrase refers to a place of mental anguish and terror in the underworld.

Second, these angels are confined until the Day of Judgment. The word "confined" is in the present passive participle tense, meaning these demons are continually kept or reserved for judgment. No "soul sleep" for angels or humans, and no annihilation.

We should note there may be other places of captivity for demons. For example, in Luke 8:31, demons possessing the man called Legion beg Jesus not to banish them to the "abyss," an unfathomable pit mentioned nine times in the New Testament. In Revelation 9, 11, 17, and 20, we see that an angel called Destroyer rules over the abyss; that it is a fiery place kept under lock and key; that the beast is released from the abyss to foment great wickedness on the earth; and that Satan is temporarily imprisoned there at some point in the future.

Finally, in Rev. 9:14, an angel is commanded to release four demons confined at the Euphrates River.

A dark recess of hell?

We might ask: Is *Tartarus* an especially dark recess of hell? Or is it a separate, temporary abode until the final judgment of Satan and his demons?

If *Tartarus* is a compartment of hell, then why are demons kept there until the Day of Judgment, only to be returned? Why are some demons released from imprisonment in the abyss and at the Euphrates River, while those in *Tartarus* are offered no parole? Finally, if there is no escape from *Tartarus*, how does this place of temporary confinement differ from the lake of fire?

While we may ponder these issues, it's always good to stick with what the Bible clearly teaches. First, Christ has defeated Satan, sin, and death for us; there is no redemption for the angels who rebelled. Second, Christ judges angels as well as people. And third, we may rest assured that Satan and all demons have a place prepared for them - the lake of fire - where they are cast one day and tormented forever.

If some especially vile fallen angels are kept in a temporary place called *Tartarus* and never allowed to carry out their evil intentions, so much the better for us.

What is the angels' "proper dwelling"?

The angels who sinned "did not keep their own position but deserted their proper dwelling" (v. 6b). We should note an important progression here. First, the angels surrendered *their own position*.

The Greek word is *oiketerion*. It means a dwelling place and, in this context, heaven. While heaven is the home of angels, it's also the temporary abode of believers until Christ returns and creates new heavens and a new earth. But redeemed mankind's permanent dwelling is on the new earth (Rev. 21:1-3). So, the angels who sinned surrendered their heavenly home. They were done with it forever. The verb is aorist in tense, thus referring to a once-for-all act.

Having abandoned the presence of Almighty God in the throne room of heaven, the angels then *deserted their proper dwelling*. The KJV renders it as their own "habitation." Another way to translate it is "first estate." The Greek is *archen*, which signifies "beginning" and leads to a secondary meaning of sovereignty, dominion, majesty, or as being in the first place of power. The Jews regarded angels as having dominion over earthly creatures; and angels sometimes are spoken of in the New Testament as *archai*, or principalities (see Rom. 8:38 KJV, NASB; Eph. 1:21 KJV). This term properly designates their dignity, which they forsook.

This certain class of angels, for reasons we are not given, sloughed off the perfection, holiness, faithfulness, and purity with which they were created because, like the evil one, they wanted to call the shots. They surrendered their privileged place around the throne of heaven and, rather than serve as agents of God in the affairs of men and women, chose to intervene directly. In so doing, they deserted the dignity ascribed to their higher being. No longer content with the grandeur assigned them under the Son of God, they aspired to take His place. In seeking to climb higher, they fell; in pursuing the upper echelons of heavenly power, they lost all influence; and in grasping at divine sovereignty, they condemned themselves to a fiery prison.

Kenneth Wuest comments, "This was apostasy with a vengeance. [The angels] had, so to speak, burnt their bridges behind them, and had descended to a new sphere, the earth, and into a foreign relationship, that with the human race, foreign, because the latter belongs to a different category of created intelligences than they."[14]

Whether one holds the view that these fallen angels engaged in sexual intercourse with human beings, or violated the boundaries of authority they were given under the Son of God, or committed the first acts of demon possession, we may conclude that these particular evil spirits are kept secure in God's maximum security prison until the day their sentence is pronounced and they are cast into the lake of fire.

Key words

In this chapter, we learned several key terms. Test your knowledge by filling in the blanks.

Sons of God. Some Bible commentators maintain that Jude draws from Gen. 6:1-4 and thus associates the "sons of God" with rebellious _____ who cohabitated with the "daughters of man," producing a race of giants that invited God's wrath in the great flood. Other commentators say the "sons of God" are humans in the godly line of _____.

Tartarus. This is a Greek name for a subterranean place of divine _____ lower than *Hades.* This may be the place to which Jude refers as "eternal _____ in darkness."

Comparing English translations of *Tartarus* (from 2 Peter 2:4):

HCSB	KJV	NIV	NASB	ESV
Tartarus	hell	hell	hell	hell

Position. The rebellious angels did not keep their own position. The Greek is *oiketerion.* It means a _____ place and, in this context, heaven.

Proper dwelling. Having abandoned the presence of Almighty God in the throne room of heaven, the angels then deserted their proper dwelling. The Greek word Jude uses is *archen*, which signifies _____ and leads to a secondary meaning of _____, dominion, majesty, or as being in the first place of _____.

Application

Questions for personal or group study

1. We have examined three interpretations of Jude 6: (a) the "angels who did not keep their own position but deserted their proper dwelling" engaged in sexual relations with women and thus invited the flood; (b) the angels, dissatisfied with their rank beneath Christ and their place in heaven, rebelled, meddling directly in human affairs (but not cohabitating with women); and (c) the angels possessed the bodies of willing earthly rulers bent on making mischief, and these rulers engaged in sexual promiscuity.

   Review the principles of biblical interpretation we examined in this chapter. Then ask yourself: Which of the three views seems most faithful to Scripture? Consider the following questions in assessing Jude 6:

   - What kind of literature is Jude: law, history, wisdom, poetry, narrative, epistle, prophecy, or apocalyptic? What difference does this make?

   - What is the context of Jude: the historical setting, intended audience, and the social and religious situations the author seeks to address?

   - What does the text plainly say? And what words or phrases make this a difficult passage?

   - How does Jude 6 compare with 2 Peter 2:4 and other passages on the interaction between angels and humans?

   - What is Jude's point in reminding us of God's work in the history of angels and humans?

   - What does Scripture clearly teach about angels?

   - Where else does the phrase "sons of God" appear in the Bible, and who does it mean in those contexts?

   - Are there key words and phrases that should be explored in the original language (Greek) to aid our understanding?

   - What is Jude telling us about God in verses 5-7?

2. Read Matt. 25:41; 1 Peter 5:8; 2 Peter 2:4; Jude 6; and Rev. 20:10 and then consider:

- What is the ultimate destiny of Satan and other rebellious angels?

- If there is no redemption for Satan and demons (Christ came in the likeness of sinful people, not in the likeness of fallen angels), then why is Satan allowed to prowl the earth like a lion? And why are some demons still permitted to tempt, torment, and even possess people? In other words, why does God delay their inevitable banishment to hell?

- Why do you think God created angels if He knew so many of them were going to rebel?

- Do you think God limits the evil that Satan and demons may perform? If so, in what ways does He restrict their evil deeds?

- If Satan and demons are bound for hell, do you think they know it? And if so, why don't they try to set things right before it's too late?

- Why are the angels of Jude 6 kept "with eternal chains in darkness," while Satan and other demons have a wide range of freedom?

- The Bible implies degrees of punishment in hell for wicked human beings. Do you think there are degrees of punishment for fallen angels as well?

- Jude writes that certain rebellious angels are kept "for the judgment of the great day." If they already are confined without hope of parole, what's the point of their being judged one day?

3. Some passages of Scripture mention other places of confinement for demons besides *Tartarus*. For example, the "abyss," an unfathomable pit, is mentioned nine times in Revelation 9, 11, 17, and 20. And in Rev. 9:14, an angel is commanded to release four demons confined at the Euphrates River. Do you think these are different depictions of the same place?

4. Finally, think about the three possible interpretations of Jude 6 offered in this chapter. Why do you think God leaves some matters unresolved for us? In a broader sense, why does He allow certain doctrinal issues to create divisions in the body of Christ - issues like divine election and Spirit baptism? Put another way, why doesn't God speak more plainly in His Word?

When false teachers stand toe-to-toe with demons and rebuke them in the power of their own flesh, they are more accurately described as foolhordy than courageous.

9

The Lord Rebuke You:
Michael and the Devil

*Nevertheless, these dreamers likewise defile their flesh,
despise authority, and blaspheme glorious beings. Yet
Michael the archangel, when he was disputing with the
Devil in a debate about Moses' body, did not dare bring
an abusive condemnation against him, but said, "The
Lord rebuke you!" But these people blaspheme anything
they don't understand, and what they know by instinct,
like unreasoning animals – they destroy themselves with
these things. (Jude 8-10 HCSB)*

Several years ago as I trimmed grass in my yard, a small garter snake slithered out from the weeds. He coiled and struck my electronic weed trimmer. This was an odd scene, as garter snakes generally flee predators and prefer to hide their heads and flail their tails rather than move aggressively. They also discharge a malodorous, musky-scented secretion to ward off danger, or simply slither away into the brush. Even when they do attack, the mild venom in the fangs in the backs of their mouths is muted by large gums in the front, making it difficult to deliver venom to larger predators.[1]

So, the sight of this relatively harmless snake, less than a foot in length, taking the fight to my weed trimmer, was curious to say the least. His open jaws were far too small to capture the housing of the trimmer, and he bounced backward after his first strike. Then, he recoiled and struck again. And again. Then he struck a final time, connecting with the whirring fishing line beneath the housing, which spun him around a couple of times and tossed him several feet into a ditch, where he gave up the fight (and ultimately, the ghost).

How remarkable was the snake's tenacity in the face of overwhelming odds. But even more notable was the realization that the snake could not distinguish between a lethal living predator and a buzzing weed whacker. It cost him his life.

We see a similar comparison in Jude, as the author likens false teachers to brute beasts who operate on instinct, are incapable of reasoning, and who bring swift and certain destruction on themselves as they speak arrogantly to demons, pollute their souls, and slough off the authority of their Creator.

Why does Jude call false teachers "dreamers"?

The false teachers leading Jude's readers astray are fearless, to say the least, but not in a good way. Jude minces no words when he calls them dreamers who destroy themselves.

It takes courage to speak truth to power. We see this in Jesus' rebuke of the scribes and Pharisees (Matthew 23); in speeches by Peter on the Day of Pentecost (Acts 2), in Solomon's Colonnade (Acts 3), and before the religious power brokers led by the high priest (Acts 4); and in Stephen's sermon to his Jewish brothers (Acts 7).

But when false teachers stand toe-to-toe with demons and rebuke them in the power of their own flesh, they are more accurately described as foolhardy than courageous. Jude informs us that these false teachers are brash - and brutish. They are "dreamers" who claim dreams and visions from God, despite the fact that their words and deeds do not match the scriptural requirements for true prophets.

In the Old Testament, the term "dreamer" is synonymous with false prophet. The Lord warns the ancient Israelites several times about the "dreamer of dreams." At one point, He advises His people to reject the dreamer as a false prophet, even if his prediction of future events comes true. The reason: The dreamer also is urging people to follow idols - a direct violation of God's commands. In such circumstances, Yahweh may be testing His people (Deut. 13:1-5).

As for false teachers depicted in Jude, John MacArthur notes, "The wicked behavior of these men often derives from their dreaming, a term that Jude used to identify the apostates as phony visionaries."[2]

In describing these dreamers, Jude chooses a form of the verb *enupniazo*, which is used only one other place in the New Testament, Acts 2:17 - "and your old men will dream dreams." In that passage, Peter draws from Joel's prophecy (Joel 2:28-32) to refer to revelatory dreams rather than normal ones. Thus, by employing the same Greek term Peter uses, Jude seems to be saying that the false teachers claim divine authority for their dreams. These dreams are promoted as new sources of truth, when in fact they are little more than unrestrained exercises of the imagination.

More than just "dreamers," these religious imposters use counterfeit revelations to justify their own sexual immorality, boastful proclamations, and claims of spiritual leadership. After all, if God has divinely appointed them as teachers, He must certainly endorse their behavior.

The apostle Paul offers the Colossians a similar warning against "dreamers," even though their doctrines are different than the ones Jude warns against: "Let no one disqualify you, insisting on ascetic practices and the worship of angels, claiming access to *a visionary realm* and inflated without cause by his fleshly mind" (Col. 2:18 - emphasis added).

Jude's "dreamers" engage in three sinful activities:

First, they **defile their flesh**, meaning they engage in immorality without restraint, fearless of opposition, and unafraid of judgment. Jude pairs the words "defile" (*miaino*) and "flesh" (*sarx*) to refer to moral and physical defilement, or sexual sin.

The word *miaino* means to dye or stain something, such as clothing or glass. It also can mean to pollute, contaminate, or corrupt. This word often designates sexual sin in the Septuagint (Greek Old

Testament - Gen. 34:13; Lev. 18:24, 27-28; Job 31:11; Jer. 3:2; Hos. 5:3; 6:10). Naturally, these false teachers do not think they are polluting their flesh. Instead, they appeal to divine visions to argue in favor of their debauchery.

Second, these false teachers **despise authority.** Perhaps Jude means human authorities such as local church leaders, the apostles, or governmental officials. However, the Greek term Jude uses for "authority" - *kyriotes* - never refers to human authorities in either the Septuagint or the New Testament. And since the next phrase likely denotes angels, Jude probably has in mind the Lordship of God and/or Christ here.[3]

Claiming divine authority, these dreamers feel empowered by God as His agents on earth. As such, they hold themselves above human and angelic accountability, while insisting that their words and deeds are as authoritative as if uttered from the lips of Christ Himself.

Third, Jude says these interlopers **blaspheme glorious beings**. The word "blaspheme" is *blasphemeo* in the Greek and means to speak evil of someone or something, especially with respect to God or sacred matters.

The term "glorious beings" comes from the Greek *doxas* - literally "glories." It's possible Jude is referring to the defamation of honorable people, such as the "dignitaries" of Ps. 149:8 or Nah. 3:10. Or, Jude may be writing of holy angels. The NASB renders *doxas* "angelic majesties," and the parallel passage in 2 Peter 2:10-11 refers to the false teachers' blasphemy of "the glorious ones ... angels." No doubt, holy angels play a special role in establishing the very moral order that Jude's false teachers openly flaunt (see Deut. 33:2; Gal. 3:19; Heb. 2:2).

But in concert with verse 9, where Michael refuses to pronounce judgment on the Devil, it may be preferable to see the false teachers' slanderous words directed at evil angels. If that's the case, Jude's argument runs as follows: These false teachers insult demons, but the archangel, Michael, does not even presume to blaspheme the Devil himself, preferring to leave his judgment to God. "If Michael as an angel with high authority did not even presume to judge Satan, how can the opponents be so filled with pride that they insult demons, who have a certain glory, even though they have subsequently sinned?"[4]

Ultimately, says Jude, these religious renegades destroy themselves. They don't understand the full implication of their words and deeds. Jude likens them to "unreasoning animals," who operate on instinct, thinking to secure their own preservation, but in fact hastening their demise.

The term translated "unreasoning" (*alogos*) means "without a word." That is, the false teachers are like animals who cannot speak intelligibly because they cannot reason. It matters not how educated these false teachers are; how many advanced degrees they hold; how eloquently they speak; how graphically they describe their dreams and visions. They are like brute beasts. Descending the spiral of ungodliness into damnation, the false teachers profess themselves wise, when in fact they are fools (Rom. 1:22).

In the end, they pronounce their own doom, for as they speak blasphemies and promote heresies, they fill up their measure of sin and invite the wrath of God (see Gen. 15:16; Matt. 23:31-32; 1 Thess. 2:16).

Who is Michael the archangel?

Jude offers one of the few references in Scripture to Michael the archangel. He is the only archangel named in the Bible, and his name means, "Who is like God?" What a contrast to Satan, who exalts himself above God, and who tempts Eve with the promise of becoming like God through disobedience to her Creator.

Though little is revealed in Scripture about Michael, we are given enough information to draw some conclusions. He is introduced in Dan. 10:13 as "one of the chief princes." He helps another angel, who has been battling the "prince of the kingdom of Persia" for 21 days, to deliver an answered prayer to Daniel. Because of the reference to Michael as "one of the chief princes," it's possible there are additional archangels, though none is named as such.

Some commentators suggest that Gabriel ("hero of God") may be an archangel. He appears to Daniel (Dan. 8:15-27; 9:20-27), and later to Zechariah (Luke 1:11-23) and Mary (Luke 1:26-38).

Michael is one of God's most powerful holy angels and the protector of God's people. He is called "the great prince" in Dan. 12:1. He leads an angelic host in a heavenly battle against the "dragon and his angels," defeating them so there is "no place for them in heaven any longer." Satan is thrown to earth, and his angels with him (Rev. 12:7-9).

No doubt, Michael is a powerful angelic being who serves primarily as the champion angel of Israel. The word "archangel" comes from a compound Greek term *archangelos* and means "ruling angel." It only occurs twice in the New Testament (1 Thess. 4:16; Jude 9) and not once in the Old Testament.

Who Michael is not

Some commentators have filled the void between biblical revelation and human imagination with fanciful views of Michael. While it's important to understand who Michael is, it's equally important to understand who he is *not*.

Michael is not Jesus. The glory, power, and majesty of Michael - and his decisive victory over Satan in the heavenly realm - lead some to conclude that Michael is in fact another name for Jesus.

Jehovah's Witnesses are perhaps the most vocal proponents of this view, teaching that Jehovah fashioned Michael in His first act of creation and then made all "other" things through him (see Col. 1:16 in the New World Translation). About 2000 years ago, according to the Watch Tower, Jehovah recreated Michael as Jesus the man. This is not an incarnation - God putting on human flesh - but the remaking of an angel into a mere human being.

Jesus later dies on a torture stake, exonerating the name of Jehovah, and ceases to exist in human form. Three days later Jehovah takes Jesus' life force and recreates it into an exalted Michael the archangel.

"[T]he Bible indicates that Michael is another name for Jesus Christ, before and after his life on earth," according to the Watch Tower's official website. Jehovah's Witnesses argue that because other individuals in the Bible are known by more than one name - Jacob/Israel and Peter/Simon, for example - it's only reasonable to see that Jesus and Michael are two names for the same person.[5]

Jehovah's Witnesses misinterpret 1 Thess. 4:16 by attaching the archangel's voice to Jesus, when in fact the New Testament never identifies Jesus as an archangel. Further, they argue that because both

Michael and Jesus lead armies of faithful angels (Matt. 13:41; 16:27; 24:31; 2 Thess. 1:7; 1 Peter 3:22; Rev. 12:7; 19:14-16), they must be the same person. But to argue from this perspective is like saying that because a CEO has authority over all employees and a manager has authority over some of the same employees, the CEO and the manager are the same person.

Unfortunately, the Watch Tower elevates a created being to the lofty position of "mighty god" while stripping away the deity of Jesus, negating His incarnation, denying His substitutionary and sacrificial death on a cross, and rejecting His physical resurrection from the dead - core elements of the gospel (1 Cor. 15:3-8).

Michael is not a patron saint to whom we pray. Roman Catholics refer to Michael as "St. Michael the Archangel," who carries out four main responsibilities: (1) To combat Satan; (2) to escort the faithful to heaven at their hour of death; (3) to be a champion of all Christians, and the church itself; and (4) to call men from life on earth to their heavenly judgment. Today, St. Michael is invoked for protection, especially from lethal enemies. He also is the patron saint of soldiers, police, and doctors.[6]

This view of Michael aligns more closely with Scripture than the view of the Watch Tower. Yet it assigns him tasks the Bible does not affirm. While Jesus mentions that angels carry the soul/spirit of Lazarus to Abraham's side (Luke 16:22), He does not name Michael among these angels.

Further, while the term "saints" may in some contexts be applied to angels, or "holy ones" (e.g., Deut. 33:2-3), Scripture never instructs us to pray to angels or to certain believers in heaven. We are to direct our petitions to God the Father in the name of Jesus, who sits at the Father's right hand as our Mediator and Intercessor (Matt. 6:9; 1 Tim. 2:5; Heb. 7:25).

Michael is not the Angel of the Lord. We should not confuse Michael with "the Angel of the Lord" (*mal'akh Yahweh*), who is identified throughout the Old Testament and at times equated with God (e.g., Gen. 22:11-12; Ex. 3:2-4). In contrast, Michael never is called "the Angel of the Lord," nor is he given divine status.

Ancient Israelites believed the Angel of the Lord to be a non-divine angel, "the angel of the countenance" and "the highest revelation of the unseen God."[7]

Catholics, for the most part, regard the Angel of the Lord as a representative of God, an actual angel, while Protestants generally believe the Angel of the Lord either is a theophany (a manifestation of Yahweh himself) or a Christophany, a pre-incarnate appearance of Christ.[8]

John Calvin writes, "I am inclined to agree with the ancient writers [the biblical authors], that in those passages wherein it is stated that the angel of the Lord appeared to Abraham, Jacob, and Moses, Christ was that angel."[9]

Zechariah 3 comes as close as any passage to identifying the Angel of the Lord with Jesus. In a vision, Zechariah sees Joshua the high priest standing before the Angel of the Lord, likely in heaven. Joshua is dressed in filthy garments, which symbolize Israel's sinful past. Satan is there as well and stands ready to accuse Joshua and the people of Israel.

But the Angel of the Lord says to those around Him, "Take off his filthy clothes!" Then, turning to Joshua, He says, "See, I have removed your guilt from you, and I will clothe you with the splendid robes" (v. 4). "This passage perfectly describes the work of Christ, who took upon himself our degradation and shame and, in an inconceivable exchange, covers us with the robes of his righteousness."[10]

It seems clear that Michael is a created angel and not God Himself. He is designated an archangel and is classified as "one of the chief princes" (Dan. 10:13), as if belonging to a group of comparable ones among angels. He is further appointed to the welfare of Israel, as other angelic beings are assigned to nations by God or by Satan (cf. Dan. 10:13, 20).

It's good to keep in mind that Jesus, the Logos - that is, the Word, the communication and revealer of God the Father (see John 1:1, 14; Rev. 19:13) - is distinct from men and angels in that He is called *monogenes* (only begotten, unique; see, for example, John 1:14, 18; 3:16, 18; 1 John 4:9). He is the Creator of all angels (Col. 1:16) and the Lord of all nations (Rev. 19:13-16).[11]

124

Where does Jude get this story?

The death of Moses is recorded in Deut. 34:1-7, but there is no mention in this passage of Michael and Satan disputing about Moses' body. There are many Jewish traditions about the death of Moses, but we should always approach non-biblical embellishments with caution.

In Jude's day, however, there is an apocryphal writing called The Assumption of Moses that records a conflict between Michael and Satan. According to this account, Satan argues over the body of Moses because Moses has killed an Egyptian overseer (Ex. 2:11-12). Satan evidently argues his right to the body because Moses is a murderer.

We should not assume that Jude has erred in quoting from an apocryphal book, nor should we declare The Assumption of Moses divinely inspired because Jude quotes from it. It may help to remember that Paul cites Greek poets and sayings without suggesting their work is authoritative (Acts 17:28; 1 Cor. 15:33; Titus 1:12).

"Jude did not intend to put a canonical stamp on *Assumption of Moses* simply because he cited it," writes Thomas Schreiner. "He viewed this story as true or helpful, or he believed it was an illustration of the truth he desired to teach."[12]

Why the debate over Moses' body?

Jude is the only writer of Scripture to mention this incident. Michael's appeal to the Lord apparently ends the dispute with Satan. But what are the archangel and the evil one fighting about? And what's the end game for each of them?

The Old Testament gives us limited information about Moses' death, recording simply, "So Moses the servant of the Lord died there in the land of Moab, as the Lord had said. He buried him in the valley in the land of Moab facing Beth-peor, and no one to this day knows where his grave is" (Deut. 34:5-6).

The terms Jude uses to describe the dispute between Michael and Satan suggest a legal row over Moses' body. By establishing Moses' guilt as a murderer, the Devil seeks to claim ownership of Moses' body and thus deprive him of an honorable burial.

What Satan would do with the body is a matter of speculation. Perhaps he would try to keep Moses from participating in a future bodily resurrection, or from appearing with Jesus on the Mount of Transfiguration (Matt. 17:1-8). Or, maybe he would offer it to the Israelites as an object of worship. Whatever the evil one's intentions, Michael's motivation is pure, and his actions reflect a desire to faithfully serve God.

Why doesn't Michael rebuke Satan?

Michael has the authority to criticize Satan because the Devil's motives are evil, and because by his very nature he is wicked. But Michael chooses instead not to utter an "abusive condemnation" against him; rather, he defers to the supreme authority in the universe.

Jude uses this angelic encounter to demonstrate the audacity of false teachers. He refers to the flippant manner in which they speak against angels, and he contrasts their behavior with that of Michael, who shows remarkable restraint when disputing with Satan over the body of Moses.

Michael knows God could grant him power over Satan (Rev. 12:7-9), yet he also is committed to curbing his own behavior within the limits God has set for him. Unlike the rebellious angels Jude mentions in verse 6, who "deserted their proper dwelling," Michael addresses Satan with a humbly devastating phrase: "The Lord rebuke you!" (v. 9).

Michael follows the example set by the Angel of the Lord in Zech. 3:2. In Zechariah's vision, Joshua the high priest stands in heaven before the Angel of the Lord. The Devil also is there at the right hand of Joshua, accusing Joshua and the people. Basically, Satan argues that, because of Israel's sinfulness, God should break His covenant promises with the people.

In response, the Angel of the Lord (likely the pre-incarnate Christ) defends Israel by deferring to God the Father and asking Him to rebuke Satan. The Father honors the Angel's request. Instead of breaking His covenant, He reaffirms His commitment to Israel's future justification, promising to forgive Israel's sins and clothe her with garments of righteousness (Zech. 3:3-5). "Those whom the Lord has chosen are vindicated in his sight."[13]

What conclusions should we draw?

We have looked in some detail at Michael's encounter with Satan and the thorny questions it raises. From this, we may make certain observations.

First, Michael understands the boundaries of his authority. As a mighty archangel who protects Israel and fights on behalf of God's people, and as one who ultimately defeats the evil one in a cosmic battle for the ages, he nevertheless submissively embraces his role as a servant of the Lord.

Second, he respects the power of Satan. Until the day he leads the charge to cast Satan out of heaven, Michael understands the freedom Satan has to roam the earth, and to steal, kill, and destroy (John 10:10; 1 Peter 5:8). Like King David awaiting the day God places him on the throne, Michael patiently bides his time and gives the Devil his due. What a contrast to the false teachers who arrogantly blaspheme demonic forces.

Third, Michael defers to God as the ultimate Judge. Telling Satan, "The Lord rebuke you!" is an object lesson for us. No matter what evil we see, and how we are called to speak against it, the exalted Christ is the Judge of all (John 5:22), and before Him all people stand one day in final judgment (2 Cor. 5:10; Rev. 20:11-15).

Last, Jude's primary point in mentioning Michael's encounter with the evil one is to illuminate the sin of false teachers, who claim divine authority yet exhibit ungodly arrogance in the way they speak against those who inhabit the unseen realm. False teachers who rail against demonic forces are playing with fire, unaware they are bound for the same eternal destiny as their unseen counterparts.

Check list

Scripture offers numerous markers to help us identify true prophets/teachers - and false ones. Here are a few.

True prophets/teachers:

- ✓ Exalt God, not themselves or idols (Deut. 13:1-4)
- ✓ Are 100 percent accurate when they speak in the Lord's name (Deut. 18:21-22)
- ✓ Tell the whole truth, not tickle the ears (Jer. 23:16-17, 31-32; Ezek. 13:22-23; 2 Tim. 4:3-4)
- ✓ Proclaim salvation by grace alone, through faith alone, in Christ alone (Gal. 1:8-9)
- ✓ Practice what they preach (2 Peter 2:1-3)

False prophets/teachers:

- ✓ Preach another Jesus - denying His virgin birth, deity, humanity, place in the Trinity, miracles, substitutionary and sacrificial death on the cross, and/or bodily resurrection (2 Cor. 11:4)
- ✓ Proclaim a different Spirit - denying His personhood, deity, place in the Godhead, and/or role in creation and salvation (2 Cor. 11:4)
- ✓ Preach a different gospel - adding to or subtracting from the finished work of Christ (2 Cor. 11:4)
- ✓ Disguise themselves as servants of righteousness (2 Cor. 11:14-15)

Key words

In this chapter, we learned several key terms. Test your knowledge by filling in the blanks.

Dreamers. Jude choses a form of the verb *enupniazo*, which is used only one other place in the New Testament. He seems to be saying that the false teachers claim divine _____ for their dreams. While promoted as new sources of truth, these dreams are in fact little more than unrestrained exercises of the _____.

Glorious beings. This term comes from the Greek word _____ - literally "glories." It's possible Jude is referring to the defamation of honorable _____, or to holy _____. But it may be preferable to see the false teachers' slanderous words directed against _____ angels.

Comparing English translations of *doxas:*

HCSB	KJV	NIV	NASB	ESV
glorious beings	dignities	celestial beings	angelic majesties	glorious ones

Unreasoning. Jude compares false teachers to "unreasoning _____." The Greek word *alogos* may also be translated "without a _____." That is, false teachers are like animals who cannot speak intelligibly because they cannot reason.

Comparing English translations of *alogos* (in reference to false teachers):

HCSB	KJV	NIV	NASB	ESV
unreasoning	brute	irrational	unreasoning	unreasoning

Archangel. This English word comes from a compound Greek term *archangelos* and means _____ _____.
This term occurs only _____ in the New Testament.

Angel of the Lord. We should not confuse Michael the archangel with the Angel of the Lord (*mal'akh Yahweh*), who is identified throughout the Old Testament and at times is equated with
_____.

Application
Questions for personal or group study

1. Jude warns against rebuking demons, offering the example of Michael the archangel, who humbly defers to the Lord in his dispute with Satan. What do you think is the harm in speaking directly to, or against, demons?

2. Consider Job 1:6-12; 2:1-6; Luke 22:31; and 1 Cor. 10:13. These verses imply that Satan and his demons may go only so far in harming or tempting God's people. Why do you think the Lord places limits on the evil one? Do these limits apply to Satan's interaction with non-believers?

3. In Acts 16:16-18, the apostle Paul casts a demon out of a slave girl, speaking directly to the "spirit of prediction." If Paul rebukes a demon, why can't we?

4. Read Acts 19:11-20. What differences do you see in the apostle Paul and the seven sons of Sceva? What impact did that event have on the people who witnessed it in Ephesus?

5. What do you make of events today, mostly on television, in which an "anointed" evangelist apparently casts out demons, heals the sick, and causes people to fall backward as he "breathes" the Holy Spirit on them? How can we know if it's real or fake?

6. Since there are so many false teachers fleecing the flock and living exorbitant lifestyles - all the while touting miracle power - is it safer for our spiritual well-being to conclude that God is not in the miracle business today? Why or why not?

7. Do you believe God still performs miracles today through a word or a touch of anointed servants? If so, why aren't miracles more common?

8. Prosperity preachers often emphasize the power of our words. Some contend that our words have creative power similar to the power God demonstrated in creating the heavens and the earth. Why is that a false doctrine?

9. Satan and his demons still have great latitude in tempting and tormenting people today. What should Christians do to protect themselves - and others?

10. A Christian friend claims the spiritual gift of discernment. She tells you that you have a "spirit" of depression and offers to lay hands on you in order to rebuke the "spirit." What should you do?

False religions and counterfeit forms of Christianity wrap themselves in elaborate ceremonies, arduous rules, and complex doctrines — all in an effort to attract God's attention and earn His favor without submitting to His authority. It is bloodless, grainy religion, and God rejects it out of hand.

10

Woe to Them!
Cain, Balaam, and Korah

Woe to them! For they have traveled in the way of Cain,
have abandoned themselves to the error of Balaam
for profit, and have perished in Korah's rebellion.
(Jude 11 HCSB)

We all have role models. Athletes, actors, and rock stars are among the most popular people we seek to mimic - even when their legendary falls from grace are captured in tabloid headlines and social-media hashtags. Unfortunately, we often take for granted those who exemplify honesty, integrity, and hard work, choosing to conform our behavior to those whose actions - no matter how outrageous - get noticed and rewarded. This is a process Susan Krauss Whitbourne, a professor of psychology at the University of Massachusetts, refers to as "vicarious reinforcement."[1]

Maybe that's why entertainers like Miley Cyrus, athletes like Dennis Rodman, and selfie-stick wielders like Kim Kardashian are so popular. It seems the more shockingly they behave, the more their celebrity grows. History takes a longer view and tends to judge such characters more harshly. After all, there aren't too many baby boomers named

Adolf. And it's doubtful that moms and dads want their little boys growing up to be like Charlie Sheen.

In a similar vein, Jude reminds his readers of some unsavory role models in Israel's past, men whose wicked deeds so overshadowed whatever good they accomplished that they are forever held up as examples of how not to live. In warning against false teachers, and in urging believers to earnestly contend for the faith, Jude reminds us of three characters who are not to be emulated. Yet the first-century false teachers unwittingly model their lives after Cain, Balaam, and Korah.

Jude already has described the false teachers in unvarnished terms. They are "certain men" that have come in by stealth, ungodly, turning God's grace into promiscuity, and denying the Lord Jesus Christ. They are dreamers who defile their flesh, despise authority, and blaspheme glorious beings. Like the unbelievers God rescued from Egypt, and like certain fallen angels and the wicked men of Sodom and Gomorrah, they are destined for destruction.

Moving on, Jude pronounces woe on these interlopers and ties their behavior to the way of Cain, the error of Balaam, and the rebellion of Korah. Let's take a closer look at these three examples and see how false teachers from the first century - and today - fall victim to the same schemes.

By the way, so-called "woe oracles" are common among Old Testament prophets, a form of public rebuke that Jesus employs in Matthew 23 to denounce the religious leaders and their wicked ways. He paints the scribes and Pharisees as "hypocrites" for locking up the kingdom of heaven from people; for devouring widows' houses and making long prayers for show; for expending great effort to make one proselyte, who then is twice as fit for hell as they are; for being blind guides; for being sticklers for the letter of the law while abandoning its spirit; for being externally righteous but inwardly vile, like whitewashed tombs; and for boastfully disregarding the fact that they are of the same mind as the leaders of old who murdered the prophets. "Snakes!" declares Jesus. "Brood of vipers! How can you escape being condemned to hell?" (v. 33).

By comparison, Jude's woe seems mild-mannered. But keep in mind that if Michael the archangel defers to the Lord in rebuking Satan, Jude is cautious not to out-reprove Jesus.

What is the way of Cain?

Perhaps Jude chooses Cain because he, like the false teachers of the first century, embraces wickedness over goodness. He thus becomes a model of sin in later writings, such as 1 John 3:12, where Cain is the antithesis of love - a murderer, a man of the evil one, and a doer of evil deeds.

Philo, a first-century Jewish philosopher, portrays Cain as a man enslaved to self-love.[2] In the Targums[3], Cain reportedly boasts, "There is no judgment, there is no Judge, there is no other world, there is no gift of good reward for the just and no punishment for the wicked."[4]

Cain, of course, is the first-born son of Adam and Eve. Perhaps hoping this child is the promised "seed" (Gen. 3:15), humanity's first parents soon discover that Cain is anything but the one who crushes the head of Satan and redeems the fallen human race. He is, as commentators note, sullen, haughty, vindictive, and defiant even in his attitude toward God.[5]

His story plays out in Genesis 4 as Cain is a tiller of the soil, while his younger brother Abel becomes a shepherd. In the course of time, possibly on the Sabbath, the two brothers present their offerings to the Lord. Abel's offering, consisting of some of the first-born of his flock, pleases the Lord. But Cain's offering from his crops fails to prompt the same divine response.

Cain is "furious" and "downcast" - literally, "his face fell" (v. 5). The Lord asks Cain, "Why are you furious? And why are you downcast? If you do right, won't you be accepted? But if you do not do right, sin is crouching at your door. Its desire is for you, but you must master it" (vv. 6-7).

Unrepentant, Cain urges his brother to "go out to the field" with him (v. 8). There, Cain attacks Abel and kills him. When the Lord inquires as to the whereabouts of Abel, Cain's notorious reply is, "Am I my brother's keeper?" (v. 9 KJV).

The Lord responds with a curse: "So now you are cursed [with alienation] from the ground that opened its mouth to receive your brother's blood you have shed. If you work the land, it will never again give you its yield. You will be a restless wanderer on the earth" (vv. 11-12).

Cain replies, "My punishment is too great to bear! ... whoever finds me will kill me" (vv. 13-14). So the Lord places a mark on Cain to protect him, threatening vengeance seven times over to anyone who kills him. Cain goes out from the Lord's presence and lives in the land of Nod, east of Eden. His descendants are enumerated to the sixth generation. Gradually, they become so corrupt that God's sends a deluge to prevent the final triumph of evil.

That's the story of Cain in a nutshell. So, in what way are the false teachers of the first century similar to the first-born son of Adam and Eve? What is "the way of Cain"?

Simply put, the way of Cain is the way of religion without faith, writes Warren Wiersbe. It is the way of pride, a man establishing his own righteousness and rejecting the righteousness of God that comes through faith in Christ. "Cain became a fugitive and tried to overcome his wretchedness by building a city and developing a civilization (Gen. 4:9ff). He ended up with everything a man could desire - everything except God, that is."[6]

Cain rejects God's way of salvation, though he is not ignorant of it. By clothing Adam and Eve with the skins of animals (Gen. 3:21), God evidently makes it clear that the only way of forgiveness is through the shedding of blood. Cain would have none of it, preferring to approach the altar with the fruits of his own labor. Why does God reject Cain's offering? Because Cain's heart is not right before Him.

The writer of Hebrews summarizes this tragic episode in early human history: "By faith Abel offered to God a better sacrifice than Cain did. By this he was approved as a righteous man, because God approved his gifts, and even though he is dead, he still speaks through this" (Heb. 11:4).

Raising Cain in the early church

Let's consider a few similarities between Cain and first-century false teachers:

They are religious. Cain brings his offering to God, just as the false teachers fully engage the early church with their doctrines. But as the apostle Paul warns Timothy, we should avoid those who are "holding to the form of religion but denying its power" (2 Tim. 3:5). Among other traits, Paul describes these religious imposters as lovers of self, without love for what is good, and lovers of pleasure rather than lovers of God. At their very core, they seek to redefine God and refashion His plan of salvation. Satan always has been an advocate of religion, as long as he's in charge; it's worship of the one true and living God that he opposes.

They are arrogant. The Lord tells Cain, "If you do right, won't you be accepted?" But rather than give God a proper offering by spilling the atoning blood of a sacrificial animal, Cain defiantly spills the blood of his innocent brother. In a similar way, the false teachers of Jude's day turn the grace of God into promiscuity and deny their only Master and Lord, Jesus Christ (Jude 4). The fact that Cain's bloodless offering is not accepted implies that God previously told him what constitutes a proper sacrifice. Similarly, the false teachers of Jude's day reject God's revelation and operate arrogantly according to their own self-styled religious practices.

They are devious. Cain deceives his brother, kills him, and then denies knowledge of Abel's whereabouts. Similarly, the false teachers of Jude's day come into the church by stealth, gain the trust of God's people, then destroy their faith - all the while insisting that their libertine dreams and visions come directly from God.

They are clever, twisting the words of God. Cain complains that he must hide himself from God's presence (Gen. 4:14), but the Scripture never records God saying that. Just as Eve adds to the warning of God by telling the serpent she is not to touch the forbidden fruit - something God never says; He only instructs her not to eat of the tree - Cain adds to the punishment God pronounces on him by making himself a victim, and crafting God as a merciless tyrant. In a similar way, Jude's first-century false teachers convince the followers of Jesus

137

that grace equals license to sin, alleged dreams and visions trump sound doctrine, and flattery is the ultimate spiritual gift.

They are spiritual rebels. Cain most certainly knows the reason his sacrifice is rejected. But rather than humbly receive the Lord's correction, he lashes out against his righteous brother and bears God's judgment without expressing the repentance it is designed to produce. Likewise, Jude's interlopers are Cain's spiritual brothers - unholy, resentful, sharp-tongued, taking the fast lane to hell so as to leave a good-looking corpse.

They are self-centered. Cain's words and conduct reveal a corrupt heart that seeks only to satisfy his sinful desires. He does not seek to abandon worship; rather, he insists on worshiping his own way, unwittingly making himself the object of his own obeisance. Similarly, the false teachers of Jude's day are all about themselves. They defile their flesh in self-indulgent living, slough off the authority of Christ and His apostles, speak arrogantly to demonic forces, nurture themselves without fear, embrace sinful desires, and flatter people for their own advantage.

Both Cain and the false teachers of Jude's day have a form of godliness, but it is an empty shell. Rejecting the revelation of God, they determine to meet Him on their own terms, and if God rejects those terms, they simply reject Him. That is the way of false religions and counterfeit forms of Christianity. They wrap themselves in elaborate ceremonies, arduous rules, and complex doctrines - all in an effort to attract God's attention and earn His favor without submitting to His authority. It is bloodless, grainy religion, and God rejects it out of hand.

In contrast, the way of Abel, like the way of the cross, is a bloody way. As the penalty of sin is death, so is the provision for sin - the death of an innocent substitute. In Old Testament times, it was a spotless animal whose shed blood atoned for, or temporarily covered, sin. Every turtle dove, every lamb, goat, or bull pointed to the day when the Lamb of God would not simply atone for sin - He would take it away. John the Baptist captures it remarkably well: "Here is the Lamb of God, who takes away the sin of the world!" (John 1:29b).

138

Despite the tragic way of Cain, we may thank God that He sent His Son to take the bloody path to Calvary, where He who knew no sin became sin for us (2 Cor. 5:21).

What is the error of Balaam?

We find the story of Balaam in Numbers 22-24, with additional information in chapter 31. It's a classic tale of a prophet for hire, someone greatly gifted by God who allows greed to drive him to "madness" (2 Peter 2:16). The Greek word translated "madness" is *paraphronia*, which literally means "beside one's own mind." In other words, Balaam's fleshly cravings are such that they overcome his ability to think and act rationally.

Interestingly, some commentators believe Balaam is portrayed as a good character in Numbers 22-24, before coming under criticism elsewhere in the Old Testament. But there are hints of his greedy motivations from the start.

Balak, king of Moab, hires Balaam to curse the people of Israel as they wander in the wilderness. Balak sees the Israelites as a military threat and seeks help from inside the Israelite camp to defeat them. Initially, it appears that Balaam is a faithful prophet, but his stall tactics "imply that he hoped to negotiate a higher payment from Balak before performing his prophetic service."[7] In the end, he accepts Balak's riches because he loves the wages of unrighteousness (cf. Prov. 11:18).

The Lord knows Balaam wants to curse Israel in exchange for treasure, so God rebukes him through his donkey, who miraculously speaks to the prophet. Balaam is empowered only to bless Israel. But he's not finished.

He also is motivated by sexual immorality. So, he tries to ruin the Israelites through moral corruption. He promotes marriage between the Israelites and their pagan neighbors, the Moabites and Midianites (Numbers 25; 31:9-20), despite God's clear warning against such marriages (Ex. 34:12-16; Deut. 7:1-4; Josh. 23:11-13; Ezra 9:12). In Num. 31:16, Moses identifies Balaam as a corrupting influence: "Yet they [Midianite women] are the ones who, at Balaam's advice, incited the Israelites to unfaithfulness against the Lord in the Peor incident [in which Balaam counsels the Moabites and Midianites to lead Israel into idolatry], so that the plague came against the Lord's community."

John MacArthur comments: "The prophet's apostasy not only assaulted God's holiness, but it also threatened the very existence of His chosen people. Although Balaam knew better, he allowed fleshly impulses to guide his choices. And, as a result, he suffered the ultimate penalty of death."[8]

In referring to Balaam, Jude exposes the motive behind the religious interests of false teachers. They do it, at least in part, for the money, exploiting people, telling them what they want to hear, making merchandise of them as they promise temporal blessings as guarantees of God's faithfulness. Consider just a few Scriptures that offer a broader perspective on the tie between greed and apostasy:

- Ps. 10:3 - "For the wicked one boasts about his own cravings; the one who is greedy curses and despises the Lord."

- Micah 3:11 - "Her [Israel's] leaders issue rulings for a bribe, her priests teach for payment, and her prophets practice divination for money. Yet they lean on the Lord, saying, 'Isn't the Lord among us?'"

- 1 Tim. 6:10 - "For the love of money is a root of all kinds of evil, and by craving it, some have wandered away from the faith and pierced themselves with many pains."

- 2 Peter 2:3a - "In their greed they [false teachers] will exploit you with deceptive words ..."

These defectors are not like God's faithful servants:

- 1 Tim. 3:2-3 - "An overseer, therefore, must be above reproach, the husband of one wife, self-controlled, sensible, respectable, hospitable, an able teacher, not addicted to wine, not a bully but gentle, not quarrelsome, not greedy ..."

- Titus 1:7 - "For an overseer, as God's manager, must be blameless, not arrogant, not quick tempered, not addicted to wine, not a bully, not greedy for money ..."

- 1 Peter 5:2 - "[S]hepherd God's flock among you, not overseeing out of compulsion but freely, according to God's will; not for the money but eagerly ..."

In short, the error of Balaam is using God-given gifts to feed fleshly desires. The false teachers seek to enrich themselves, as Balaam does, and to satisfy their lustful passions - all the while claiming God as the source of their messages. They propagate error in order to make money, and yet they may be deceived to such an extent that they actually believe their own messages. While they may not teach their false doctrines in exchange for sexual favors, they likely promote the ungodly view that sexual license is a gift of God's grace, and thus they lead many astray.

In the parallel passage in 2 Peter 2:15-16, we see a more detailed summary of Balaam's transgression: "By abandoning the straight path, they [false teachers] have gone astray and have followed the path of Balaam, the son of Bosor, who loved the wages of unrighteousness, but received a rebuke for his transgression: a speechless donkey spoke with a human voice and restrained the prophet's madness."

A note in the Scofield Reference Bible adds this thought: "The 'error' of Balaam was that, reasoning from natural morality, and seeing the evil in Israel, he supposed a righteous God must curse them. He was blind to the higher morality of the Cross, through which God maintains and enforces the authority and awful sanctions of His law, so that He can be just and the justifier of a believing sinner."[9]

In Rev. 2:14, Jesus chastens the church at Pergamum for tolerating some who "hold to the teaching of Balaam, who taught Balak to place a stumbling block in front of the sons of Israel." The sexual sin at Baal Peor, which snares the Israelites, is attributed to Balaam's advice (see Num. 31:16). Pseudo-Philo, a Jewish work from the first or second century, portrays Balaam's advice this way: "Pick out the beautiful women who are among us and in Midian, and station them naked and adorned with gold and precious stones before them. And when they see them and lie with them, they will sin against their Lord and fall into your hands."[10]

For Balaam, it is all for naught and ends quite badly. In Numbers 31, the Lord instructs Moses to take vengeance on behalf of the Israelites against the Midianites. Moses obediently sends 1,000 men from each of the twelve tribes into battle, where they rout the enemy, killing every male. Among those slain are the five kings of Midian, along with Balaam, son of Beor, who succumbs to the sword (Num. 31:8). A shameful end to a wasted life.

What is Korah's rebellion?

Korah is a Levite from the Kohathite clan, which enjoys a favored position among the three clans of Levi in the assignment of priestly responsibilities (Num. 3:27-32; 4:1-20). But Korah wants more. So, he incites 250 prominent Israelites to rebel against Moses and Aaron. Together, they challenge God's appointed leaders, accusing Moses and Aaron of exalting themselves above the Lord's assembly.

Moses tells Korah and his followers to appear before the Lord the next morning, along with Aaron. Each is to take his firepan, place incense in it, and present his firepan before the Lord, who will choose the true leaders of Israel. When the sun rises, Korah assembles the whole community at the entrance of the tabernacle. The Lord instructs Moses and Aaron to tell the people to get away from the dwellings of Korah, along with the tents of two other rebels, Dathan and Abiram.

Immediately after Moses' warning, the Lord intervenes in dramatic fashion: "Just as he finished speaking all these words, the ground beneath them split open. The earth opened its mouth and swallowed them and their households, all Korah's people, and all their possessions. They went down alive into Sheol with all that belonged to them. The earth closed over them, and they vanished from the assembly.... Fire also came out from the Lord and consumed the 250 men who were presenting the incense" (Num. 16:31-33, 35).

If that isn't enough, the next day the entire Israelite community complains that Moses has killed the Lord's people. Immediately, the Shekinah glory appears, covering the tabernacle. God sends a plague that takes the lives of 14,700 - a number that would have been greater had Moses and Aaron not intervened on the people's behalf.

Korah's rebellion is not so much against God's anointed leaders as it is against God Himself. By rejecting Moses and Aaron, and by embracing arrogant substitutes who foolishly portray themselves as eminently qualified, the people become eyewitnesses of God's judgment and then suffer the consequences of their hard-hearted rebellion.

In a similar manner, the false teachers in Jude's day rebel against God's authority in the local church and thus poke their fingers in the eye of their offended God. As a result, they will be destroyed as suddenly as Korah and his apostate followers. Jude is so certain of the false teachers' destruction that he states it in the past tense.

Korah's words against Moses and Aaron should serve to remind us that we are held accountable for how we speak about those in authority over us. Paul writes to Titus with these instructions: "Remind them [God's people] to be submissive to rulers and authorities, to obey, to be ready for every good work, to slander no one, to avoid fighting, and to be kind, always showing gentleness to all people. For we too were once foolish, disobedient, deceived, captives of various passions and pleasures, living in malice and envy, hateful, detesting one another" (Titus 3:1-3).

Paul then assures Titus of God's redeeming mercy and grace, which naturally prompt His people to good works. He follows up with a final warning: "But avoid foolish debates, genealogies, quarrels, and disputes about the law, for they are unprofitable and worthless. Reject a divisive person after a first and second warning, knowing that such a person is perverted and sins, being self-condemned" (Titus 3:9-11).

In summarizing the triad of rascals from Israel's past, Jude reminds his readers that opposing God's chosen leaders is a dangerous game. The false teachers of the first century have carved out a place of service in the church, but they are not satisfied to submit to the God-ordained authority over them. In their arrogance, they speak against the apostles and other church leaders and, like the "super apostles" of 2 Corinthians 11-12, maneuver for positions of higher influence.

While castigating true servants of the Lord, these renegades are oblivious to the ground splitting open beneath their feet and the great white throne awaiting their arrival.

Warren Wiersbe summarizes Jude 11 with great insight: "Cain rebelled against God's authority in *salvation*, for he refused to bring a blood sacrifice as God had commanded. Balaam rebelled against God's authority in *separation*, for he prostituted his gifts for money and led Israel to mix with the other nations. Korah rebelled against God's authority in *service*, denying that Moses was God's appointed servant and attempting to usurp his authority."[11]

Is the rebel spirit alive today?

False teachers in the 21st century have much in common with Cain, Balaam, and Korah. They redefine God's work of salvation, peddle prophecy for profits, and exalt themselves above the authorities Christ has ordained for His church. While many examples could be cited, let's consider proponents of today's Word of Faith movement - a vast and varied brand of apostate Christianity that shamelessly follows in the footsteps of ancient Israel's unholy triumvirate. The central teaching of the Word of Faith movement - also known as the prosperity gospel and the health and wealth gospel - is that God wills our prosperity and health; therefore, to be a Christian in poverty or sickness is to be outside the will of God.

Take note of the following Word of Faith teachings and see if you can trace them to the way of Cain (self-centered religion), the error of Balaam (a gospel of greed), or the rebellion of Korah (mutiny against divinely appointed authorities):

Human beings are little gods. Human nature consists of body, soul, and spirit, but the spirit is the real person made in God's image; therefore, human beings are exact duplicates of God, or little gods. Our problem is that we allow our bodies and souls to control our lives rather than our own divine spirits.

God is like us. He is a God that possesses faith. He created the world by faith and accomplishes His will by believing things in His heart and speaking words of faith, thereby bringing things into existence. We may do the same.

Jesus came to restore our godhood. When Adam fell, he forfeited his status as the god of this world by obeying Satan, who in turn gained legal dominion over this world and passed Satan's nature of death, along with sickness and poverty, down to the rest of humanity. Jesus came to create a new race of humans who, like Jesus, would be God incarnate.

Jesus went to hell. In dying spiritually on the cross, Jesus took on Satan's nature and went to hell, where He was "born again," rising from the dead with God's nature. In hell, not on the cross, Jesus secured our salvation. This paved the way for us to be born again and exhibit God's nature in our lives.

Faith is believing we have whatever we say. Faith is speaking to things and circumstances - like check books and illnesses - and commanding them to do as we say. This is the basis of positive and negative confession, the idea that what we believe and say, whether good or bad, comes to pass.

Our divine birthright is financial prosperity and good health. Since we are divine spirits created and redeemed to rule our circumstances by speaking words of faith, we are to obtain health and wealth. Believers need not accept sickness or poverty into our lives.[12]

What's wrong with today's prosperity preachers?

The champions of today's Word of Faith movement boast of special holy anointing. They base doctrines on alleged dreams and visions, exalt themselves, and pursue fleshly desires. Briefly, here are five errors of the Word of Faith movement:

It abuses the Bible. Specifically, promoters of the Word of Faith movement commit three common errors of biblical interpretation:

- First, they ignore the context. Take 3 John 2, a commonly claimed passage in support of Christian prosperity: "Dear friend, I pray that you may prosper in every way and be in good health, just as your soul prospers." This verse must be read as part of the full narrative, and the full narrative must be considered in light of the intended audience, and in comparison with the rest of Scripture. John's words are a common greeting used in first-century letters and therefore should not be taken as a promise of health and wealth, either in the first century or today. We must bear in mind that the Bible was written to certain people at specific times. That doesn't mean the Scriptures are less authoritative or less relevant today. It simply means we cannot disregard the historical setting of each book. The primary audience was never intended to be 21st century Americans.

- Second, they rely on extra-biblical experiences to establish their interpretations of Scripture. It is not uncommon to hear prosperity preachers say God spoke to them in an audible voice, or appeared to them in dreams and visions. This is not to deny that the Lord uses dreams and visions to speak to people today, but it's not the norm. Further, we must lay all experiences against the yardstick of Scripture. The canon is closed, and we must take pains not to add to or take away from God's Word. As a caution, Mormonism is based largely on the alleged visions of Joseph Smith. These visions led to false doctrines concerning the nature of God, the finished work of Jesus on the cross, and the ultimate destiny of human beings.

- Third, they begin with doctrine rather than with the Bible. Based on dreams, visions, prophecies, and other subjective experiences, they formulate new teachings that tickle the ear rather than lead to godliness (2 Tim. 4:3). Many counterfeit forms of Christianity begin this way. Charles Taze Russell, who established a Bible study that morphed into the Watch Tower Bible and Tract Society (the Jehovah's Witnesses), rejected the Trinity, the deity of Christ, and the doctrine of an eternal hell because he found them unreasonable. The end result is a worldwide organization that follows the teachings of the Watch Tower rather than the truth of God's Word.

It is man-centered rather than God-centered. Some Word of Faith leaders go so far as to describe God as having a body similar to that of man, and conversely describe humans as "little gods." We are exact duplicates of God, say several prosperity preachers. This deifies people and demotes God to a subservient role in which He waits for us to grant Him permission to work in the world.

It promotes a false theology of giving. God's gifts to us - for example, His creation, grace, mercy, and eternal life - are unmerited; they cannot be bought, bartered, or inherited. The Word of Faith movement, however, pursues a *quid pro quo* approach to stewardship. In other words, if Christians say and do certain things, God is honor-bound to grant their wishes.

146

It oppresses the poor and the sick. Since prosperity preachers insist that our words of faith create wealth and healing, a lack of these blessings is due to an absence of faith. People in poverty, for example, are there by their own doing, while people who are disabled, ill, or riddled with cancer are failing to appropriate the faith that would make them well.

It denies the cost of discipleship. Jesus is an itinerant teacher who places little value on an earthly home, warning those who seek to follow Him that "the Son of Man has no place to lay his head" (Matt. 8:20b). He further tells His followers that those who cling to possessions fail to be kingdom-minded: "I assure you: It will be hard for a rich person to enter the kingdom of heaven! Again I tell you, it is easier for a camel to go through the eye of a needle than for a rich person to enter the kingdom of God" (Matt. 19:23-24).

The disciples react in amazement. Peter responds to Jesus, "Look, we have left everything and followed you. So what will there be for us?" (Matt. 19:27). Jesus assures the apostles that when the Son of Man sits on His glorious throne, they also will sit on twelve thrones. He further promises that "everyone who has left houses, brothers or sisters, father or mother, children, or fields because of My name will receive 100 times more and will inherit eternal life" (Matt. 19:28-29).

Our Lord makes no promises of prosperity and comfort in this life. Those who claim that "100 times more" means a hundred-fold increase of material blessings on earth are guilty of taking the Savior's words out of context and twisting them to enlarge their own tents.

If the health and wealth gospel is true, the apostles are miserable failures. According to biblical accounts, tradition, and church history, it's likely that all of the apostles suffer martyrs' deaths with the exception of John, who is boiled in oil and, after surviving the ordeal, is exiled to Patmos. This is hardly a rousing endorsement of the prosperity gospel.

Finally, the Bible tells us that all true followers of Jesus are to expect hardship - not wealth, health, and leisure - as a result of their faith. Writing about his "persecutions and sufferings" at Antioch, Iconium, and Lystra, Paul warns, "In fact, all those who want to live a godly life in Christ Jesus will be persecuted" (2 Tim. 3:12).

Paul writes to the Philippians that his goal is "to know Him and the power of His resurrection and *the fellowship of His sufferings*, being conformed to His death" (Phil. 3:10 - emphasis added).

After being stoned, dragged outside the city of Lystra, and left for dead, Paul returns to the city, strengthening the hearts of the disciples and "encouraging them to continue in the faith, and by telling them, 'It is necessary to pass through many troubles on our way into the kingdom of God'" (Acts 14:22).

Writing to believers in the provinces of Pontus, Galatia, Cappadocia, Asia, and Bithynia, Peter reminds his readers to expect suffering for the sake of Christ: "Dear friends, when the fiery ordeal arises among you to test you, don't be surprised by it, as if something unusual were happening to you. Instead, as you share in the sufferings of the Messiah rejoice, so that you may also rejoice with great joy at the revelation of His glory. If you are ridiculed for the name of Christ, you are blessed, because the Spirit of glory and of God rests on you. None of you, however, should suffer as a murderer, a thief, an evildoer, or as a meddler. But if anyone suffers as a Christian, he should not be ashamed, but should glorify God with that name" (1 Peter 4:12-16).

Other passages of Scripture could be cited, but the point is this: Even a casual reader of the New Testament finds that suffering, persecution, and poverty are far more prevalent among believers than riches and comfort.

This is not to say wealth is evil; it is, in fact, morally neutral. However, the desire for riches is a snare that leads many believers down a path of destruction, as Paul notes: "For *the love of money* is a root of all kinds of evil, and by craving it, some have wandered away from the faith and pierced themselves with many pains" (1 Tim. 6:10 - emphasis added).

What should be our attitude toward wealth and health?

So, how should Christians respond to the prosperity gospel and its false teachings about money and comfort?

We should be content with what we have. Paul experiences many hardships in his ministry - beatings, being left for dead, shipwreck, hunger, cold, imprisonment, and much more. Yet he writes that he has "learned" to be content (see Phil 4:11-12). Further, he reminds Timothy that "godliness with contentment is great gain" (1 Tim. 6:6).

We should be indifferent toward wealth. Prosperity is neither good nor evil. But our attitude toward it reveals a great deal about us (see 1 Tim. 6:6-10, 17-19). Agur's request of the Lord in Prov. 30:8b-9 expresses a proper attitude toward worldly gain: "Give me neither poverty nor wealth; feed me with the food I need. Otherwise, I might have too much and deny You, saying 'Who is the Lord?' or I might have nothing and steal, profaning the name of my God."

Jesus specifically warns us against laying up treasures on earth (Matt. 6:19-21), and reminds us that we cannot be slaves to both God and money (Matt. 6:24).

We should see poverty and sickness in light of the Fall. Sin and its consequences affect all people. Our mortal bodies are subject to the ravages of the curse. We get sick, contract diseases, suffer injuries, grow old, and ultimately die. Poverty may afflict us if we are slothful, disadvantaged, or oppressed. Jesus' story of Lazarus and the rich man tells us that the wicked sometimes prosper and the righteous sometimes suffer, but in the end God, who sees the heart, sets everything right (Luke 16:19-31).

It is important to note that God entrusts every human being with an ability to make choices for which we experience consequences. Oftentimes, these choices reflect an eternal perspective (see, for example, Matt. 19:16-22; Luke 12:16-21). We also should remember that God sometimes uses sickness and death as acts of divine discipline (see Acts 5:1-11; 1 Cor. 11:27-32).

Signs, wonders, and miracles accompany Paul's ministry (Rom. 15:19; 2 Cor. 12:12). Yet neither he nor his associates experience health at all times. "And *never* is their sickness attributed to a lack of faith, nor their recovery to great faith," writes Gordon. D. Fee.[13]

For example, Epaphroditus falls ill and nearly dies, yet "God had mercy on him" (Phil. 2:27). Paul leaves Trophimus sick in Melitus (2 Tim. 4:20). When Timothy suffers frequent stomach ailments, Paul does not tell the young pastor to claim healing but to "use a little wine" (1 Tim. 5:23).

We should look ahead. For Christians, a day is coming when God wipes every tear from our eyes. Death exists no longer. Grief, crying, and pain are gone "because the previous things have passed away" (Rev. 21:4).

A day of health and prosperity is coming for all who call upon the Lord. As adopted children of God and joint-heirs with Jesus, we are to dwell in the heavenly city that knows nothing of darkness or doom. The Father and the Lamb light the New Jerusalem with Their presence, and nothing profane ever enters it.

While faithful saints on this side of heaven may endure torture, mocking, scourging, bonds, imprisonment, stoning, death by the saw and sword, destitution, affliction, mistreatment, sheepskins for clothing, living in caves and holes in the ground, they are "approved through their faith," and in heaven one day they walk the streets of gold (see Heb. 11:35-40; Revelation 21-22).

We should understand that God deals harshly with false teachers. Like Cain, Balaam, Korah, and first-century false teachers, peddlers of the prosperity gospel will give an account before God one day for the degree to which they fleeced the flock.

Jesus tells His disciples, "Much will be required of everyone who has been given much. And even more will be expected of the one who has been entrusted with more" (Luke 12:48b). No doubt the Word of Faith hawkers are gifted communicators with worldwide platforms to proclaim the gospel. Unfortunately, they misuse their gifts and abuse the Word of God, keeping many from the kingdom, and driving believers away in despair because they lack the "faith" to see their dreams come true.

Jesus calls the scribes and Pharisees "hypocrites" and tells them, "You lock up the kingdom of heaven from people. For you don't go in, and you don't allow those entering to go in.... Snakes! Brood of vipers! How can you escape being condemned to hell?" (Matt. 23:13, 33). In a similar manner, today's prosperity preachers prevent their followers from entering the kingdom by proclaiming "another Jesus ... a different spirit ... a different gospel" (2 Cor. 11:4).

In the Sermon on the Mount, Jesus warns of false prophets who come in sheep's clothing, but inwardly are ravaging wolves. "You'll recognize them by their fruit," He says; that is, their unbiblical doctrine exposes their true nature. Jesus describes their day of reckoning: "On that day many will say to Me, 'Lord, Lord, didn't we prophesy in Your name, drive out demons in Your name, and do many miracles in Your name?' Then I will announce to them, 'I never knew you! Depart from Me, you lawbreakers!'" (Matt. 7:15-22).

The apostle Peter writes, "But there were also false prophets among the people, just as there will be false teachers among you. They will secretly bring in destructive heresies, even denying the Master who bought them, and will bring swift destruction on themselves. Many will follow their unrestrained ways, and because of them the way of truth will be blasphemed. In their greed they will exploit you with deceptive words. Their condemnation, pronounced long ago, is not idle, and their destruction does not sleep" (2 Peter 2:1-3).

It's not too late for false teachers to repent. Meanwhile, faithful teachers are urged to remain true to the Lord. Peter exhorts elders of the Dispersion to "shepherd God's flock among you, not overseeing out of compulsion but freely, according to God's will; not for the money but eagerly; not lording it over those entrusted to you, but being examples to the flock. And when the chief Shepherd appears, you will receive the unfading crown of glory" (1 Peter 5:2-4).

Key words

In this chapter, we learned several key terms. Test your knowledge by filling in the blanks.

Way of Cain. The way of Cain is the way of religion without _____. It is the way of pride, a man establishing his own _____ and rejecting the righteousness of God that comes through _____.

Error of Balaam. The error of Balaam is using God-given _____ to feed fleshly desires. The false teachers of Jude's day seek to _____ themselves, as Balaam does, and to satisfy their lustful passions - all the while claiming _____ as the source of their messages.

Korah's rebellion. Korah leads a revolt against _____ and _____, but even more against _____ Himself. In a similar manner, the false teachers of whom Jude speaks rebel against God's authority in the local _____ and thus poke their fingers in the eye of their offended God.

Word of Faith. Also known as the prosperity gospel and the health and wealth gospel, the Word of Faith movement teaches that God wills our _____ and _____; therefore, to be a Christian in _____ or _____ is to be outside the will of God.

Comparing English translations of *paraphronia*, used to describe the mindset of Balaam in 2 Peter 2:16, and literally meaning "beside one's own mind":

HCSB	KJV	NIV	NASB	ESV
madness / irrationality	madness	madness	madness	madness

Application
Questions for personal or group study

Your good friend Lisa picks you up in her new BMW and treats you to dinner at a pricey bistro. As a captive audience of one, you listen to her describe her "spiritual breakthrough" in which she now possesses the same faith God had when He spoke the universe into existence.

"I've learned to speak words of faith over my life," she says, "and now everything is possible for me." Lisa is in excellent health and seems to fall into money the way people trip over bad carpeting. She is a rabid follower of several internationally acclaimed Word of Faith teachers and says she has applied their spiritual insights to her life - with dramatic results.

Pausing to scan the dessert menu, she says, "So, what do you think?"

First, tell Lisa you'll have the crème brulee. Then, consider asking her the following questions, while grounding your answers in Scripture:

1. **Little gods?** Are you aware that many Word of Faith teachers proclaim that we are "little gods"? Do you believe the Bible teaches this? If so, in what way are you a little god? Are you equal with Jesus in divinity? Do you realize that Satan tempted Eve with the promise of becoming like God?

2. **How much is enough?** How much wealth are you entitled to as a child of God? How much is enough, and when will you know you are there? What do you think God wants you to do with your financial blessings?

3. **Why did Jesus die?** Did Jesus die because He made "negative confessions" about going to the cross? Why couldn't He defeat Satan through "positive confessions" rather than through His suffering and death? Are you aware that many Word of Faith leaders say Jesus suffered in hell for three days at the hands of Satan and his demons? How is this possible when Jesus said hell was created for Satan and demons as a place for *their* punishment, not His (Matt. 25:41)? And are you aware that Satan is not in hell yet? He will be sent there at the return of Jesus (Rev. 20:10). Today, Satan is roaming the earth, according to the apostle Peter (1 Peter 5:8).

4. **Can God discipline us?** Do you believe God has a right to discipline us for sin? If so, might that discipline include illness, or even death (see Acts 5:1-11; 1 Cor. 11:27-32)?

5. **Does God have faith?** Are you aware that prosperity preachers claim God has faith, which He uses to create reality? If God has faith, how can He be all-knowing and all-powerful, since faith implies an absence of knowledge and/or power?

6. **Who creates wealth?** Where do prosperity preachers get their wealth? Do they follow the same rules they impose on you? For example, has a prosperity preacher ever given away all of his or her earthly wealth in order to claim a "hundredfold increase" from God? Then why do some of them ask you to give your last dollar to their ministry while they live in luxury?

7. **Whose fault is poverty and sickness?** If you get sick or become poor, is it due to your lack of faith? Are you aware that many Word of Faith leaders suffer illness and disease, and all of them eventually die? Could the actions of other people make you sick or poor, even though you positively confess health and prosperity? Whose lack of faith leads to the suffering and death of children, and to the abortion of unborn babies?

8. **Does God have a body?** Did you know that many Word of Faith leaders teach that God has a physical body? Are you aware that Mormons teach the same doctrine, but the Bible does not?

9. **What is your motive?** Do you love God for who He is or for what He can do for you? Is it possible that you embrace the Word of Faith movement because you like the idea of being healthy and prosperous, not because it's true? Is God a means to an end for you - that end being wealth, health, comfort, and exaltation in the eyes of other people?

10. **What does the Bible really say?** How carefully have you tested the prosperity preachers' doctrines according to the Bible? When they claim out-of-body experiences or personal

encounters with Jesus, do you test their alleged experiences by the Word of God? If their "revelations" are contrary to Scripture, which one do you believe?

One final consideration: If you pose these questions to Lisa, be prepared to split the check (and download the Uber app; you may need a ride home).

In the end, the apostate strikes a fatal blow to himself, for he has passed the point of no return and – like the scribes and Pharisees of Jesus' day – brings upon himself "greater damnation."

11

Crossing the Line:
Can Apostates Be Christians?

Of all the terms Jude uses to describe false teachers - ungodly, dreamers, dangerous reefs, waterless clouds, wild waves of the sea, wandering stars, and discontented grumblers, to name a few - he stops short of calling them apostates. Yet that is what they are. Hey Jude, what gives?

A closer look at the New Testament's sparing use of this term may prove helpful, particularly as we broach the thorny subject of apostates' standing with God. Are apostates backslidden Christians? Shameless pretenders? Or people who once knew Christ but now have willfully rejected Him, thus losing their salvation?

Originally, the Greek word *apostasia* meant rebellion against government. The Apocryphal book of 1 Esdras describes the Jews as "rebels" against King Artaxerxes (1 Esdras 2:23). Later, the term "apostate" is applied to "one who rebels against God."[1]

As Eugene E. Carpenter and Philip W. Comfort note, "Apostasy, therefore, is serious business. People who commit apostasy abandon their faith and repudiate their former beliefs. It is not heresy (denial of part of the faith), or the transfer of allegiance from one religious body to another within the same faith. Apostasy is a complete and final rejection of God."[2]

John MacArthur defines apostasy as "the sin of rejecting the gospel for which there is no forgiveness." He further describes it as "an intentional falling away or withdrawal, a defection." Apostates, he writes, "are people who move toward Christ, right up to the edge of saving belief," but then "their interest in the things of God begins to wane, and the pressures and attractions of the world distract them further still, until they have no interest at all. They may turn to another religion or to no religion at all. Apostasy is determined by what you leave, not where you go after you leave. After a person leaves God, it makes little difference where he then goes."[3]

An apostate, then, is someone who has received the knowledge of the truth, but willfully and decisively rejects it.

Apostasia appears only twice in the New Testament. The apostle Paul is accused of apostasy for teaching others to "*abandon* Moses, by telling them [Jews living among Gentiles] not to circumcise their children or to walk in our customs" (Acts 21:21b - emphasis added). And Paul warns the Thessalonians not to be deceived by those claiming that the Day of the Lord has already come. "Don't let anyone deceive you in any way," he writes. "For that day will not come unless the *apostasy* comes first and the man of lawlessness is revealed, the son of destruction" (2 Thess. 2:3 - emphasis added).

Many other passages of Scripture describe people who abandon the faith, never to return. The apostle John writes of "antichrists" who "went out from us, but they did not belong to us; for if they had belonged to us, they would have remained with us. However, they went out so that it might be made clear that none of them belongs to us" (1 John 2:19).

Paul points to Hymenaeus and Alexander as examples of those who have rejected "faith and a good conscience" and thus "have suffered the shipwreck of their faith." The apostle informs Timothy that he has "delivered them to Satan, so that they may be taught not to blaspheme" (1 Tim. 1:19-20).

Peter warns that those who profess faith in Christ and then walk away are like dogs returning to their vomit, and like sows who, after being washed, wallow in the mud. He writes, "For it would have been better for them not to have known the way of righteousness than, after knowing it, to turn back from the holy commandment delivered to them" (2 Peter 2:21).

The writer of Hebrews describes certain professing Jewish Christians who are beyond repentance because they have returned to the practice of offering animal sacrifices for the forgiveness of sins (Heb. 6:1-6). This is the same as trampling on the Son of God and regarding as profane the blood of the covenant (Heb. 10:1-31).

Distinguishing marks

These passages, and others like them, illuminate certain qualities that distinguish apostates from backslidden believers, as well as from unbelievers who have yet to hear the gospel.

First, apostates possess knowledge of the truth of the gospel and often initially profess belief in Christ. Like the seed cast on rocky soil, they spring up quickly, only to wilt under the scorching rays of pressure or persecution (Matt. 13:3-9, 18-23).

Second, apostates willfully reject the gospel. They go beyond sincere doubt and deny the very doctrines that define true Christianity - particularly those beliefs having to do with the person and work of Jesus. It's fair to say that all apostates are unbelievers, but not all unbelievers are apostates. Some unbelievers have yet to hear the gospel, and others are in various stages of wrestling with its truth.

Third, apostates have passed the point of no return. In particularly graphic terms, Peter describes them as dogs returning to their vomit, and sows returning to the muck. The writer of Hebrews says it is impossible to bring them back to the point of repentance (Heb. 6:4). Jesus and Paul at times speak of an apostate's measure of sin that, once full, brings a swift and certain end to mercy, as well as the full weight of divine wrath (Matt. 23:31-32; 1 Thess. 2:16). And Jude speaks of the apostates' damnation as already secured (Jude 4).

Finally, apostates are most dangerous when they remain in the church. John describes those who went *out* from among believers - to paganism, the cult of Caesar, vain philosophy, or some other false belief system (see 1 John 2:19). While their departure is tragic, these apostates no longer pose a direct threat to the body of Christ. However, those who have fully and finally rejected the faith, and yet continue to profess it, are apostates of the most dangerous kind.

As Ralph Earle writes in a commentary on 2 Thess. 2:3, "This emphasis on an apostasy from within takes on added significance in the light of recent developments in the church world. There was a day when the Bob Ingersolls railed and ranted against Christianity. [Ingersoll was a 19th century American orator known as 'The Great Agnostic.'] Now this opposition comes from within the church. When teachers of theology in leading theological seminaries in America tell their ministerial students that God is dead, and when a prominent denominational leader declares that it is a sin to believe in individual salvation, it would seem that 'The Apostasy' has come."[4]

While passages such as Heb. 6:1-6 are difficult to interpret and are much debated, it nevertheless seems faithful to Scripture to conclude that apostates are unbelievers who were never justified by faith to begin with, and who, because of the collateral damage they cause to the church, are to be severely judged.

What causes apostasy?

But what factors contribute to a person's "falling away"? There appear to be several. Certainly, one cause is the influence of false teachers in the church. Jesus tells His disciples, "Many false prophets will rise up and deceive many" (Matt. 24:11). Paul similarly warns Timothy of a coming day when people will not tolerate sound doctrine, "but according to their own desires, will accumulate teachers for themselves because they have an itch to hear something new" (2 Tim. 4:3b).

Persecution is another contributor. "Then they will hand you over for persecution, and they will kill you," says Jesus. "You will be hated by all nations because of My name. Then many will take offense, betray one another and hate one another" (Matt. 24:9-10).

Another cause of apostasy is temptation, particularly the temptation to pursue the things of this world. In explaining the parable of the sower, Jesus says, "As for the seed that fell among thorns, these are the ones who, when they have heard, go on their way and are choked with worries, riches, and pleasures of life, and produce no mature fruit" (Luke 8:14). Paul urges young Timothy to come to him soon, "for Demas has deserted me, because he loved this present world" (2 Tim. 4:10a).

Still another factor is resisting the Holy Spirit, or neglecting His call. Stephen speaks boldly to the religious leaders of his day, "You stiff-necked people with uncircumcised hearts and ears! You are always resisting the Holy Spirit; as your forefathers did, so do you" (Acts 7:51). And the writer of Hebrews asks rhetorically, "[H]ow will we escape if we neglect such a great salvation?" (Heb. 2:3a).

The apostate is more than a danger to the church, and more than a danger to the unbeliever who otherwise may be drawn to the gospel. In the end, the apostate strikes a fatal blow to himself, for he has passed the point of no return and - like the scribes and Pharisees of Jesus' day - brings upon himself "greater damnation" (Matt. 23:14b KJV).

Many passages on final judgment of the ungodly could be cited, but Paul's depiction is a concise summary: "... it is righteous for God to repay with affliction those who afflict you ... This will take place at the revelation of the Lord Jesus from heaven with His powerful angels, taking vengeance with flaming fire on those who don't know God and on those who don't obey the gospel of our Lord Jesus. These will pay the penalty of everlasting destruction, away from the Lord's presence and from His glorious strength" (2 Thess. 1:6-9).

Proportion and punishment

It appears that judgment of the wicked is in proportion to sin. For example, Jesus tells Pilate, "This is why the one who handed Me over to you has the greater sin" (John 19:11b). Both Pilate and Judas are unbelievers, but Judas is an apostate; therefore, his sin is greater than Pilate's and carries harsher consequences.

In Luke 12:47-48, Jesus tells His disciples that judgment also is in proportion to knowledge and obedience: "And that slave who knew his master's will and didn't prepare himself or do it will be severely beaten. But the one who did not know and did things deserving of blows will be beaten lightly. Much will be required of everyone who has been given much. And even more will be expected of the one who has been entrusted with more."

The writer of Hebrews adds, "How much worse punishment, do you think one will deserve who has trampled on the Son of God, regarded as profane the blood of the covenant by which he was sanctified, and insulted the spirit of grace?" (Heb. 10:29).

Wayne Grudem, addressing the topic of the "unpardonable sin," refers to Heb. 6:4-6 and writes, "There the persons who 'commit apostasy' have had all sorts of knowledge and conviction of the truth: they have 'been enlightened' and have 'tasted the heavenly gift'; they have participated in some ways in the work of the Holy Spirit and 'have tasted the goodness of the word of God and the powers of the age to come,' yet they then willfully turn away from Christ and 'hold him up to contempt' (Heb. 6:6). They too have put themselves beyond the reach of God's ordinary means of bringing people to repentance and faith. Knowing and being convinced of the truth, they willfully reject it."[5]

While "crossing the line" into apostasy is a troubling topic to consider, we should not allow the condemnation of those who have fallen away to drag us into despair about our own sincere doubts and spiritual setbacks. As Grudem cautions, "The fact that the unpardonable sin involves such extreme hardness of heart and lack of repentance indicates that those who fear they have committed it, yet still have sorrow for sin in their heart and desire to seek after God, certainly do not fall in the category of those who are guilty of it."[6]

A final thought: It may be difficult at times to distinguish between an apostate and a backslidden believer. But ultimately, the role of deciding who's in God's kingdom and who's not isn't ours; it belongs to our sovereign Lord. For our part, we should concern ourselves first of all with our own relationship with Christ. As Paul writes, "Test yourselves to see if you are in the faith. Examine yourselves. Or do you not recognize for yourselves that Jesus Christ is in you? - unless you fail the test" (2 Cor. 13:5).

Next, we should embrace sound doctrine, earnestly contending for the faith delivered to the saints once for all (Jude 3). We should always be ready to give a defense to anyone who asks us for a reason for the hope that is in us - doing so with gentleness and respect (1 Peter 3:15-16). And we should proclaim the message of Christ, persisting in it whether convenient or not, rebuking, correcting, and encouraging with great patience and teaching (2 Tim. 4:2).

The apostates among us will never turn back; the gloom of eternal darkness awaits them (2 Peter 2:17b). Meanwhile, backslidden believers will never be lost, although they should be subject to church discipline and may fall under divine discipline, even to the point of premature death (see Matt. 18:15-20; 1 Cor. 11:27-32; Heb. 12:3-12). In the end, we can't judge the human heart, but we can recognize apostates by their fruit - that is, their doctrines and lifestyles (Matt. 7:15-20).

Key word

In this chapter, we learned a key term that is used sparingly in the New Testament. Test your knowledge by filling in the blanks.

Apostasia. This Greek word appears only _____ in the New Testament. The apostle Paul is accused of _____ for teaching others to "abandon Moses, by telling them [Jews living among Gentiles] not to circumcise their children or to walk in our customs" (Acts 21:21).

Paul warns the Thessalonians not to be _____ by those claiming that the Day of the Lord has already come. "Don't let anyone deceive you in any way," he writes. "For that day will not come unless the _____ comes first and the man of lawlessness is revealed, the son of destruction" (2 Thess. 2:3).

An apostate is someone who has _____ the knowledge of the truth, but willfully and decisively _____ it.

Comparing English translations of *apostasia* in 2 Thess. 2:3:

HCSB	KJV	NIV	NASB	ESV
apostasy (rebellion)	falling away	rebellion	apostasy	rebellion

Application
Questions for personal or group study

1. Jude depicts the false teachers of his day as apostates - unbelievers who have passed the point of no return. How does he use verses 4, 10, 11, 13, and 19 to build his case?

2. Jesus instructs us not to judge hypocritically (Matt. 7:1-6). And none of us can say with certainty that a person is beyond redemption. So, why does Jude boldly state, in so many words, that the false teachers he describes in his epistle are bound for hell? Who is he to judge?

3. Read Gen. 15:13-16. What do you think the Lord means when He tells Abram, "the iniquity of the Amorites has not yet reached its full measure"? And why would God make Abram's descendants suffer for 400 years in Egyptian bondage while He waits in vain on the Amorites to repent?

4. Consider Jesus' harsh words to the scribes and Pharisees in Matt. 23:29-32. In what way are their sins tied to the sins of their forefathers? To what future event is Jesus referring when He says, "Fill up, then, the measure of your fathers' sins!"?

5. Read 1 Thess. 2:13-16. Who, specifically, is "adding to the number of their sins"? And what is their standing with God?

6. Scripture indicates that a person may pass a "point of no return" in his or her rebellion against God. How does Paul describe this descending spiral of ungodliness in Romans 1? What does Paul say is God's response to the unrepentant sinner?

7. Why do you think God lets some people drift so far away from Him that they are beyond repentance? Is there a limit to His grace and mercy?

8. Do you think only God knows when people have filled up their measure of sins? Is it possible they don't even know? And if they do know, why *can't* they - or why *won't* they - do anything about it?

9. Compare Matt. 12:22-32 with Heb. 6:4-8. How is the so-called "unpardonable sin" of which Jesus speaks similar to the apostasy that the writer of Hebrews describes?

10. How would you counsel someone who fears he or she has committed the unpardonable sin?

12

Wild Waves and Wandering Stars:
The Doom of False Teachers

*These are the ones who are like dangerous reefs at
your love feasts. They feast with you, nurturing only
themselves without fear. They are waterless clouds
carried along by winds; trees in late autumn – fruitless,
twice dead, pulled out by the roots; wild waves of the
sea, foaming up their shameful deeds; wandering stars
for whom is reserved the blackness of darkness forever!
(Jude 12-13 HCSB)*

Driving west on a county road in central Missouri, I watched in fascination as a meteor streaked brilliantly against the predawn blackness of a moonless sky. Meteors, or shooting stars, are fairly common. They are fragments of rock or iron from outer space that enter the earth's atmosphere. They range in size from less than a gram to more than 60 tons, and if they survive their fiery journey across our skies and thus become meteorites, they can strike the earth with enough force to leave huge craters, destroy property, and injure people.[1]

The most destructive meteorite strike of the 20th century occurred in a remote area of Siberia in 1908. The so-called Tunguska Event leveled more than 80 million trees and covered almost 850 miles. Astoundingly, no one was injured.[2]

More recently, the Chelyabinsk meteor that entered earth's atmosphere over Russia in 2013 was brighter than the sun, exploding about 18 miles above the earth and producing a hot cloud of dust and gas, with an atmospheric impact so intense that it resulted in a large shock wave, damaging 7,200 buildings and injuring 1,500 people.[3]

The meteor I witnessed that dark morning was nothing like the Siberian event or the Chelyabinsk fireball, but it was the brightest shooting star I had ever seen. It seemed to hang in the sky for a long time before dimming and then vanishing on the horizon. It seemed so big, so bright, and so close that I expected it to strike the earth, create a fireball on impact, and shake the ground. But nothing happened. I explored for signs of an impact but saw none. I even checked the news; surely someone else had seen this brilliant meteor paint the sky. Nothing. No news reports. No trending social media. Silence. And blackness.

The apostates of Jude's day are like meteors. They seemingly come out of nowhere. Stealthily, they slip into the church. And when they gain a foothold as teachers, they blaze above the Christian landscape - bright, striking, dazzling, eclipsing local church leaders who labor in obscurity for the kingdom. And then, after attracting so much attention, they are gone. The blackness from which they came returns to them - or rather, they return to it. A flash in the predawn sky of the first century is traded for an eternity in outer darkness.

Natural phenomena often make good object lessons. Jesus frequently uses commonly known articles from nature to drive home spiritual points. In the parable of the wheat and tares, for example, He illustrates the counterfeit work of Satan in this present evil age (Matt. 13:24-30, 36-43). In the story of the mustard seed, He shows His disciples how the kingdom of heaven advances from humble beginnings to towering majesty (Matt. 13:31-32; Mark 4:30-32; Luke 13:18-19). And in the parable of the dragnet full of fish, Jesus makes it clear that, in the age to come, God separates the citizens of the kingdom of heaven from those in Satan's domain (Matt. 13:47-50).

Jude follows this style of teaching. He compares false teachers to five phenomena from nature: dangerous reefs; waterless clouds; fruitless trees; wild waves; and wandering stars.

How are false teachers like natural phenomena?

Dangerous reefs

First, Jude likens false teachers to dangerous reefs[4] that present a very real threat to doctrinal integrity. Reefs are ridges of jagged rock, coral, or sand just above or below the surface of the sea. Often they are beautiful, colorful formations that teem with sea life and attract snorkelers. But they also feature sharp outcroppings that can rip open the hull of a ship or pierce the flesh of an unsuspecting diver.

In like manner, false teachers project attractive personas that lure immature believers with promises of sexual freedom and personal autonomy. But in the end, the apostates' rejection of sound doctrine, and their renunciation of a good conscience, cause them to suffer the shipwreck of their faith. But that is not the end. Like sirens - the mythological half-bird, half-woman creatures who lure sailors to destruction by the sweetness of their songs - these false teachers entice their pupils to join them on the rocks of spiritual destruction (1 Tim. 1:19).

Jude writes that false teachers attend the congregation's "love feasts," nurturing only themselves. Initially, love feasts are intended to be regular church gatherings where fellowship, encouragement, instruction, and care are experienced. "The feast was similar to a contemporary potluck dinner held on the Lord's Day," writes John MacArthur. "Believers would gather to worship, hear the teaching of Scripture, celebrate Communion, and then share their common love meal."[5]

Over time, however, false teachers so taint the love feasts, and so corrupt their attendees, that the feasts cease to be held. In 1 Cor. 11:17-22, the apostle Paul chastens the Corinthians for turning the Lord's Supper, observed during these times, into a drunken and gluttonous event. He reminds the Corinthians that because of this, some among the congregation are experiencing the chastening of Christ through sickness, weakness, and even death (vv. 27-30).

Even so, the false teachers fearlessly seek to satisfy their fleshly desires at these communal gatherings. Shrugging off any sense of Christian conscience, and sloughing off the mantle of authority, they illustrate the excesses of a libertine lifestyle with complete disregard of the consequences. These false teachers, writes Kenneth Wuest, "have no compunctions of conscience about participating in the fellowship of evangelical believers, posing as Christians."[6]

Paul warns Timothy that some false teachers are "liars whose consciences are seared." They have rejected the truth for so long, and have embraced "teachings of demons" to such an extent, that they are incapable of experiencing remorse for the damage they do to the spiritual well-being of others (1 Tim. 4:1-2). When professors of the Christian faith trade the fruit of the Spirit for the god of their bellies, the false teachers who lead them astray celebrate victory rather than bemoan defeat. The love feasts are designed for Christian fellowship and selfless ministry, but false teachers have twisted them into opportunities for self-indulgence.

Jude describes the apostates as "nurturing only themselves." The word "nurturing" is from *poimaino*, which means "to shepherd." Unfortunately, they care for no one but themselves. Jude may have in mind Ezek. 34:2b-4, which reads, "Woe to the shepherds of Israel, who have been feeding themselves! Shouldn't the shepherds feed their flock? You eat the fat, wear the wool, and butcher the fatlings, but you do not tend the flock. You have not strengthened the weak, healed the sick, bandaged the injured, brought back the strays, or sought the lost. Instead, you have ruled them with violence and cruelty."

As a result, the Lord declares, "Look, I am against the shepherds. I will demand My flock from them and prevent them from shepherding the flock. The shepherds will no longer feed themselves, for I will rescue My flock from their mouths so that they will not be food for them" (Ezek. 34:10).

As Thomas R. Schreiner notes, "The reference to shepherds indicates that the opponents were leaders, claiming that they had the ability to guide and lead God's people. But they had no concern for anyone but themselves. They did not exert effort and care for the flock but instead used their positions of leadership to establish a comfortable life for themselves."[7]

It is a solemn calling to be a shepherd over God's flock. Christ serves as the consummate example. He is the good shepherd who lays down His life for His sheep (John 10:11). In contrast, as Warren Wiersbe points out, false shepherds "use and abuse people in order to get what they want, and yet all the while, *the people love it!* Paul marveled at this when he wrote 2 Corinthians 11:20 - You don't mind, do you, if a man takes away your liberty, spends your money, takes advantage of you, puts on airs, or even smacks your face?"[8]

Like tropical reefs, adding continuously to their heft as coral and algae attach to them, false teachers indulge their flesh at the expense of unsuspecting pupils. They shepherd no one else as they grow larger and ever more dangerous. Jude sounds an alarm to the church: These charming, charismatic leaders are not who they seem, and their false doctrines only entice gullible followers to shipwreck themselves on the reefs of demonic teachings.

We should note in Jude 12 that the words "without fear," rendered "without the slightest qualm" in the NIV, come from the Greek *aphobos*, which means "shamelessly." The false teachers experience no pangs of conscience when they fill their bellies and puff out their chests at the expense of those they steer toward the rocks of spiritual destruction.

Waterless clouds

Nothing brings more anticipation in times of drought than gathering thunderheads above the horizon. How discouraging it is, however, when the only products of these swirling clouds are flashes of lightning and the rumbling of thunder. The clouds billow overhead and cast their shadows, display their sound and fury, and then drift away.

Palestine boasts an arid climate. Its people depend on rain at key times to sustain life, and perhaps nothing is more disappointing than mounting storm clouds that pass overhead without surrendering a drop of water.

Perhaps Solomon has this in mind when he writes, "The man who boasts about a gift that does not exist is like clouds and wind without rain" (Prov. 25:14).

Jude likens false teachers to clouds that tease us with the promise of rain but leave us high and dry. In a parallel passage, Peter likens them to "mists driven by a whirlwind" as they utter "bombastic, empty words," promising freedom while being unwitting "slaves of corruption" (2 Peter 2:17-19). They promote indulgence in the flesh as a gift of God's grace. In the end, however, libertine behavior fails to produce the promised spiritual satisfaction. Like rainless clouds, false teachers cast wide shadows but cannot quench their pupils' spiritual thirst.

The word translated "waterless" in Jude 12 (*anudros*) also appears in Matt. 12:43, where Jesus describes an unclean spirit coming out of a man. The spirit roams through "waterless places" looking in vain for rest. "By describing false teachers in the same way that Luke describes demons, Jude reiterated the connection between the apostates and their satanic sources."[9]

If Jesus' reference to "waterless places" seems elusive to us, it may help to know that this reflects a popular idea in His day that the parched deserts of Syria, Arabia, and Egypt are haunted by demons, who from these places launch invasions against unsuspecting people. In the apocryphal Book of Tobit, the demon Asmodeus flees to the upper parts of Egypt (8:3). And in Rev. 18:2, we're told that Babylon the Great, now fallen, is a dwelling for demons and a haunt for every unclean spirit.

Perhaps demons prefer barren places over lush landscapes because they don't want to be reminded of the beauty of God's creation, or because, like waterless places, they are void of spiritual nourishment. It also may be argued that desolate places symbolize those locations on earth that have not been well watered by the gospel; therefore, they make fertile ground for demonic influences.

Fruitless trees

Orchard workers labor year-round to ensure a bumper crop. They tend the soil, prune the limbs, ward off destructive pests, and use creative methods to keep unseasonable frosts at bay. Despite their best efforts, orchardists sometimes discover at harvest time that certain trees drop their leaves without ever producing fruit. The promise of a harvest goes unfulfilled, and the orchard worker must decide whether to labor another year with this tree or pull it up by its roots.

In Luke 13:6-9, Jesus tells a parable about a barren fig tree. The owner of the tree complains to the vinedresser that he has sought fruit for three consecutive years on this tree but has found none, and he instructs the vinedresser to cut it down. The vinedresser asks for one more year, promising to dig around the tree, fertilize it, and nurture a good crop if at all possible. "Perhaps it will bear fruit next year," says the vinedresser, "but if not, you can cut it down."

The parable is in reference to the nation of Israel, which has proven unresponsive to the Word of God. The Lord is patient, but there is a limit to His forbearance. Like the prophets of old, the Jewish people in first-century Israel reject God's message - and further, reject God's Son, the promised Messiah.

The analogy of fruitless trees finds an even broader application to the nation of Israel in the account of Jesus cursing the fig tree (Matt. 21:18-22; Mark 11:12-14, 20-25). Jesus comes upon a fig tree with leaves but no fruit. Alfred Edersheim explains that, in Palestine, fruit appears *before* the leaves. Therefore, this tree offered the promise of fruit but failed to deliver.[10]

It was a perfect object lesson for Jesus to share with His disciples. The nation of Israel, led by prophets, scribes, and interpreters of Scripture, is spiritually dead. As proof, the people are on the verge of calling for the crucifixion of the very Messiah they were raised up to worship. Now, the Savior's longsuffering is slowly turning to judgment, which falls hard on Jerusalem about 40 years after this encounter. In A.D. 70, the Roman general Titus besieges the great city, destroys the Temple, kills roughly one million Jews, and scatters the rest.

Though the Temple has not yet fallen at the time of Jude's epistle, the author writes of a similar spiritual barrenness displayed by false teachers who have infiltrated the early church. He describes them as "trees in late autumn - fruitless, twice dead, pulled up by the roots." What a contrast to the godly man whose delight is in the Lord's instruction. As the psalmist notes, "He is like a tree planted beside streams of water that bears its fruit in season and whose leaf does not wither. Whatever he does prospers" (Psalm 1:3).

The word "fruitless" in Jude 12 comes from the Greek *phthinoporina*, a compound term that captures the idea of waning, or wasting away, in late autumn. Jude's reference is to autumn trees without fruit at the precise time they are expected to bear fruit. Not only do they fail to produce a crop; they are incapable of doing so, and thus they are fit only to be pulled up by their roots and burned. In like manner, these false teachers are as devoid of spiritual fruit as twice-dead autumn trees.

In the Sermon on the Mount, Jesus provides His disciples a similar warning about false prophets. They appear as sheep, although inwardly they are ravaging wolves. "You'll recognize them by their fruit," He says. "Are grapes gathered from thorn bushes or figs from thistles? In the same way, every good tree produces good fruit, but a bad tree produces bad fruit. A good tree can't produce bad fruit; neither can a bad tree produce good fruit" (Matt. 7:16-18).

Of course, thorn bushes and thistles are incapable of producing nutritious food; it is not their nature to do so. Similarly, false prophets, who are spiritually dead, bear only the nonedible fruit of false doctrine. And what becomes of them? "Every tree that doesn't produce good fruit is cut down and thrown into the fire. So you'll recognize them by their fruit" (Matt. 7:19-20).

If there is any doubt about Christ's comparison of false prophets to fruitless trees, He goes on to explain that some false prophets are so heavily invested in deceiving others, they have deceived themselves: "Not everyone who says to Me, 'Lord, Lord!' will enter the kingdom of heaven, but only the one who does the will of My Father in heaven. On that day many will say to Me, 'Lord, Lord, didn't we prophesy in Your name, drive out demons in Your name, and do many miracles in Your name?'" Jesus does not deny that the false prophets did these things. He simply responds, "I never knew you! Depart from Me, you lawbreakers!" (Matt. 7:21-23).

For Jude, the false teachers who infiltrate the church must seem very much like the Jewish religious leaders about whom Jesus warns the apostles. They promise rich and satisfying spiritual food but produce nothing edible. Like twice-dead trees that farmers pull up by their roots and use for firewood, false teachers are destined for outer darkness, where the fires of judgment are never quenched.

Edward Pentecost writes, "The dead condition of apostate leaders was indicated by two things: (a) they did not bear spiritual fruit in others, and (b) they were without spiritual roots themselves, and thus faced judgment."[11] As Jesus tells His disciples concerning the Pharisees, "Every plant that My heavenly Father didn't plant will be uprooted" (Matt. 15:13).

Wild waves

The sea has a way of revealing its secrets. Deep ocean currents, plate tectonics, violent storms, salt water tides, and other natural phenomena combine to churn up history from the ocean floor and deposit it on our shores. Usually, these once-hidden relics are messy, chaotic, and corroded - but always, they are revealing. In a similar way, over time, false teachers expose their true nature - unredeemed, vile, narcissistic, greedy, lustful, unfulfilled. Jude likens these interlopers to the wild waves of the sea, foaming up their shameful deeds.

The word translated "wild" in Jude 13 is *agrios*, meaning fierce, untamed. Like churning ocean waves, false teachers not only lack good works; they produce evil ones. What they do is likened to "the grimy foam that coats a beach, leaving a sticky residue of shame behind."[12]

Scripture often uses the sea as a symbol for those who don't know God. In that vein, Jude may be building his case on a statement from the prophet Isaiah: "But the wicked are like the storm-tossed sea, for it cannot be still, and its waters churn up mire and muck" (Isa. 57:20).

As false teachers pontificate with great, swelling rhetoric, they inexplicably dredge up the wretched refuse of their hearts. Their arrogance, immorality, irreverence, and insubordination wash up on the shores of God's kingdom and reveal their true character. As Jesus reminds us, "A good man produces good out of the good storeroom of his heart. An evil man produces evil out of the evil storeroom, for his mouth speaks from the overflow of the heart" (Luke 6:45).

In the apostle John's glimpse of the future, from his exiled perspective on Patmos, he reports, "Then I saw a new heaven and a new earth, for the first heaven and the first earth had passed away, and *the sea existed no longer*" (Rev. 21:1 - emphasis added). The Greek word John uses for "new" is *kainos*, which means "different from the usual, better than the old, superior in value or attraction." In other words, God does not simply annihilate the old order of things and start again from scratch; He purges the sinful and fallen cosmos and restores it to its pristine beauty.

But why does the sea vanish? One possible interpretation is that John likens the sea to the earth's unredeemed people and their legacy of sin. Once Christ returns and sets things right, only the saved of all time remain. The wicked are resurrected and summoned before the great white throne, then cast into the lake of fire, leaving the glory of God to fill the earth: "For the earth will be filled with the knowledge of the Lord's glory, as the waters cover the sea" (Hab. 2:14).

Drawing from the influence of Daniel's vision of the four beasts on early Christianity, N.T. Wright notes, "The sea has become the dark, fearsome place from which evil emerges, threatening God's people like a giant tidal wave threatening those who live near the coast. For the people of ancient Israel, who were not for the most part seafarers, the sea came to represent evil and chaos, the dark power that might do to God's people what the flood had done to the whole world, unless God rescued them as he rescued Noah."[13]

Charles Swindoll offers these thoughts: "To people of the ancient world ... the sea was a mysterious, frightening, and dangerous place, characterized by chaos and possessing the power to kill without warning.... In the book of Revelation, the sea also served as a symbol ... of disorder, violence, or unrest that marks the old creation. John's imagery of the sea elsewhere in Revelation designates it as an origin of all kinds of cosmic evil. It could also represent the unbelieving nations who persecuted God's people. Clearly, in ancient times, the sea stood for chaos and calamity, disorder and destruction."[14]

Perhaps Jude, in referring to false teachers as "wild waves of the sea, foaming up their shameful deeds," seeks to connect them to the earth's wicked, who ultimately find themselves in the lake of fire. The chaos and carnage their apostate lives have produced return to them in hell and become their everlasting companions.

Wandering stars

Jude has used illustrations from the natural world - the sky, the earth, and the water - to describe the evil deeds of false teachers. Now, he offers one final example - this one from outer space. He writes that apostates are like "wandering stars." The phrase could signify planets in their elliptical orbits, which make them appear to wander. But more likely, Jude is referring to meteors, oddly shaped chunks of asteroids or comets that flash brightly as they invade the earth's atmosphere.

We should note the parallel between verse 12 and Jude 6, where gloomy darkness is the holding cell of certain fallen angels. Ultimately, Satan, demons, and false teachers all punch their tickets for the same everlasting terminus: outer darkness, eternal fire, hell. It is a place specifically created for the Devil and his angels (Matt. 25:41). However, people who reject the revelation of God and refuse His gracious offer of eternal life find themselves spending eternity the way they lived their earthly lives: independently of God. While Satan masquerades as an angel of light, and his minions disguise themselves as ministers of righteousness, their self-made brilliance flames out, and their once-lofty trajectory wobbles toward a dark eternity where no flint is struck and no light is created.

Note the manner in which several New Testament passages depict the final judgment of the wicked:

- Describing the "sons of the kingdom" - Israelites who reject the Messiah - Jesus says they "will be thrown into the outer darkness. In that place there will be weeping and gnashing of teeth" (Matt. 8:12).

- In the parable of the wedding banquet for the king's son, Jesus describes a man invited to the feast who arrives in his own clothing (the filthy rags of his own righteousness), having refused the wedding garment offered freely by the host (the righteousness of Christ). The king responds to the man's insolence the only way he can to protect his son's honor and to ensure the delight of his guests. He commands his servants, "Tie him up hand and foot, and throw him into the outer darkness, where there will be weeping and gnashing of teeth" (Matt. 22:13).

- In the parable of the talents, Jesus describes an "evil, lazy slave" who rejects his master's grace and squanders his call to serve. The master tells his servants, "And throw this good-for-nothing slave into the outer darkness. In that place there will be weeping and gnashing of teeth" (Matt. 25:26, 30).

- Lastly, the apostle John sees a great white throne in heaven, and Jesus seated on it. The "dead, the great and the small," stand before the throne and are judged according to their works. Books are opened - most significantly, the book of life, in which Christ searches in vain for their names. "And anyone not found written in the book of life was thrown into the lake of fire" (Rev. 20:11-15).

Fire and darkness await the wandering stars. Although we may rightly wonder how flames and blackness can coexist, it appears that Jesus and the New Testament writers use these two natural elements as symbols of the wicked person's indescribable suffering through an endless night, far from the inviting glow of the banquet hall, and banished from the feast spread across the king's table.

Unlike meteors, fixed stars guide navigators through treacherous waters and into safe harbors. Our Lord is "the Bright Morning Star" (Rev. 22:16), and Christians are called to "shine like stars in the world" (Phil. 2:15). Anyone foolish enough to fix his course by the cascading light of a falling star is bound to be led astray. Similarly, as Edward Pentecost notes, "the prominence of apostate leaders is short-lived, useless, and false. They do lead unwary followers astray, pretending to be what they are not. They will therefore be swallowed up into the blackest darkness forever; eternal judgment is certain for them."[15]

John MacArthur writes, "Apostates often appear for a short time on the stage of Christianity. They promise enduring spiritual light and direction but deliver nothing but an erratic, aimless, worthless flash. The utter blackness and darkness of hell has been reserved forever for them."[16]

Key words

In this chapter, we learned several key terms. Fill in the blanks to test your knowledge.

Nurturing. This word comes from the Greek *poimaino*, which means "to _____." Only, the false teachers care for no one but themselves. How different they are from Jesus, who is the good _____.

Comparing English translations of *poimaino*:

HCSB	KJV	NIV	NASB	ESV
nurturing	feeding	who only feed	caring	feeding

Without fear. Rendered "without the slightest qualm" in the NIV, this phrase comes from the Greek *aphobos*, meaning "_____." The false teachers experience no pangs of _____ when they fill their bellies and puff out their chests at the expense of those they steer toward the rocks of _____ destruction.

Comparing English translations of *aphobos*:

HCSB	KJV	NIV	NASB	ESV
without fear	without fear	without the slightest qualm	without fear	without fear

Waterless. The Greek word *anudros* describes the empty promises of _____ _____. Like clouds with no _____, these apostates cast shadows of promise but drift off without delivering the goods.

Fruitless. The Greek *phthinoporina* is a compound term that captures the idea of waning, or _____ away, in late autumn. Like twice-dead fruit trees, false teachers not only _____ to produce a crop; they are incapable of doing so and thus are fit only to be pulled up by their roots and _____ .

Wild. The Greek word *agrios* means _____ , untamed. Like the wild _____ waves, false teachers not only lack _____ works; they produce evil ones.

Application
Questions for personal or group study

In verses 12-13, Jude likens false teachers to five different natural phenomena: dangerous reefs, waterless clouds, fruitless trees, wild waves, and wandering stars. Consider each word picture and answer the accompanying questions.

1. **Dangerous reefs.** Several leading prosperity preachers say our words have creative power similar to the creative power in the voice of God. Faith is not just believing what God says; it's believing we have whatever we say. Therefore, we must "positively confess" that our cancer is gone, that our daughters are head cheerleaders, and that our check books are bulging with credit.

   • In what ways are these teachers "dangerous reefs"?

   • What do we say to the friend who has just emptied his checking account in order to offer a "seed faith" gift to a television evangelist?

   • How do we explain the biblical reality that faithful servants of the Lord suffer, get sick, and sometimes die painful deaths?

   • Where do you think a person gets the idea that he is a "little god" with the power to create his own reality?

   • What is a biblically faithful understanding of the power of the tongue?

2. **Waterless clouds.** Some popular television evangelists say the believer's divine birthright is financial prosperity and good health. Since Christ became a curse for us, we no longer need to accept sickness or poverty in our lives. Therefore, we ought to live in divine health and wealth as a testimony to the power of God and as evidence that we are children of God.

    -   How are these evangelists like "waterless clouds" - promising showers of blessing but delivering only passing shadows?

    -   If financial prosperity and good health are indicators of a person's faith in God, how do we explain Kim Jong-un and Mother Teresa?

    -   Would you say that this teaching makes God a means to an end, rather than the end of faith Himself? Why or why not?

    -   What is a more biblically faithful understanding of our birthright as children of God?

    -   How and when are God's promises of wealth and healing fulfilled?

3. **Fruitless trees.** Latter-day Saints founder Joseph Smith taught that godhood is attainable to those who follow a proscribed path of good works.

    -   Who makes a similar promise in Genesis 3?

    -   Why is the lure of becoming divine so seductive?

    -   What does the Bible teach about "glorification"?

    -   In what ways are Joseph Smith and other LDS leaders, who proclaim the doctrine of "exaltation" (godhood), twice dead? Think carefully about Jude's analogy of trees in late autumn - "fruitless, twice dead, pulled out by the roots."

    -   The word *Elohim* is found 2,602 times in the Old Testament.[17] It is the word used most often for God, but it also depicts false gods, angels, and human leaders. How does the context of the following passages help us determine the intended meaning?

And why can we say with confidence that the Bible argues against the LDS concept of human beings as "gods in embryo"?

- » Gen. 1:1; Ps. 50:1; Isa. 2:3
- » Ex. 20:3; 32:1
- » Ps. 8:5; 97:7; 138:1
- » Ex. 4:16; 7:1
- » Ex. 21:6
- » Ps. 45:7

4. **Wild waves.** Stories abound of Christian leaders who have lost their ministries (and in some cases their freedom) due to sex scandals, financial impropriety, or abusive leadership styles. In some cases, these leaders are evangelical Christians teaching sound doctrine. At the heart of their "fall from grace" is pride - the idea that they are too big to fail, too important to be held accountable, or too smart to get caught.

- How are these leaders like "wild waves"?

- Even though some fallen Christian leaders taught sound doctrine, their moral failures or insatiable thirst for power did more than just damage their reputation; they injured the cause of Christ. How are these types of failures just as dangerous as false doctrine?

- Read 1 Tim. 3:1-13 and Titus 1:5-9. Why are these standards important for church leaders? And how strictly should we interpret them? For example, how do we determine whether someone manages his household well? Is not given to much wine? Has a good reputation?

- In your view, which of the following would prompt you to seek church discipline for a leader in your congregation:
  - » Drinks a beer once in a while at home
  - » Was seen dining at a popular restaurant with a woman who was not his wife
  - » Teaches a pre-millennial view of the last days
  - » Divorces his wife, claiming God told him to do so

» Announces his belief that the miracles of the Bible are not true

» Confesses an addiction to online pornography

- Why are a leader's words so important in understanding his or her heart?

5. **Wandering stars.** Charles Taze Russell, whose Bible study morphed into The Watch Tower Bible and Tract Society (Jehovah's Witnesses), taught that the wicked are annihilated in hell; they do not suffer endless torment apart from Christ.

- What makes Russell's teaching an attractive doctrine?

- How would you argue against it?

- In what ways can you reconcile a loving God with everlasting punishment in hell?

- Consider the following beliefs and practices of The Watch Tower[18] and ask: (1) Which are contrary to Scripture? And, (2) Which are potentially the most spiritually devastating?

  » "We do not practice tithing, and no collections are ever taken at our meetings. All our activities are supported by anonymous donations."

  » "People who die pass out of existence. They do not suffer in a fiery hell of torment."

  » "Jehovah God, Jesus Christ, and the faithful angels reside in the spirit realm. A relatively small number of people - 144,000 - will be resurrected to life in heaven to rule with Jesus in the Kingdom."

  » "We remain strictly neutral in political affairs and avoid affiliation with other religions."

  » "Deliverance from sin and death is possible through the ransom sacrifice of Jesus. To benefit from that sacrifice, people must not only exercise faith in Jesus but also change their course of life and get baptized."

  » "We have learned from the Bible that Jesus is not Almighty God and that there is no Scriptural basis for the Trinity doctrine."

The Holy Spirit enables Enoch to look through the telescoping lens of time, compressing the span over which false prophets and false teachers deceive people. Ultimately, they stand before the returning Christ and are held accountable for the wreckage their destructive ministries have wrought.

13

Look! The Lord Comes:
The Prophecy of Enoch

And Enoch, in the seventh [generation] from Adam,
prophesied about them:
Look! The lord comes
with thousands of His holy ones
to execute judgment on all,
and to convict them
of all their ungodly deeds
that they have done
in an ungodly way,
and of all the harsh things
ungodly sinners
have said against Him.

These people are discontented grumblers, walking
according to their desires; their mouths utter arrogant
words, flattering people for their own advantage.
(Jude 14-16 HCSB)

Most people who profess belief in Jesus anticipate His return. But *when* and *how* - and even in *what form* - He comes back is a matter of considerable debate.

Muslims, for example, believe Jesus is returning one day to destroy the Dajjal (Antichrist); break the cross as a declaration against the notion he was ever crucified; kill the pig, thus making pork universally prohibited; and abolish the *Jizyah* tax on Christians and Jews, as these former unbelievers now universally embrace Islam.[1]

Jehovah's Witnesses believe Jesus (an exalted Michael the archangel) returned invisibly in 1914, began ruling as king over the whole earth, and now is preparing for his invisible "revelation" in the events of Armageddon and the beginning of the Millennium.[2]

Baha'is teach that Baha'u'llah, a 19th-century Iranian prophet, is both a manifestation of God and the second coming of Christ. In addition, he is the promised Holy Spirit, the Day of God, the Maiytrea (from Buddhism) and the Krishna (from Hinduism).[3]

The Indian guru Paramahansa Yogananda offers a mystical interpretation of the Second Coming, in which it is understood as an inner experience that takes place within a person's heart. The true Second Coming, he writes, is the resurrection within you of the Infinite Christ Consciousness.[4]

Evangelical Christians hold a variety of views about the Second Coming. Some believe Jesus steps into the heavens to rapture His church either before, during, or at the end of a seven-year tribulation period, followed by His glorious, personal return to earth, which ushers in a 1,000-year period in which He sits on the throne of David and rules the world in righteousness. Others say that Jesus returns only after the world essentially becomes Christianized. Still others believe He simply returns one day to raise the dead, judge all people, and create new heavens and a new earth; Scriptures referring to tribulation periods and millennial kingdoms are to be taken figuratively.

While these pre-, post-, and amillennial views are distinct in their details, evangelicals are united in their beliefs that Jesus is returning personally, visibly, and physically one day to set things right; to resurrect and judge all people; to fully establish His kingdom on earth; and to restore the created order to sinless perfection.

There are many biblical prophecies about the return of Christ. No doubt, some are easier than others to fathom. But the Bible always has been the ultimate authority for evangelicals. So, with a rich tapestry of Old Testament insights into the Day of the Lord, why does Jude quote a prophecy of Christ's return from a non-biblical source?

As we are about to discover, the prophecy of Enoch, while drawn from an apocryphal source, is consistent with prophecies of the Day of the Lord in Scripture. Further, quoting from non-biblical sources is neither unprecedented nor wrong for those writing under divine inspiration. But first things first.

Who is Enoch?

We must be careful not to confuse the Enoch to whom Jude refers with the eldest son of Cain. Cain builds a city east of Eden in the land of Nod and names the city Enoch after his son (Gen. 4:17). Enoch's great-great grandson, Lamech, is the first recorded polygamist in the Bible, illustrating the corrupt progeny of Cain.

In contrast, the Enoch mentioned in the Book of Jude hails from the line of Seth. He is the son of Jared and the father of Methuselah (Gen. 5:21; Luke 3:37). Enoch is 65 years old when Methuselah is born. Then, according to Moses, Enoch "walks with God" 300 years and produces other sons and daughters. Finally, at the age of 365 - relatively young by comparison with Jared, who lives to be 962, and with Methuselah, who dies at 969 - we encounter one of the most unusual endings to an earthly life recorded in Scripture: "Enoch walked with God, and he was not there, because God took him" (Gen. 5:24).

Thus, Enoch shares with Elijah the distinction of being one of two biblical characters caught up into heaven without experiencing physical death. Enoch is featured in the Faith Hall of Fame in Heb. 11:5 - "By faith, Enoch was taken away so that he did not experience death, and he was not to be found because God took him away. For prior to his transformation he was approved, having pleased God." The writer of Hebrews then launches into one of the great statements about faith: "Now without faith it is impossible to please God, for the one who draws near to Him must believe that He exists and rewards those who seek Him" (Heb. 11:6).

And then we come to the final mention of Enoch in Scripture - his prophecy recorded in Jude 14-15:

> And Enoch, in the seventh [generation] from Adam, prophesied about them: Look! The Lord comes with thousands of His holy ones to execute judgment on all, and to convict them of all their ungodly deeds that they have done in an ungodly way, and of all the harsh things ungodly sinners have said against Him.

Where can we find Enoch's prophecy?

Nowhere in Scripture does Enoch's prophecy appear, leading some to dispute the inspiration of the Book of Jude. After all, it is argued, if a writer inspired by the Holy Spirit shares an ancient prophesy about the end of days, why not select a prophecy that already has found its way into the canon? However, there is good reason to accept the prophecy of Enoch as the very words of God.

The quotation is from the Book of Enoch, a pseudepigraphical work attributed to the great-grandfather of Noah.[5] This book is not considered canonical by any religious group, whether Judaism, Roman Catholicism, the Greek or Russian Orthodox Church, or Protestantism.[6] Possibly written in the second century B.C., and familiar to Jewish Christians,[7] the book certainly is known to the church fathers of the second century. In fact, Justin Martyr, Irenaeus, Clement of Alexandria, and others quote from it.[8]

The book is part of Jewish history and tradition, and rabbinical allusions to it are not uncommon.[9] The Book of Enoch is then lost for some centuries, with the exception of a few fragments, before being rediscovered in its entirety in a copy of the Ethiopic Bible in the 18th century. Noah and Enoch are purportedly given revelations aimed at vindicating the ways of God, setting forth retribution reserved for sinners, and declaring that the world is under the sovereign rule of the Lord.[10]

Specifically, Jude draws from Enoch 1:9, which reads:

> And behold! He cometh with ten thousands of His holy ones
> To execute judgment upon all,
> And to destroy all the ungodly:

And to convict all flesh
Of all the works of the ungodliness which they have
ungodly committed,
And of all the hard things which ungodly sinners have
spoken against Him.[11]

Jude's quotation is similar but not identical to Enoch 1:9. Perhaps this is because Jude cites a portion of the Book of Enoch the Spirit confirms as genuine, tightening up the language from its non-inspired source. As Edward Pentecost writes, "If Jude quoted the apocryphal book, he was affirming only the truth of that prophecy and not endorsing the book in its entirety."[12]

As a side note, Jude says that Enoch "prophesied," not "wrote." Jude may be referring to a God-given prophetic word and not specifically to a book. We should not automatically conclude from the phrase "Enoch ... prophesied" that Jude is citing a written work, or further, a written work considered Scripture.

In any case, it may help to consider the background of the Book of Enoch, which appears to be a secondary source that draws from the Old Testament. By quoting Enoch, then, Jude indirectly quotes the passages to which the Book of Enoch alludes. But which Hebrew Scriptures are Enoch's primary sources?

James VanderKam, a professor of Hebrew Scriptures and a noted expert on the literature of Enoch, writes that Enoch's reference to the "holy ones" derives from Job 5:1 and 15:15, as well as from Daniel 4. This reference to God's celestial band recalls Deut. 33:2, while Zech. 14:5 envisions an advent of God along with His holy ones. Further, Dan. 7:10 pictures God as surrounded by myriads of heavenly attendants at the time of judgment.[13]

Author George W.E. Nickelsburg adds that three other Old Testament passages may have influenced the writing of Enoch 1:3-5, 9. They are: Genesis 6-9, which repeatedly speaks of the corruption of all flesh and of the judgment that falls on all but a few people; Isa. 66:15-16; and Jer. 25:30-32.[14]

The point here is that Jude does not simply snatch a convenient text from a non-canonical book in order to build his case. Rather, in quoting from the Book of Enoch, he affirms the Old Testament texts from which the book is drawn. There appears to be solid alignment between the Old Testament, Enoch 1:9, and Jude. Thus, drawing from Enoch and Old Testament passages, Jude applies Enoch's prophecy to the false teachers of the last days, which include the interlopers of the first century.

W.M. Dunnett writes, "Jude clearly accepted it [Enoch 1:9] as an inspired, apparently historical, and true utterance, without necessarily placing approval on the entire content of the Book of Enoch."[15]

Although not included in the biblical record until Jude captures it, Enoch's prophecy is the earliest human prophecy found anywhere in Scripture. Only the prophetic promise of God regarding the "seed of woman" is earlier (Gen. 3:15). In fact, Enoch's message predates the words of Moses, Samuel, and the Hebrew prophets by many centuries.[16]

Why trust a prophecy that doesn't come from the Bible?

Still, we might ask why Jude draws from this material in the first place. Isn't it better to quote directly from Deuteronomy, Job, Daniel, or another canonical book to make the point that the Lord is coming to execute judgment, and that He's not coming alone? Perhaps. But Enoch's prophecy is consistent with the others. Further, it argues the point in a concise and straightforward manner.

Equally important, Jude may be using this quotation because it comes from ancient literature his opponents favor. Thus, he turns their venerated scriptures against them, much as Jesus does to the Sadducees, who think they've wrestled Him to the ground on the issue of the resurrection with their hypothetical case of a woman married consecutively to seven brothers (Matt. 22:23-33). They ask, "[I]n the resurrection, whose wife will she be of the seven? For they all had married her" (v. 28).

Jesus responds, in part, by taking them back to the Torah, which they regard as sacred. He could have cited Job 19:25-27 or Dan. 12:2, but instead He quotes from Exodus 3: "Now concerning the resurrection of the dead, haven't you read what was spoken to you by God: I am the God of Abraham and the God of Isaac and the God of Jacob? He is not the God of the dead, but of the living" (vv. 31-32; quotation from Ex. 3:6, 15-16).

Perhaps in a similar way, Jude silences his critics by drawing from their vaunted texts to show that they are the objects of God's future wrath.

We also should keep in mind that Jude's quotation of a non-biblical source has a precedent in the apostle Paul. For example, in several separate passages, he quotes Greek poets (Epimenides and Aratus in Acts 17:28; Aeschylus in Acts 26:14; Menander and/or Euripides in 1 Cor. 15:33; and Epimenides in Titus 1:12). And in 2 Tim. 3:8, he alludes to ancient Jewish traditions. Yet Paul doesn't endorse everything in these works, nor does he consider them Scripture. Like Paul, Jude cites familiar works to make a point. (See the nearby table, "Non-biblical Sources Cited by Paul and Jude.")

While the sources from which Paul and Jude draw lack divine inspiration, they become part of inspired Scripture in the context of their epistles, written under the direction of the Holy Spirit. As one commentary notes, "As to the book of Enoch, if quoted by Jude, his quotation of a passage from it gives an inspired sanction only to the truth of that passage, not to the whole book; just as Paul, by inspiration, sanctions particular sentiments from Aratus, Epimenides, and Menander, but not all their writings."[17]

Who are the "holy ones" coming to execute judgment?

Who does Enoch have in mind when he prophesies that the Lord is coming with His "holy ones"? Most likely Enoch is thinking of angels, since they serve as agents of judgment at the return of Christ. In addition, the coming of Christ is patterned after the Lord's appearance on Sinai, where He "came with ten thousand holy ones" (Deut. 33:2). But we should not discount the promise of God that the saints also accompany Jesus in His glorious appearing.

Jesus assures His followers that He is going to prepare for them a place in heaven, where they will live in His presence between death and resurrection (John 14:2-3). In addition, believers are promised a part in the judgment of the world and evil angels (1 Cor. 6:2-3), as well as a place of authority and service in the new heavens and earth (Rev. 22:1-5). Therefore, even if Enoch makes reference only to angels as "holy ones," those who trust in Christ may rest assured that when He comes again, we return with Him.

It might be helpful to survey a few of the many Scriptures relating to the return of Christ, and the supporting role of angels and redeemed people:

Dan. 7:9-27. Daniel sees "thousands upon thousands" serving the Ancient of Days, and "ten thousand times ten thousand" standing before Him. Perhaps this is a reference to angels, or to people, or both. However, the rest of the chapter refers to *people* as "holy ones." Daniel is told that "the holy ones of the Most High will receive the kingdom and possess it forever, yes, forever and ever" (v. 18). He sees the Ancient of Days arrive, and a judgment given in favor of "the holy ones of the Most High," who take "possession of the kingdom" (v. 22). An evil king speaks words against the Most High, and oppresses "the holy ones of the Most High" (v. 25). But ultimately his dominion is taken away. "The kingdom, dominion, and greatness of the kingdoms under all of heaven will be given to the people, the holy ones of the Most High. His kingdom will be an everlasting kingdom, and all rulers will serve and obey Him" (v. 27).

Zech. 14:5. Zechariah prophesies a "day of the Lord" (v. 1) in which Yahweh becomes King over all the earth. On that day, "the Lord my God will come and all the holy ones with Him." As with Daniel, this could be a reference to angels, saints, or both.

Matt. 13:39-41, 49-50. Jesus interprets the parable of the wheat and tares for His disciples and explains that "The harvest is the end of the age, and the harvesters are angels.... The Son of Man will send out His angels, and they will gather from His kingdom everything that causes sin and those guilty of lawlessness." Then, in the parable of the net, our Lord remarks, "So it will be at the end of the age. The angels will go out, separate the evil people from the righteous, and throw them into the blazing furnace. In that place there will be weeping and gnashing of teeth."

Matt. 16:27. Jesus tells His disciples, "For the Son of Man is going to come with His angels in the glory of His Father, and then He will reward each [person] according to what he has done."

Matt. 24:30-31; 25:31. Foretelling His coming in judgment, Jesus says, "Then the sign of the Son of Man will appear in the sky; and then all the peoples of the earth will mourn; and they will see the Son of Man coming on the clouds of heaven with power and great glory. He will send out His angels with a loud trumpet, and they will gather His elect from the four winds, from one end of the sky to the other.... When the Son of Man comes in His glory, and all the angels with Him, then He will sit on the throne of His glory."

Mark 8:38. Jesus has summoned a crowd, along with His disciples. He admonishes them to take up their crosses and follow Him. Then He adds, "For whoever is ashamed of Me and of My words in this adulterous and sinful generation, the Son of Man will also be ashamed of him when He comes in the glory of His Father with the holy angels."

1 Cor. 6:2-3. Paul writes, "Or do you not know that the saints will judge the world? And if the world is judged by you, are you unworthy to judge the smallest cases? Do you not know that we will judge angels - not to speak of things pertaining to this life?"

1 Thess. 3:13. In Paul's prayer for the church at Thessalonica, he writes, "May He make your hearts blameless in holiness before our God and Father at the coming of our Lord Jesus with all His saints."

2 Thess. 1:7-10. Writing of God's judgment and glory, Paul notes, "This [the saints being counted worthy of God's kingdom] will take place at the revelation of the Lord Jesus from heaven with His powerful angels ... in that day when He comes to be glorified by His saints and to be admired by all those who have believed ..."

Rev. 2:26; 3:21. Jesus assures the faithful in Thyatira and Laodicea that they will judge and rule with Him: "The victor and the one who keeps My works to the end: I will give him authority over the nations ... The victor: I will give him the right to sit with Me on My throne."

Angels and saints play complementary roles in the coming Day of the Lord. But we should keep in mind that it is His day, nor ours. And we should fix our gaze on the King of kings and Lord of lords.

One final note: The phrase "The Lord comes" (Jude 14) also may be translated "The Lord came." In this sense, we may see Enoch's vision as so convincing that he speaks of it as if it already has come to pass.

The apostle Paul writes in much the same way about our salvation in Romans 8: "For those He foreknew He also predestined to be conformed to the image of His Son, so that He would be the firstborn among many brothers. And those He predestined, He also called; and those He called, He also justified; and those He justified, He also glorified" (vv. 29-30).

While the saints already have been predestined, called, and justified, we have not yet been glorified; that occurs at our resurrection. Yet Paul sees God's work of salvation from an eternal perspective. He is so certain of our future glorification that he describes it as already accomplished.

How does Enoch's prophecy apply to false teachers?

Jude writes that Enoch's prophecy, made centuries earlier, applies to the judgment of false teachers throughout the ages, including first-century apostates. His use of "these" (Greek *houtoi*) indicates that Jude's opponents are those about whom Enoch prophesies. The Holy Spirit enables Enoch to look through the telescoping lens of time, compressing the span over which false prophets and false teachers deceive people. Ultimately, they stand before the returning Christ and are held accountable for the wreckage their destructive ministries have wrought.

Christ comes, not only to execute judgment on false teachers, but to "convict" them of their ungodly deeds. The verb translated "to convict" is *elegcho* in the Greek and means "to expose," "rebuke," or "prove guilty." The Lord lays out His case, presenting the evidence in such a way that a guilty verdict is inescapable and indisputable.

This day of reckoning may feature several events:

- A review of God's grace, sufficient in depth and scope to lead even the vilest sinner to repentance (Rom. 2:4)

- A recounting of the incremental steps whereby the guilty reject the truth and descend a spiraling staircase of ungodliness (Rom. 1:18-32)

- A reminder of the many lives these false teachers ruined, and the damage they did to the kingdom of God (Acts 20:29-30)

- A rebuke for passing the point of no return, having filled up their measure of sin (Matt. 23:32; 1 Thess. 2:16)

- And a rejection of their false deeds done in the name of Christ (Matt. 7:21-23)

The false teachers may protest, "Lord, Lord, didn't we prophesy in Your name, drive out demons in Your name, and do many miracles in Your name?" But the Lord announces to them, "I never knew you! Depart from Me, you lawbreakers!" (Matt. 7:22-23). Jesus does not deny that the apostates spoke in His name, or even that they performed miraculous deeds (by the power of Christ's name and by God's permissive will). But He is clear in His sentence: "I never knew you!" They never had a personal relationship with Christ, and thus their deeds never were for His glory. Thus, they must depart - to the lake of fire, to outer darkness, where there is weeping and gnashing of teeth.

Jude is clear that false teachers are not backslidden believers who have drifted from their biblical moorings. In quoting Enoch, he establishes that they are unregenerate. He quotes the word "ungodly" several times.[18] Their deeds are *ungodly*. They have performed them in *ungodly* ways. And they have spoken harsh words against the Lord, revealing themselves as *ungodly* sinners.

Enoch's multiple use of "ungodly" (Greek *asebes* – "godlessness" or "impiety") targets their sinful brashness. They refuse to hold a reverent attitude toward God. With every deceitful word, every selfish deed, every demonstration of spiritual arrogance, they store up divine wrath for the day of judgment. As the apostle Paul warns Romans who are self-seeking and disobey the truth, "But because of your hardness and unrepentant heart you are storing up wrath for yourself in the day of wrath, when God's righteous judgment is revealed" (2:5).

Jude expands on Enoch's prophecy in verse 16, focusing particularly on the sinful words spewing from their mouths. He calls them "discontented grumblers, walking according to their desires." The word "grumblers" (Greek *gongystai*) is used only here in the New Testament. It's the same term the Septuagint (the Greek translation of the Old Testament) uses to describe the murmuring of the Israelites against God (see, for example, Ex. 16:7-9; Num. 14:27).

Like the ancient people of God, whose complaints against Moses and Aaron are in fact grumblings against Yahweh, the false teachers of Jude's day prefer a spiritual Egypt to the Promised Land. And, like the unbelieving Israelites whose corpses littered the desert, the false teachers of Jude's day are assured of a day of reckoning, when they are separated eternally from the light and warmth of the Shekinah glory.

The word "discontented" in Jude 16 is rendered "complainers" in the KJV, "fault finders" in the NIV, and "malcontents" in the ESV. It means "to blame," and it describes someone habitually dissatisfied. Despite being well-fed, celebrated, and preferred, the false teachers want more. They cannot find contentment because they seek to fill the spiritual void in their lives with fleshly comforts, thus revealing their true nature as unregenerate grumblers.

Jude's depiction of false teachers, "walking according to their desires," is similar to Peter's words for apostates. They "follow the polluting desires of the flesh" (2 Peter 2:10); exhibit "fleshly desires and debauchery" (2:18); and "scoff, following their own lusts" (3:3). From their blackened hearts, they utter arrogant words, flattering people for their own advantage. They make merchandise of people (2 Peter 2:3), telling them what they want to hear.

As the apostle Paul writes to Timothy, "For the time will come when they will not tolerate sound doctrine, but according to their own desires, will accumulate teachers for themselves because they have an itch to hear something new. They will turn away from hearing the truth and will turn aside to myths" (2 Tim. 4:3-4).

All of this illustrates what Jesus says in Matt. 15:18, "But what comes out of the mouth comes from the heart, and this defiles a man." By their words, false teachers unearth their spiritual death and betray the corruption of their unregenerate hearts. Rather than proclaim the truth of God's Word and edify His people, they reveal their discontentment, arrogance, hypocrisy, lust, and self-worship. As Enoch foretells, there is nothing left for them but a day of reckoning, when the Lord comes with His holy ones to set things right.

Non-biblical Sources Cited by Paul and Jude

Scripture Passage	Text	Non-biblical Source
Acts 17:28a	For in Him we live and move and exist ... (Paul speaking on Mars Hill)	Epimenides, a seventh- or sixth-century B.C. philosopher-poet. Quoted from *Criteca* and originally applied to Zeus; Paul applies it to God.
Acts 17:28b	... as even some of your own poets have said, "For we are also His offspring." (Paul speaking on Mars Hill)	Aratus, a third-century B.C. Greek poet. Quoted from *Phainomena 5*, in which humanity is attributed to Zeus.
Acts 26:14	When we had all fallen to the ground, I heard a voice speaking to me in the Hebrew language, "Saul, Saul, why are you persecuting Me? *It is hard for you to kick against the goads*" (emphasis added). (Paul speaking before Agrippa)	Aeschylus, a Greek playwright (B.C. 523-426). Quoted from the play *Agamemnon 1624*.
1 Cor. 15:33	Do not be deceived: "Bad company corrupts good morals."	Menander (B.C. 342-291). Quoted from the play *Thais*. Also quoted from Euripides' (B.C. 480-406) play *Aiolos*.

Scripture Passage	Text	Non-biblical Source
2 Tim. 3:8	Just as Jannes and Jambres resisted Moses, so these also resist the truth, men who are corrupt in mind, worthless in regard to the faith.	Ancient Jewish traditions (Targum of Pseudo-Jonathan, Qumran scrolls, and rabbinic writings) identify these magicians by name, although the Old Testament does not.
Titus 1:12	One of their very own prophets said, Cretans are always liars, evil beasts, lazy gluttons.	Epimenides, a sixth-century B.C. Cretan poet. The lie to which he refers is the claim that Zeus is mortal, which evidently is believed on Crete.
Jude 14-15	And Enoch, in the seventh [generation] from Adam, prophesied about them: Look! The Lord comes with thousands of His holy ones to execute judgment on all, and to convict them of all their ungodly deeds that they have done in an ungodly way, and of all the harsh things ungodly sinners have said against Him.	Book of Enoch 1:9 (also known as 1 Enoch 1:9).

Key words

In this chapter, we learned several key terms. Fill in the blanks to test your knowledge.

Pseudepigraphical. This word refers to falsely attributed works, whose claim to authorship is unfounded. It's a term used to describe the Book of _____, from which Jude quotes. This book is not considered _____ by any religious group, whether Judaism, Roman Catholicism, the Greek or Russian Orthodox Church, or Protestantism.

Holy ones. When Enoch prophesies that the Lord comes with thousands of His "holy ones," most likely he is thinking of _____, since they serve as agents of judgment at the return of Christ. But we should not discount the promise of God that the _____ also accompany Jesus in His glorious appearing.

These people. Jude's use of "these" (from the Greek *houtoi*) in verse 16 indicates that the false teachers of his day are the people to whom _____ refers in his prophecy.

Comparing English translations of *elegcho* (referring to the work of Christ when He returns in judgment):

HCSB	KJV	NIV	NASB	ESV
to convict	to convince	to convict	to convict	to convict

Comparing English translations of *gongystai* (in reference to false teachers):

HCSB	KJV	NIV	NASB	ESV
grumblers	murmurers	grumblers	grumblers	grumblers

Application

1. In quoting Enoch 1:9, Jude says the Lord is coming with His "holy ones," most likely a reference to angels. But Scripture promises the saints that they, too, return with Jesus. Read again the passages cited in this chapter (and listed below) that speak of the return of Christ. Then mark whether the verses speak of angels or people (or perhaps of both), and what role they play.

Scripture	Angels or People?	Role in Christ's Return
Dan. 7:9-27		
Zech. 14:5		
Matt. 13:39-41, 49-50		
Matt. 16:27		
Matt. 24:30-31; 25:31		
Mark 8:38		
1 Cor. 6:2-3		
1 Thess. 3:13		
2 Thess. 1:7-10		
Rev. 2:26; 3:21		

2. Why do you think Jude quotes from a pseudepigraphical book (the Book of Enoch) when he could have quoted from any number of Old Testament passages to describe the future return of Christ with His "holy ones"?

3. Critics may argue that Jude's epistle should be excluded from the canon of Scripture because he quotes from the pseudepigraphical Book of Enoch. How would you defend the inspiration of Jude against this charge?

4. Jude applies the prophecy of Enoch to false teachers in his day. Do you think it's fair to carry that prophecy forward and pin it on today's religious renegades as well? Why or why not?

5. In his book, *Can We Still Believe the Bible?*, Craig L. Blomberg notes three main criteria the early church used to determine whether a book belonged in the New Testament canon: (1) Apostolicity - that is, was the book written while the apostles were alive? (2) Catholicity - were believers throughout the world to which Christianity was spreading in agreement on these books, and using them? And (3) Orthodoxy - were the books faithful to the teachings of Jesus and the apostles?[19] Does the epistle of Jude meet these criteria?

6. Both Jude and the apostle Paul quote from non-biblical sources, yet their writings are considered inspired. In contrast, the *Book of Mormon* duplicates extensive passages from the Bible, yet most Christians deny that the writings of Joseph Smith are inspired. Is that fair? Why or why not?

7. How will some false teachers defend themselves before Christ on the day of judgment, according to Matt. 7:22? Do you think they actually believe what they are saying? And if so, does that mean unbelievers can become so deceived that they think they are faithful followers of Jesus, when in fact they are enemies of His kingdom?

8. In his ancient prophecy about the end times, Enoch uses the phrase "ungodly" several times to describe false teachers. In what ways, specifically, are the words and deeds of false teachers in the church ungodly?

9. Why do you think the Lord waits so long to bring judgment on false teachers, many of whom live out their days in good health and great comfort?

10. In 2 Corinthians, Paul must defend himself against so-called "super apostles," who are, in fact, false apostles. Read 2 Cor. 11:4. What three doctrinal errors are the "super apostles" promoting? Think about Mormonism, the Watch Tower, and Islam. In what ways do they teach "another Jesus ... a different spirit ... a different gospel?"

14

Merely Natural:
Scoffers without the Spirit

But you, dear friends, remember the words foretold by the apostles of our Lord Jesus Christ; they told you, "In the end time there will be scoffers walking according to their own ungodly desires." These people create divisions and are merely natural, not having the Spirit.

(Jude 17-19 HCSB)

William MacLeod Raine (1871 - 1954) was a newspaper man and author of a number of western adventure novels. In a feature about Dodge City, Kansas, Raine wrote that practical jokes fueled the city's "good spirits" in the late 19th century - and the wilder the joke, the better.

Enter "Mysterious Dave," also known as Dave Mathers, one of the nastiest characters to walk the sawdust trail. Raine called him "the worst of bad men and a notorious scoffer."

It so happened that an evangelist known as Brother Johnson came to town and led a series of meetings so successful that the crowds outgrew the church and adjourned to a local dance hall, thus attracting Mysterious Dave. He listened to Brother Johnson preach several times, admiring the evangelist's fiery sermons against sin. Perhaps, the preacher thought, there was hope for this Dodge City scoundrel.

So, Brother Johnson preached directly at Dave, leveraging the full weight of his message against the sinner's stubborn resistance. And then it happened. Dave buried his head in his hands and sobbed. The preacher boldly exclaimed that he was willing to die if he could convert this one vile sinner. The deacons in the congregation agreed that they, too, would not resist going straight to heaven if Mysterious Dave were converted.

At last Dave rose to his feet and said, "I've got yore company, friends. Now, while we're all saved I reckon we better start straight for heaven. First off, the preacher; then the deacons; me last." Dave pulled out his "whoppin' big gun" and started shooting.

The preacher dove through a window to avoid the gunfire. His deacons scattered in search of cover. Raine concluded, "Seemed like they was willin' to postpone taking that ticket to heaven. After that they never did worry any more about Dave's soul."[1]

Notorious scoffers like Dave Mathers eventually reveal their true character. They are incorrigible and unrepentant. At some point, people may fairly conclude that they have passed the point of no return. Nothing successfully prompts a change in their behavior because their character is fully corrupted.

But scoffers in the Old West are nothing new. First-century false teachers honed the art of ridicule long before the first brigands rode into Dodge City. Jude reminds his readers that the apostles warned us of such people. We should be on guard but not surprised.

What is the end time?

Jude exhorts his readers to "remember the words foretold by the apostles of our Lord Jesus Christ; they told you, 'In the *end time* there will be scoffers walking according to their own ungodly desires'" (vv. 17-18 - emphasis added). Most English translations render "end time" as "last times" or "last time." In the parallel passage in 2 Peter

3:3, Peter uses a phrase that nearly every English version translates as "last days." So, if the "end time" is the same as "last time" and "last days," how are we to understand the time frame to which Jude refers?

Since Jude mentions the apostles' end-time prophecies, and these prophecies describe the work of scoffers after the death, burial, and resurrection of Christ - yet prior to His return - we must conclude that the "end time" describes the days between the Lord's first coming and His second coming.

In other words, Jude reminds his readers that throughout the church age, Satan sows tares in Christ's wheat fields (Matt. 13:24-30, 36-43). False teachers play a key role in Satan's plan to spoil the crop. But when Jesus returns with His holy angels, He casts those who cause sin and are guilty of lawlessness into the blazing furnace, where there is weeping and gnashing of teeth. With judgment completed, "the righteous will shine like the sun in their Father's kingdom" (Matt. 13:43a).

As with the prophecy of Enoch, Jude applies the apostles' foresight to his own day. The fulfillment of these prophecies is not reserved for some far-away date. Rather, it unfolds before the very eyes of Jude's readers. This is an important reminder to those who read Bible prophecy by the light of today's headlines. We may rightly expect the world to become more wicked as the return of Christ draws nearer, but we have no right to claim for the 21st century alone the fulfillment of New Testament end-times prophecies. Things already are pretty bad in the first generation of the church age.

Even so, it may prove helpful to step back and look at the last days from a broader perspective. There is a connection between the New Testament teaching on the "end time" and the Old Testament concept of the "day of the Lord."

To ancient Israelites, the Messianic age was completely in the future and encompassed everything related to the Anointed One suffering for our sins, rising from the dead, sitting on the throne of David, and ruling the world in righteousness. When Jesus appears and fulfills the Messianic prophecies relating to His passion, but not to His glorious reign in Jerusalem, it becomes necessary to see the Old Testament prophecies in a new light - as an already-but-not-yet fulfillment of the Messiah's kingdom work.

The "day of the Lord" in the Old Testament, as it refers to final judgment and restoration, is yet to come. Meanwhile, it merges with the "end time" of the New Testament and anticipates the glorious return of the Son of Man, when He sets things right and creates new heavens and a new earth. With that in mind, let's review a few related biblical terms and corresponding passages.

Last days

The term "last days" refers to the final period in history when the Messiah comes to establish God's kingdom. The Old Testament writers envision a time when God makes good on His promises, delivers His people from their enemies, and blesses them. "The fulfillment of the last days is also tied directly to the coming ruler from David's line" (Isa. 9:6-7; 11:1-9; Jer. 30:9; 33:15).[2]

The New Testament writers understand that the "last days" began with the first coming of Jesus and will be completed when He returns at a future unknown time. The apostles warn us that rebellion and ungodliness characterize the last days (1 Tim. 4:1; 2 Tim. 3:1 - 4:5; 2 Peter 3:3). The writer of Hebrews understands that he and his audience are living in this time frame: "Long ago God spoke to the fathers by the prophets at different times and in different ways. In these *last days*, He has spoken to us by His Son ..." (Heb. 1:1-2a - emphasis added).

While Christians live in these "last days," we are to remain faithful (2 Tim. 3:10, 14-15); prepare to face persecution (2 Tim. 3:12); persevere in ministry (2 Tim. 4:1-2, 5); live holy lives (2 Peter 3:11, 14); prepare ourselves, for we do not know the day or the hour of Christ's return (Matt. 25:13); and be positive in our outlook because He is going to set things right (Revelation 21-22).

The last day

"The last day" refers in some New Testament contexts to future resurrection and judgment. After the death of her brother, Martha expresses to Jesus her confidence that Lazarus will "rise again in the resurrection at the last day" (John 11:24).

Jesus uses the term "last day" in the same manner in John 6:39-40: "This is the will of Him who sent Me: that I should lose none of those He has given Me but should raise them up on the *last day*. For this is the will of My Father: that everyone who sees the Son and believes in Him may have eternal life, and I will raise him up on the *last day*" (emphasis added; see also vv. 44, 54.)

There is an already-but-not-yet tension in which Christians live today - a joyful tension, if it may be so described - that anticipates a coming day in which all God's promises are fulfilled. The one who believes in Jesus has eternal life (already), and will be resurrected and fully conformed to the image of Christ on the last day (not yet).

In John 12:48, Jesus foretells the future destiny of those who rebuff His gracious call to salvation: "The one who rejects Me and doesn't accept My sayings has this as his judge: the word I have spoken will judge him on the *last day*" (emphasis added).

The already-but-not-yet reality of the kingdom affects all people. The unbeliever stands condemned (the already; John 3:18), and faces future resurrection and judgment (not yet; Rev. 20:11-15).

Last time, end of times, last hour

The New Testament writers use the phrases "last time," "end of times," and "last hour" to further depict the already-but-not-yet nature of God's kingdom.

In 1 Peter 1:3-5, Peter writes, "Blessed be the God and Father of our Lord Jesus Christ. According to His great mercy, He has given us a new birth into a living hope through the resurrection of Jesus Christ from the dead, and into an inheritance that is imperishable, uncorrupted, and unfading, kept in heaven for you, who are being protected by God's power through faith for a salvation that is ready to be revealed in the *last time*" (emphasis added).

So, we have a new birth, a living hope, and a promised inheritance now (the already), to be realized in the future (not yet).

Peter further says in 1 Peter 1:20-21, "He [Christ] was destined before the foundation of the world, but was revealed at the *end of the times* for you who through Him are believers in God, who raised Him from the dead and gave Him glory, so that your faith and hope are in God" (emphasis added).

Our salvation is anchored in eternity past to the election of God the Father and the foreordination of Christ, who was revealed at the "end of the times" for us (the already), so that our present-day faith and hope in God assures future fulfillment of all His promises (not yet).

John writes in 1 John 2:18, "Children, it is the *last hour*. And as you have heard, 'Antichrist is coming,' even now many antichrists have come. We know from this that it is the *last hour*" (emphasis added).

Many "antichrists" - those opposed to Christ, including some who presume to take His place - already have come, proving that we are in the last hour (the already). This serves as a prelude to the coming Antichrist (not yet).

Day of the Lord

The expression "day of the Lord" in Scripture often refers to events at the end of human history. Sometimes it's associated with the words "that day." A key to understanding these phrases is to note that "they always identify a span of time during which God personally intervenes in history, directly or indirectly, to accomplish some specific aspect of His plan."[3]

To the ancient Israelites, "the day of the Lord" sometimes meant the day Yahweh would intervene to put Israel at the head of the nations, irrespective of their faithfulness to Him. But prophets like Isaiah, Ezekiel, Amos, Joel, Zephaniah, and Zechariah make it clear that "the day" also means judgment upon God's people. Other spokesmen, fully aware of the sinfulness of surrounding nations, prophesy that the day (or "that day") is one of judgment on other nations for their wickedness, such as Babylon (Isa. 13:6, 9), Egypt (Jer. 46:10), and even "all the nations" (Oba. 15).

J.S. Wright summarizes it well: "The Day of the Lord is thus the occasion when Yahweh actively intervenes to punish sin that has come to a climax. This punishment may come through an invasion (Am. 5-6; Is. 13; Ezk. 13:5), or through some natural disaster, such as a locust invasion (Joel 1-2). All lesser interventions come to a head in the actual coming of the Lord himself. At this Day there are truly repentant believers who are saved (Joel 2:28-32), while those who remain enemies of the Lord, whether Jews or Gentiles, are punished."[4]

Concerning the end of human history, scholars are divided as to whether the day of the Lord is an instantaneous event in which Christ returns to reward His children and banish the wicked to hell, or a series of events featuring Christ's glorious return, the resurrection and final judgment of all people, an extended reign of Christ on earth, and the creation of new heavens and a new earth.

Old Testament passages often convey a sense of expectation, proclaiming that the day of the Lord is near (Isa. 13:6; Ezek. 30:3; Zeph. 1:7). Some passages about the day of the Lord describe historical judgments that already have been fulfilled to some degree (for example, Isa. 13:6-22; Ezek. 30:2-19; and Zeph. 1:14-18), while others refer to divine intervention further into the future (such as Joel 2:30-32; Zech. 14:1-21; Mal. 4:1, 5). This is because the Old Testament prophets often are given a telescopic view of the future, when, from their perspective, the events encompassing God's intervention in human history are compressed.

New Testament passages refer to the day of the Lord as a day of wrath, a day of visitation, and even "the great day of God, the Almighty" (Rev. 16:14), a future time when God's wrath and His salvation are fully revealed. The day of the Lord comes quickly (2 Thess. 2:2; compare Zeph. 1:14-15), and so we must keep ourselves prepared and watchful.

Ultimately, the day of the Lord is fulfilled when all that God's Word promises takes place. Christ returns, resurrects and judges all people, casts Satan and his demons into the lake of fire, and creates new heavens and a new earth. The day of the Lord is a day of vengeance, salvation, restoration, and completion. Believers should look forward to it; the wicked should fear it and repent while there is still time.

Where does Jude get the quote about scoffers?

Nowhere in the New Testament is an apostle quoted exactly as saying, "In the end time there will be scoffers walking according to their own ungodly desires" (Jude 18). However, Jude's words approximate what Peter writes in a parallel passage: "First, be aware of this: scoffers will come in the last days to scoff, following their own lusts ..." (2 Peter 3:3). No doubt, Jude makes reference to Peter's words, lending credence to the view that Jude is written after 2 Peter. Peter warns of a coming day when false teachers infiltrate the church. Jude sounds the alarm that the false teachers have arrived.

Even before Peter, though, Paul offers similar warnings. In his farewell address to the Ephesian elders, he says, "I know that after my departure savage wolves will come in among you, not sparing the flock. And men from among yourselves will rise up with deviant doctrines to lure the disciples into following them" (Acts 20:29-30).

And to Timothy, Paul offers these exhortations:

"Now the Spirit expressly says that in the latter times some will depart from the faith, paying attention to deceitful spirits and the teachings of demons, through the hypocrisy of liars whose consciences are seared" (1 Tim. 4:1-2).

And, "But know this: difficult times will come in the last days. For people will be lovers of self, lovers of money, boastful, proud, blasphemers, disobedient to parents, ungrateful, unholy, unloving, irreconcilable, slanderous, without self-control, brutal, without love for what is good, traitors, reckless, conceited, lovers of pleasure rather than lovers of God, holding to the form of religion but denying its power. Avoid these people!" (2 Tim. 3:1-5).

John further contributes (years after the epistle of Jude is written): "Children, it is the last hour. And as you have heard, 'Antichrist is coming,' even now many antichrists have come. We know from this that it is the last hour" (1 John 2:18).

Other passages could be cited, but Jude's point is clear: His contemporaries, the leaders of the early church, provide abundant warning about arrogant, unrepentant, blasphemous scoffers. Jude lends his voice to their clarion call for followers of Jesus to be on guard.

Jude's use of the term "scoffers" stands with Peter's (2 Peter 3:3) as the only places in the New Testament where this word is used as a noun.[5] The Greek word *empaiktai* refers to those who deride or mock. In the Septuagint (the Greek translation of the Old Testament), the word appears in Isa. 3:4, where the Lord warns Judah, "I will make youths their leaders, and the *unstable* (or mischief makers) will govern them" (emphasis added).

210

The verb *empaizo* - which means to play like a child; to sport, jest, or ridicule - is used in the synoptic Gospels by Jesus as He prophesies His impending sufferings, and by the Jewish leaders and Roman soldiers who inflict these sufferings.[6]

Clearly, Jude's reference to scoffers should be applied to the false teachers of his day. But who, or what, are they mocking?

In Peter's use of "scoffers," he describes the dismissive way people mock the message of Christ's return. "Where is the promise of his coming?" these scoffers ask derisively. "For ever since the fathers fell asleep [died], all things continue as they have been since the beginning of creation" (2 Peter 3:4). Peter responds by reminding his readers that these mockers ignore God's judgment of the world by water in the days of Noah, and thus they cannot see the impending judgment of this world by fire.

Peter then offers a word of encouragement: "Dear friends, don't let this one thing escape you: with the Lord one day is like 1,000 years, and 1,000 years like one day. The Lord does not delay His promise, as some understand delay, but is patient with you, not wanting any to perish, but all to come to repentance.... But based on His promise, we wait for new heavens and a new earth, where righteousness will dwell" (2 Peter 3:8-9, 13).

Jude's use of "scoffers" is different. While no doubt he would stand in full agreement with Peter and the other apostles about the imminent return of Christ, and those who refuse to see it coming, Jude's point seems to be that these false teachers mock the law of God. These ideas are related. After all, those who mock God's revealed will for all people naturally reject the idea that they must give an account one day before the divine Moral Lawgiver.

Jude puts a finer point on this when he caps what he already has written. These teachers are "ungodly, turning the grace of our God into promiscuity and denying our only Master and Lord, Jesus Christ" (v. 4). They commit "ungodly deeds" in an "ungodly way," and say "harsh things" against God (v. 15). They are "discontented grumblers" who walk "according to their desires," and their mouths "utter arrogant words" (v. 16). Now, Jude writes, the result of this ungodliness is that "These people create divisions and are merely natural, not having the Spirit"(v. 19).

What "divisions" do these false teachers create?

Jude writes that false teachers "create divisions" (v. 19). The Greek word *apodiorizo* refers not only to divisions, but to the motives behind them and the results they produce. The term means "to make a distinction." It describes these interlopers as ones who present themselves as superior to other leaders in the church. Marvin Vincent, the Presbyterian minister best known for his *Word Studies in the New Testament*, writes that these false teachers "draw a line through the Church and set off one part from another."[7]

In this regard, they are like the Pharisees, lovers of money who, while listening to Jesus, are "scoffing at Him" (Luke 16:14). Jesus tells them, "You are the ones who justify yourselves in the sight of others, but God knows your hearts. For what is highly admired by people is revolting in God's sight" (v. 15).

The religious leaders demonstrate hypocrisy, saying one thing and doing another. Jesus tells the crowds not to do what the scribes and Pharisees do because "they don't practice what they teach. They tie up heavy loads that are hard to carry and put them on people's shoulders, but they themselves aren't willing to lift a finger to move them. They do everything to be observed by others: They enlarge their phylacteries and lengthen their tassels. They love the place of honor at banquets, the front seats in the synagogues, greetings in the marketplaces, and to be called 'Rabbi' by people" (Matt. 23:3b-7).

Finally, the religious leaders of Jesus' day concoct their own twisted view of the Hebrew Scriptures. Jesus warns His disciples to "beware of the yeast of the Pharisees and Sadducees," meaning their false teaching (Matt. 16:6, 11-12).

Unfortunately, this "yeast" rises in the early church and manifests itself in many forms. Paul, for example, is forced to defend his true apostleship against those who have come into Corinth behind him, professing to be "super apostles" (2 Cor. 11:5; 12:11). Paul calls them what they are: "false apostles, deceitful workers, disguising themselves as apostles of Christ" (2 Cor. 11:13). Specifically, he identifies three areas of false teaching; the "super apostles" preach "another Jesus ... a different spirit ... a different gospel" (2 Cor. 11:4).

The "dreamers" about whom Jude writes are cut from the same cloth. Their arrogance, flattery, self-indulgence, and corrupt doctrines create strife within the body of Christ. Imagine the questions their false teaching has aroused among new converts and poorly grounded followers of Christ:

- "Can I truly compartmentalize my life in such a way that my sensual appetites don't affect my spiritual walk?"

- "Is the grace of God a license to indulge my baser desires?"

- "Does my freedom in Christ mean there are no consequences for my behavior?"

- "Are the apostles' doctrines outmoded?"

- "Which teachers should I follow?"

- "Should I rebuke demons - or even curse the Devil?"

- "Are prosperity and good health signs of God's blessing?"

- And many others.

It may be that the false teachers compete with one another for prominence, much as some modern-day television evangelists attempt to out-sensationalize one another in a battle for ratings - and revenues. Paul faces a similar situation in Corinth, where some are saying "I'm with Paul," "I'm with Apollos," "I'm with Cephas," or "I'm with Christ." Such divisions grieve the apostle, who writes, "Now I urge you, brothers, in the name of our Lord Jesus Christ, that you all say the same thing, that there be no divisions among you, and that you be united with the same understanding and the same conviction" (1 Cor. 1:10).

There may be a tendency in some local churches to exalt one leader over others and, perhaps unintentionally, to surrender extra-biblical authority to that man or woman. The cult of personality is dangerous for a congregation. And it's damaging to the venerated leader, who may succumb to pride, ultimately shipwrecking his ministry, not to mention the spiritual confidence of others. Jude sees this danger, and he exhorts his readers to avoid the divisions caused when God's people idolize anyone claiming divine authority.

As the apostle John warns, "Dear friends, do not believe every spirit [a person claiming divine gifting for service], but test the spirits to determine if they are from God" (1 John 4:1).

Edward Pentecost writes, "Wherever there is the authentic, the counterfeit will appear; this happened in the early church. False apostles and teachers began to appear, and it was necessary to develop a system to protect the church against false prophecies and forged letters. Since Christ had committed 'the faith' to His Apostles, one of the main tests in the early church was, 'Is that what the Apostles taught?' When the church assembled the New Testament books, it was required that each book be written either by an apostle or by someone closely associated with an apostle. Apostolic teaching was, and still is, the test of truth."[8]

How can Jude say false teachers are unbelievers?

Jude describes false teachers as "merely natural, not having the Spirit" (v. 19).[9] He seems to be stating plainly that these professing Christians are unbelievers. How can he make such a judgment? Doesn't Jesus say, "Do not judge, so that you won't be judged" (Matt. 7:1)? Isn't God the only one who may rightly search the hearts of people (Jer. 17:10)? How can Jude possibly know that these interlopers are lost? Isn't it possible they are merely deceived, or backslidden?

First, we should note that Jude describes these particular false teachers as "natural." Literally, this means "animal-souled" and stands in contrast with "spiritual," or "having the Spirit." The apostle Paul describes the unbeliever as a "natural man" who "does not welcome what comes from God's Spirit, because it is foolishness to him; he is not able to know it since it is evaluated spiritually" (1 Cor. 2:14).

Clearly, these New Testament authors are depicting people outside the kingdom of God. Jude's use of the term *psuchikos* - soulish, sensual, animal-souled - depicts them in strictly physical terms. As John MacArthur states bluntly, "His [Jude's] materialistic description exposed them for who they really were - religious terrorists who lacked such internal qualities as a proper self-perception, the ability to reason, and a true knowledge of God. Even though the false teachers claimed a transcendental understanding of God, they did not know Him at all."[10]

214

It may help our understanding to consider the three-fold nature of all people.[11] God created us with body, soul, and spirit. The body, of course, is the physical part of us. Through our five senses, we relate to the natural world in which we live. Next, there is the soul, which is the unseen, conscious life consisting of mind, emotion, and will. Finally comes the spirit, the innermost part of us with which we relate to God, who is Spirit.

The "natural man," as Paul and Jude depict him, is certainly alive in body and soul, but spiritually dead (Eph. 2:1). That is, he can think, emote, and make decisions. But because he has rejected Christ, the Holy Spirit does not inhabit his human spirit. Therefore, his life is directed by what he experiences through his five senses, what he thinks about, and what he reasons from a mind that Satan has blinded and the Spirit has not renewed (Rom. 12:2; 2 Cor. 4:4).

In essence, the "natural man" is only two-thirds alive. Being spiritually dead, he cannot know God or benefit from God's presence in his life. It takes the regeneration of the Holy Spirit to make a person fully alive and able to live in a manner pleasing to God (John 3:3, 5; Rom. 8:9; 1 John 3:24; 4:13). Paul makes this distinction between the believer and the unregenerate person in Titus 1:15-16: "To the pure, everything is pure, but to those who are defiled and unbelieving nothing is pure; in fact, both their mind and conscience are defiled. They profess to know God, but they deny Him by their works. They are detestable, disobedient, and disqualified for any good work."

All right, you may say. So unbelievers are spiritually dead, natural, animal-soulish. But that doesn't address the issue of how Jude, or any other apostle, could know that a false teacher is lost. How can they make such judgments? Several observations may prove helpful.

First, Jude and other New Testament writers pen their words under the divine direction of the Holy Spirit. Concerning the doctrine of inspiration, it is biblically faithful to say that the words of Jude are not Jude's alone; they are the very words of God. Jude determines that the false teachers about whom he writes are outside the kingdom of God because the Holy Spirit already has made that determination and thus inspires Jude to confirm it in writing.

Second, the oft-quoted words of Jesus - "Do not judge, so that you won't be judged" (Matt. 7:1) - should be taken in context. In this portion of the Sermon on the Mount, Jesus warns against hypocritical judgment. Only when we remove the log from our own eye are we sufficiently clear-eyed to remove the speck from our brother's eye.

Jesus' command does not preclude discernment. Immediately after Jesus says, "Do not judge," He warns, "Don't give what is holy to dogs or toss your pearls before pigs" (Matt. 7:6). Not much later, He warns, "Beware of false prophets who come to you in sheep's clothing but inwardly are ravaging wolves. You'll recognize them by their fruit" (vv. 15-16a). How are we to identify those who oppose the gospel or peddle false doctrines unless we "judge according to righteous judgment" (John 7:24)?

We are to be discerning (Col. 1:9; 1 Thess. 5:21). We are to preach the whole counsel of God, including the Bible's teaching on sin (Acts 20:27; 2 Tim. 4:2). We are to gently confront erring brothers and sisters in Christ (Gal. 6:1). We are to practice church discipline (Matt. 18:15-17). And we are always to speak the truth in love (Eph. 4:15).[12]

Finally, we may discover that certain people are unsaved based on their fruit - that is, their words and deeds. Some may boldly proclaim their defiance against Christ and their rejection of His finished work on the cross. Others may expose their need of redemption by professing Jesus, while revealing an unbiblical view of who He is and what He accomplished through His earthly ministry. Still others, like the false teachers to whom Jude refers, infiltrate the church and claim divine gifting for service. But their arrogant words and false doctrines, and their self-indulgent lifestyles, belie the depths of their depravity.

Christians always should stand boldly in the truth. At times, this means confronting false teachers in our midst. Even so, we should defend the faith with gentleness and respect, keeping our conscience clear so that when we are accused - of judging falsely, for example - those who denounce us are put to shame (1 Peter 3:16).

We may think a landowner's tree is dead when it bears no fruit, and our role as neighbor is well-served when we point this out. But we have no right to make firewood of the tree. Who is to say the gardener won't dig a trench around it, and fertilize its soil for one more season?

Perhaps next year it springs to life, or failing to do so, the landowner cuts it down (Luke 13:6-9).

Ultimately, final judgment is in the hands of Jesus (John 5:22). Only He knows when individuals have filled up their measure of sin, thus passing the point of no return (Matt. 23:32-33; 1 Thess. 2:16). A person may offer clear evidence that he is lost, and it is no sin for us to grasp the obvious. However, we move beyond the bounds of judging rightly when we conclude he has fallen so far that he cannot be redeemed.

Jude declares the false teachers of his day to be "merely natural, not having the Spirit" (v. 19), confirming the reason they were "designated for this judgment long ago" (v. 4). Under divine direction, Jude reveals the condition of their hearts and their ultimate destiny, a judgment God determined in eternity past.

Key words

In this chapter, we learned several key terms. Fill in the blanks to test your knowledge.

Last days. This term refers to the final period in _____ when the Messiah comes to establish God's _____.

The last day. In some New Testament contexts, "the last day" refers to future _____ and _____.

Last time, end of times, last hour. The New Testament writers use these phrases to further depict the already-but-not yet nature of God's _____.

Day of the Lord. The phrase "day of the Lord" in Scripture often refers to _____ at the end of human history. Sometimes it's associated with the words "_____ _____."

Comparing English translations of *empaiktai* (referring to false teachers who deride or mock):

	HCSB	KJV	NIV	NASB	ESV
Jude 18	scoffers	mockers	scoffers	mockers	scoffers
2 Peter 3:3	scoffers	scoffers	scoffers	mockers	scoffers

Comparing English translations of *apodiorizo* (referring to divisions that false teachers cause):

HCSB	KJV	NIV	NASB	ESV
divisions	separate	divide	divisions	divisions

Application

Questions for personal or group study

1. Paul, Peter, and John offer many warnings about false teachers (see question 3). Why is the authoritative word of the apostles so important to first-century Christians? And why should their writings continue to be heeded today?

2. Look up the following Scriptures and note the unique qualifications required of an apostle:

Scripture	Qualifications
Matt. 10:1-25	
Acts 1:21-22	
Rom. 15:15-19	
1 Cor. 9:1-2	
2 Cor. 1:1	
2 Cor. 12:11-13	
Gal. 1:15-16	
Eph. 1:1	
Col. 1:1	
1 Tim. 1:1	
2 Tim. 1:1	
Heb. 2:2-4	

3. Consider the following passages and identify, as best you can: (a) the warning given, (b) any specific area of doctrine or behavior addressed, and (c) how believers should respond.

Scripture	Warning	Doctrine / Behavior	Appropriate Response
Acts 20:28-31			
Col. 2:16-19			
1 Thess. 2:14-16			
2 Thess. 2:3-12			
1 Tim. 4:1-5			
1 Tim. 6:20-21			
2 Tim. 2:15-19			
2 Tim. 3:1-9			
2 Tim. 4:1-5			
2 Peter 2:1-3			
1 John 4:1-6			
Rev. 2:1-7			
Rev. 2:12-17			
Rev. 2:18-29			
Rev. 3:1-6			
Rev. 3:14-22			

4. Do the biblical terms "last days," "the last day," "last time," "end of times," "last hour," and "day of the Lord" seem confusing to you? Why do you think the Holy Spirit inspired the human authors to use so many different terms? In what ways do these terms describe the same events? And how does the context of these phrases help us see unique ways the Lord works in human history?

5. Jesus and the New Testament writers describe the kingdom of God as already here, yet not fully revealed. In what ways is the kingdom of God an accomplished fact? And what remains to be done for the kingdom to come in its fullness?

6. Jude declares the false teachers of his day to be unbelievers. They are "merely natural, not having the Spirit" (v. 19b). Since only God knows the human heart, how can Jude make such a bold declaration?

7. Jude writes that false teachers "create divisions" in the church. In what ways do you think these apostate leaders caused problems in the first-century church? What are some schisms that false apostles, false prophets, and false teachers cause in today's church?

We should never shy away from preaching the reality of hell – not with a gleeful glint in our eyes, but through the watery lens of our tears. Perhaps some may be snatched from the fire.

15

But You, Dear Friends:
Hating the Garment Defiled by the Flesh

*But you, dear friends, building yourselves up in your most
holy faith and praying in the Holy Spirit, keep yourselves
in the love of God, expecting the mercy of our Lord Jesus
Christ for eternal life. Have mercy on some who doubt;
save others by snatching them from the fire; on others have
mercy in fear, hating even the garment defiled by the flesh.*

(Jude 20-23 HCSB)

Fans of the phenomenally popular sit-com *Seinfeld* may recall the
episode that first aired April 15, 1993. "The Smelly Car" revolves
around a parking valet's excessive body odor, which attaches itself to
the interior of Jerry's BMW. The malignant scent clings to Jerry's
clothing, and it lingers in Elaine's hair, ruining her romantic life.

Exasperated, Jerry tells his friend Kramer, "Don't you see what's
happening here? It's attached itself to me! It's alive! ... This is not
just an odor - you need a priest to get rid of this thing!"

Determined to get satisfaction, Jerry drives back to the restaurant
where the valet soiled his car and demands that the maître d' pay

for detailing. When the maître d' refuses, Jerry locks him in the car until, overcome by the stench, he relents. Jerry has the car thoroughly cleaned, but to no avail; the B.O. remains. So, he tries returning the car, but the dealership won't take it back due to the invasive stench.

At last, Jerry drives into a rough neighborhood, leaves the car unlocked, and sets the keys in plain sight. At this point, he just wants to be rid of the vehicle at any cost. A young thief waits for Jerry to walk away, then seizes the opportunity to take the BMW for a joyride. Once inside the befouled car, he changes his mind.

Co-writer Peter Melhman reportedly got the idea for the episode from the real-life experience of a friend.[1]

It's not uncommon to find ourselves in situations where flop sweat, the smoke of burning trash, or a run-in with a skunk produces a malodorous companion to our hair and clothing, attracting unwanted attention and requiring a thorough remedy. The polluting effects of soiled garments are in Jude's mind when he writes the final verses of his epistle, for he warns his readers to beware of the collateral damage done by those engaged in ungodly behavior. He instructs followers of Jesus to "have mercy in fear, hating even the garment defiled by the flesh" (v. 23).

Fortunately, the One who is able to make us "stand in the presence of His glory, blameless and with great joy" (v. 24), is the same One who walks through a Babylonian furnace with three Hebrew men and delivers them safely without so much as a hint of smoke on their clothing.

Now that Jude has equipped us to recognize false teachers by what they say and how they live - and to rest assured that God deals harshly with them - he caps his epistle with practical advice.

Jude begins the final segment of his letter with four exhortations for erecting a defensive perimeter around our spiritual lives: We are to build ourselves up in our faith, pray in the Holy Spirit, keep ourselves in the love of God, and expect the mercy of Christ for eternal life.

Next, we are to deal shrewdly with those who have surrendered ground to false teachers in the church. Some are in doubt; some are in peril; and some have become a danger to the rest.

Finally, as we see in the next chapter, covering verses 24-25, Jude offers a rich doxology that exalts God, who protects us from stumbling, and ensures that we stand blameless and joyful in His presence one day.

What do we do about false teachers?

Thomas Schreiner writes, "Jude recognized that his readers would not continue to be devoted to the faith if they concentrated only on resisting the opponents, as important as that was. The readers must also grow in the Christian faith themselves and keep themselves in the sphere of God's love."[2]

Jude directs us to build a defensive perimeter around our spiritual lives. There are four key elements.[3]

Build yourselves up

First, Jude encourages his readers to stay doctrinally strong, "building yourselves up in your most holy faith" (v. 20). That "faith" is the same as "the faith that was delivered to the saints once for all" (v. 3). Right actions spring from right beliefs, which are based on a right knowledge of God's Word. This means "rightly dividing the word of truth" (2 Tim. 2:15b KJV). In practical terms, spiritual edification must be grounded in a study of God's Word.

Paul tells the Ephesian elders, "And now I commit you to God and to the message of His grace, which is able to build you up and to give you an inheritance among all who are sanctified" (Acts 20:32). And he writes to Timothy, "All Scripture is inspired by God and is profitable for teaching, for rebuking, for correcting, for training in righteousness, so that the man of God may be complete, equipped for every good work" (2 Tim. 3:16-17).

The idea of building is a consistent one throughout the New Testament. Consider:

- Our bodies are temples of the Holy Spirit (1 Cor. 3:16-17; 6:15-20).

- The church is the sanctuary of the living God (2 Cor. 6:14-18).

- Believers are members of God's household, built on the foundation of the apostles and prophets, with Christ as the cornerstone (Eph. 2:19-22).

- Christians are "living stones," being built into a spiritual house for a holy priesthood to offer spiritual sacrifices acceptable to God (1 Peter 2:5).

Further, Paul writes that the only foundation of the church is Christ. We must build on that foundation to receive a reward when we stand before the judgment seat of Christ (Rom. 14:10-12; 1 Cor. 3:10 - 4:5; 2 Cor. 5:1-10). If we build on that foundation with gold, silver, and costly stones - that is, good works grounded in sound doctrine - we receive a reward. But if we build with wood, hay, or straw - dead works rooted in the flesh - our works are consumed in the fires of judgment. Our salvation remains intact, but we exit the judgment like a man escaping a house fire with only the shirt on his back (1 Cor. 3:12-15).

Every Christian builds upon his or her faith in Christ. But what and how we build depends on our grasp of the Word of God. And, in the end, it all passes through the purging fires of the believer's judgment. The good is purified; the dross is destroyed.

Pray in the Spirit

Second, Jude encourages us to pray in the Holy Spirit. This is not a reference to speaking in tongues, which would limit such prayers to those the Spirit has so gifted. Rather, it means to pray in a manner consistent with the Holy Spirit's will.

Praying in or with the Spirit (or spirit) is mentioned three times in Scripture. In his commentary on the gift of tongues, Paul writes, "I will pray with the spirit [note the lower case, indicating the inner person, not the Holy Spirit], and I will also pray with my understanding. I will sing with the spirit, and I will also sing with my understanding" (1 Cor. 14:15). Paul does not forbid the Corinthians to pray or sing in unlearned languages (v. 39), but he argues that it's better to include the mind and thus understand what is being communicated so as to benefit the congregation (vv. 15-19). This clearly is a different context than the one in which Jude writes.

The second reference to praying in the Spirit/spirit is Eph. 6:18, where Paul writes, "With every prayer and request, pray at all times in the Spirit, and stay alert in this, with all perseverance and intercession for all the saints." This passage identifies the Holy Spirit's role as our helper in prayer. As Kenneth Wuest points out, all true prayer is exercised in the sphere of the Holy Spirit, motivated and empowered by Him. "That means that if the saint expects to really pray, he must be Spirit-filled or Spirit-controlled. The fullness of the Holy Spirit is the prerequisite to effectual praying.... We pray by means of the Holy Spirit, in dependence on Him."[4]

The final reference to praying in the Holy Spirit, of course, is Jude 20. Praying in the Spirit here means praying in harmony with the Word of God, and with the will of God, for the glory of God. The Lord reveals His will in His Word (see, for example, Deut. 17:19-20; Ps. 119:11, 105, 130; Matt. 4:4; Rom. 15:4; 2 Tim. 3:16-17), but often we lack the ability to apply His will to circumstances in our lives.

That's where the Spirit helps us. He intercedes for us before the Father with sympathy and urgency (Rom. 8:26-27). Writing to the Ephesians, Paul exhorts his readers to put on the full armor of God so they may stand against the wiles of Satan. He follows this immediately by writing, "With every prayer and request, pray at all times in the Spirit, and stay alert in this, with all perseverance and intercession for all the saints" (Eph. 6:18). The Holy Spirit teaches what we are to pray for, and how.

Praying in the Holy Spirit means praying according to the leading of the Spirit. Warren Wiersbe points out, "As Christians, we may pray in solitude (Matt. 6:6), but we never pray *alone*; the Spirit of God joins with us as we pray because He knows the mind of God and can direct us.... When the believer is yielded to the Spirit, then the Spirit will assist him in his prayer life, and God will answer prayer."[5]

Put another way, praying in the Spirit includes realizing that our prayers are carried along by the third person of the triune Godhead, in the name of Jesus Christ, to the throne room where the Father sits in glory. "True prayer," writes Samuel M. Zwemer, "is God the Holy Spirit talking to God the Father in the name of God the Son, and the believer's heart in the prayer-room."[6]

In his classic book, *Prayer Power Unlimited*, J. Oswald Sanders writes, "In this prayer life, the believer has the aid of two Advocates who continually make themselves available and plead his cause.... The Son of God intercedes for us before the throne of glory, securing for us the benefits of His mediatorial work.... The Spirit of God is Christ's Advocate in our hearts to meet our deepest needs."[7]

Sanders lists six ways the Spirit helps us in prayer:

1. He introduces us into the presence of the Father (Eph. 2:18).

2. He overcomes our reluctance, working in us the desire to pray (Zech. 12:10).

3. He imparts a sense of sonship and acceptance that creates freedom and confidence in the presence of God (Gal. 4:6).

4. He helps us in the ignorance of our minds and in the infirmities of our bodies, as well as the maladies of the soul (Rom. 8:26).

5. He takes our faltering and imperfect prayers, adds to them the incense of the merits of Christ, and puts them in a form acceptable to the Father (Rev. 8:3).

6. He lays special burdens of prayer on believers who are walking in fellowship with Him (Dan. 10:2-3).[8]

Keep in the love of God

Third, Jude urges his readers to keep themselves in the love of God. Of course, God always loves us. His love is unconditional and enduring. In verse 1, Jude tells followers of Jesus they are "loved by God the Father." As the apostle John notes, it is "not that we loved God, but that He loved us and sent His Son to be the propitiation for our sins" (1 John 4:10). The word translated "propitiation" is *hilasmos* in the Greek and conveys the idea of satisfaction. That is, while God's justice demands satisfaction for our sins, His love provided that satisfaction in the sacrificial and substitutionary death of His Son on the cross, thus restoring a peaceful relationship between holy God and sinful humans.

Jude's instruction, then, seems to be that we operate in the sphere of His love as obedient children. It's within that sphere that we experience divine blessing. Paul encourages Roman believers about the triumph of their faith in God, whose love has been poured out in their hearts through the Holy Spirit. He goes on to remind them that "God proves His own love for us in that while we were still sinners Christ died for us!" (Rom. 5:5, 8).

Later in his epistle, Paul brings the believer's triumph of faith to a climax by asking and answering a key question: "Who can separate us from the love of Christ? ... For I am persuaded that neither death nor life, nor angels nor rulers, nor things present, nor things to come, nor powers, nor height, nor depth, nor any other created thing will have the power to separate us from the love of God that is in Christ Jesus our Lord!" (Rom. 8:35a, 38-39).

Jesus tells His disciples, "As the Father has loved Me, I have also loved you. Remain in My love. If you keep My commands you will remain in My love, just as I have kept My Father's commands and remain in His love." As a result, "I have spoken these things to you so that My joy may be in you and your joy may be complete" (John 15:9-11).

The depth of our love for Jesus is measured by the degree of our obedience to Him. If we remain in His love, taking up our crosses daily, and being led by the indwelling Spirit, we bear much fruit for the kingdom of heaven and enjoy divine blessings. However, if we become disobedient children, we move from blessing to chastening, as the writer of Hebrews reminds us: "And you have forgotten the exhortation that addresses you as sons: My son, do not take the Lord's discipline lightly, or faint when you are reproved by Him; for the Lord disciplines the one He loves, and punishes every son whom He receives" (Heb. 12:5-6).

The Lord's chastening matches our measure of rebellion. It is intended for our good as He conforms us to His image. And it serves to protect His kingdom from internal corruption. For some, the still, small voice of the Spirit is sufficient to prompt repentance. For others, rebuke comes through Christ's servants in the form of personal intervention or church discipline. Paul, for example, confronts Peter about his duplicity with respect to treatment of Jewish and Gentile believers (Gal. 2:11-15). And he instructs the church at Corinth to remove from fellowship a man having sexual relations with his stepmother (1 Cor. 5:1-5). Sometimes, the chastening is severe. Peter delivers words of death to Ananias and Sapphira for lying to the Holy Spirit (Acts 5:1-11). And Paul reminds the Corinthian believers that failure to conduct a thorough self-examination before partaking of the Lord's table may result in sickness, and even death (1 Cor. 11:27-32).

Thomas Schreiner writes, "God keeps his own, and yet believers must keep themselves in God's love. Jude represented well the biblical tension between divine sovereignty and human responsibility. On the one hand, believers only avoid apostasy because of the grace of God. On the other hand, the grace of God does not cancel out the need for believers to exert all their energy to remain in God's love."[9]

Expect the mercy of Christ

Jude tells us to expect the mercy of our Lord Jesus Christ for eternal life. The New American Standard Bible challenges Christians to be "waiting anxiously." The New Revised Standard Version urges us to "look forward to" the Lord's mercy, while The Message has Jude telling readers they should be "keeping your arms open and outstretched, ready."

The bottom line is that all Christians should live in the light of eternity, eagerly awaiting the return of our Lord. At the circumcision of Jesus, Simeon takes the child in his arms and offers prophetic praise to God. Luke describes Simeon as "righteous and devout, looking forward to Israel's consolation" (Luke 2:25b). Immediately after this, a prophetess named Anna steps forward and speaks about the Lord to all who are looking forward to the redemption of Jerusalem (Luke 2:36-38).

After Jesus' death, Pilate grants Joseph of Arimathea permission to bury the crucified body of the Savior. Mark depicts Joseph as "a prominent member of the Sanhedrin who was himself looking forward to the kingdom of God" (Mark 15:43a). No doubt, righteous Israelites faithfully anticipated the coming of the Messiah, and they rejoiced in His appearance as Jesus of Nazareth.

Today, Christians look back, with grateful hearts, at the finished work of Christ on the cross. Equally important, we keep our arms open and outstretched as we anticipate His glorious return. Calls to wait expectantly dot the New Testament epistles. Paul admonishes the Corinthians to "eagerly wait for the revelation of our Lord Jesus Christ" (1 Cor. 1:7b). He reminds the Philippian saints, "our citizenship is in heaven, from which we also eagerly wait for a Savior, the Lord Jesus Christ" (Phil. 3:20). And he applauds the Thessalonians for turning from idols to God, and for waiting "for His Son from heaven, whom He raised from the dead - Jesus, who rescues us from the coming wrath" (1 Thess. 1:10).

Further, Paul tells us there is a reward - a "crown of righteousness" - reserved for the day of judgment for "all those who have loved His appearing" (2 Tim. 4:8). And he urges Titus to consider how the grace of God instructs us to deny godlessness and worldly lusts, and to live in a sensible, righteous, and godly way in the present age, "while we wait for the blessed hope and the appearing of the glory of our great God and Savior, Jesus Christ" (Titus 2:13).

Jude, in the context of his letter, conceives of mercy as something future - something yet to be received at the coming of the Lord. This does not negate the benefits of His present mercy; rather, it stresses that at His coming, when we are glorified and the effects of the Fall are reversed, we possess the full and final benefits of His mercy. This includes both the removal of what we actually deserve - everlasting separation from God in hell - and full conformity to His image.

We see Jesus as He is, and we are like Him, reflecting His holiness, purity, and love. We serve Him on a fully renovated earth and experience sinless perfection throughout the coming ages. This is true life, everlasting life, as God created it and intended it to be. The fallen world in which we live is crumbling beneath the weight of sin. It cannot endure. But the One who became sin for us tells us to wait, watch, and be ready. "I have told you these things so that in Me you may have peace," He tells His disciples. "You will have suffering in this world. Be courageous! I have conquered the world" (John 16:33).

Who are those under the spell of false teachers?

Now that we have built a protective perimeter around our hearts by shoring up our doctrinal infrastructure, praying in the Spirit, keeping ourselves in the love of God, and waiting eagerly for the return of Christ, Jude instructs us to rescue those under the spell of false teachers.

Specifically, he addresses three groups of people: doubters, deceived, and departed. As John MacArthur writes, "Those who pose the greatest threat to the church also constitute part of its mission field."[10] We must do more than erect a defensive wall around us. Like those who have put on the full armor of God, we must engage in battle against "the world powers of this darkness, against the spiritual forces of evil in the heavens" (Eph. 6:12).

The doubters

The first group of people Jude addresses consists of those who doubt. That is, they are not able to discern between true doctrine and false doctrine. These may be the same folks Peter describes as "unstable people" that prove to be easy marks for false teachers (2 Peter 2:14). Likely, the doubters are immature believers who are not well-grounded in the faith, although Jude also could be describing unbelievers who are being drawn to Christ, but who must contend with the obstacles of false doctrine. Jude hints that false teachers also prey on disgruntled church members because the false teachers themselves are "discontented grumblers" (v. 16).

False teachers are clever. Often attractive, articulate, and persuasive, they profess to speak for God - even using Scripture and biblical terms - yet they deny the central beliefs of historical Christianity. How can someone seeking the truth, whether an unbeliever or an immature Christian, tell the difference between true doctrine and false doctrine? This is the front line of battle where Jude has challenged us to be, contending for the faith that was delivered to the saints once for all (v. 3).

Jude is not the only first-century church leader wrestling with this assault on the kingdom of heaven. The apostle Paul writes to the Corinthians, "But I fear that, as the serpent deceived Eve by his cunning, your minds may be corrupted from a complete and pure devotion to Christ" (2 Cor. 11:3). Paul then goes on to identify three specific doctrines that the "super-apostles" (whom he later calls "false apostles") are promoting. They teach "another Jesus ... a different spirit ... a different gospel" (v. 4).

Today, these three markers continue to help us separate true Christianity from false belief systems. It is noteworthy that three of the most popular and prolific false religious organizations in the world today - the Church of Jesus Christ of Latter-day Saints, the Watch Tower Bible and Tract Society, and Islam - all proclaim non-biblical views of Jesus, the Holy Spirit, and the gospel. If we as Christians did little more than ground ourselves in these three core biblical doctrines (concerning Jesus, the Holy Spirit, and the gospel), we would go a long way in protecting ourselves and others from the wiles of many false teachers.

Paul also grapples with Judaizers in Galatia. Judaizers promote a mixture of grace, through Christ, and works, through the keeping of the Law. He writes, "You foolish Galatians! Who has hypnotized you, before whose eyes Jesus Christ was vividly portrayed as crucified? I only want to learn this from you: Did you receive the Spirit by the works of the law or by hearing with faith? Are you so foolish? After beginning with the Spirit, are you now going to be made complete by the flesh? Did you suffer so much for nothing - if in fact it was for nothing? So then, does God supply you with the Spirit and work miracles among you by the works of the law or by hearing with faith?" (Gal. 3:1-5).

James, the brother of Jude, urges his readers to ask God for wisdom. "But let him ask in faith without doubting," says James. "For the doubter is like the surging sea, driven and tossed by the wind…. An indecisive man is unstable in all his ways" (James 1:6, 8).

For Jude's readers, the issues largely are pride and prosperity - speaking arrogantly to demonic forces while living a hedonistic lifestyle. The false teachers are bold, persuasive, and evidently unchallenged. As a result, many people in the church, whether unbelieving seekers or new believers, are confused. They simply cannot discern whether the pure gospel, preached by the apostles, or this new gospel, proclaimed by charismatic false teachers, is the true gospel. So those who are strong in the faith must show mercy to those torn between truth and error.

Showing mercy does not mean ignoring the serious nature of false doctrine. Nor does it mean commending doubters for their sincerity. Rather, it means extending to those who vacillate between truth and error the same patience, kindness, and perseverance that God shows to us. If the Lord delays His coming in order to grant unbelievers more time to repent (2 Peter 3:9), shouldn't we also labor patiently with those earnestly seeking the truth?

The deceived

The second group under the spell of false teachers consists of those who have gone beyond doubt into deception. These people still may be in the local church, although fully engaged in "the teachings of demons" (1 Tim. 4:1). Or, perhaps they have left the fellowship of the local church and now are immersed in the companionship of an apostate group. In either case, Thomas Schreiner argues that these people are "close to being captured by the teaching and behavior of the opponents. Believers should not give up on them. Their lives could still be salvaged, and they could be snatched from the fire that threatened to destroy them."[11]

While the first group - the doubters - may include true followers of Jesus, it appears the second group is characterized primarily by those who do not know Christ. Perhaps they call Jesus "Lord," as many do on the day of judgment, self-deceived into a false sense of security (Matt. 7:21-23). Or, it could be that they knowingly have left the faith, cleaving to false teachings to satisfy their fallen natures.

Like Esau, the immoral and irreverent son of Abraham who sold his birthright for a single meal, these unbelievers do not value the things of God and are dangling over the precipice of outer darkness (see Gen. 25:27-34; Heb. 12:16-17). It is possible, however, that some of the deceived to which Jude refers are indeed Christians who have never become grounded in the faith and thus, like little children, are "tossed by the waves and blown around by every wind of teaching" (Eph. 4:14).

What are we to do with such unwitting, or willing, victims of deception? Jude exhorts us to "save" these folks by "snatching them from the fire" (v. 23). What does he mean by "save"? Save them from damnation? Save them from drifting into apostasy? Save them from the consequences of their actions? Jude may be addressing all of these scenarios. But his primary focus seems to be on rescuing those on the brink of spiritual danger before they pass the point of no return.

As Warren Wiersbe writes about Christians in this dangerous predicament, "The angels took Lot by the hand and pulled him out of Sodom (Gen. 19:16), and sometimes that must be done in order to rescue ignorant and unstable believers from the clutches of false teachers."[12]

The verb "snatching" (Greek *harpazo*) means to seize, carry off, or take something or someone by force. It's the same Greek word Paul uses to describe what happens to Christians on earth on the day of resurrection. They are "caught up" with the resurrected saints to meet the Lord in the air (1 Thess. 4:17). The phrase "caught up" is rendered *rapio* in Latin, which lends itself to the modern term "Rapture" to describe this glorious day.

Jude likely borrows this imagery from the prophets, however. For example, consider what the Lord says through Amos about unrepentant Israel: "I overthrew some of you as I overthrew Sodom and Gomorrah, and you were like a burning stick snatched from a fire, yet you did not return to Me" (Amos 4:11).

A similar phrase is used in a different context in Zechariah, who sees Joshua the high priest standing before the Angel of the Lord, with Satan there to accuse Joshua. The Angel of the Lord says to Satan, "The Lord rebuke you, Satan! May the Lord who has chosen Jerusalem rebuke you! Isn't this man a burning stick snatched from the fire?" (Zech. 3:2). The Angel - the pre-incarnate Christ - proclaims Joshua's sins forgiven and orders that his filthy clothes be replaced with clean garments and a clean turban. All of this foreshadows the finished work of Christ, and offers both encouragement and incentive to Joshua and Zerubbabel as they lead the Israelites returning to their homeland after the Babylonian captivity.[13]

With these images in mind, Jude may be picturing those who have embraced the doctrines of the false teachers and thus figuratively are singed by the very fires of hell. It is not too late for them, but they must be made to understand how little time is left for them to repent.

Notice how Jesus deals with people in various stages of unbelief. To the confused or unsure, like the woman at the well (John 4), He exhibits exceptional kindness and patience as He corrects their false beliefs. But to those fully embracing man-made doctrines that oppose the purity and simplicity of Scripture, like the scribes and Pharisees, He pulls no punches, calling them hypocrites, blind guides, blind fools, and snakes. He warns them they are filling up the measure of their father's sins. And He wonders aloud how they can escape being condemned to hell (Matthew 23).

We cannot search the hearts of men and women, or say with certainty whether they are saved or lost. However, for those openly proclaiming "another Jesus," "a different spirit," or "a different gospel," we should confront them with biblical truth, which includes the real and present danger of eternal separation from God in hell for those who reject their only hope of salvation.

Jesus does not hold the reality of hell over the heads of the scribes and Pharisees for the purpose of magnifying His sovereign power, but to make clear the truth that our choices now have everlasting consequences. We, too, should never shy away from preaching the reality of hell - not with a gleeful glint in our eyes, but through the watery lens of our tears. Perhaps some may be snatched from the fire.

It seems quite likely that the fire to which Jude refers in this passage is future judgment in hell. That imagery runs consistently throughout the New Testament. John the Baptist tells the Pharisees and Sadducees - whom he calls, "Brood of vipers!" - to show they are truly repentant by producing good fruit. And he warns them, "Therefore every tree that doesn't produce good fruit will be cut down and thrown into the fire" (see Matt. 3:7-10). He goes on to proclaim the coming of Messiah, whose winnowing shovel is in His hand. "He will clear His threshing floor and gather His wheat into the barn. But the chaff He will burn up with fire that never goes out" (v. 12).

Jesus often uses fiery images to depict hell. In the parable of the dragnet, He tells His listeners, "So it will be at the end of the age. The angels will go out, separate the evil people from the righteous, and throw them into the blazing furnace. In that place there will be weeping and gnashing of teeth" (Matt. 13:49-50). And in warnings about hell, He says, "And if your eye causes your downfall, gouge it out. It is better for you to enter the kingdom of God with one eye than to have two eyes and be thrown into hell, where *Their worm does not die, and the fire is not quenched*" (Mark 9:47-48; quotation from Isa. 66:24).

236

Addressing the Thessalonians about God's judgment and glory, Paul writes that "it is righteous for God to repay with affliction those who afflict you, and to reward with rest you who are afflicted, along with us. This will take place at the revelation of the Lord Jesus from heaven with His powerful angels, taking vengeance with flaming fire on those who don't know God and on those who don't obey the gospel of our Lord Jesus" (2 Thess. 1:6-8).

Warning Jewish unbelievers, who only partially embrace the gospel, the writer of Hebrews declares, "For if we deliberately sin after receiving the knowledge of the truth, there no longer remains a sacrifice for sins, but a terrifying expectation of judgment, and the fury of a fire about to consume the adversaries" (Heb. 10:26-27).

Perhaps the most graphic, and terrifying, picture of hell fire comes in John's vision of the great white throne judgment, where all unbelievers have their day in court. The Lord Jesus, who sits in judgment upon the throne, opens various books, most significantly the book of life. John solemnly records, "And anyone not found written in the book of life was thrown into the lake of fire" (Rev. 20:15).

So, if Jude implores us to snatch the deceived from the fires of hell, what does that mean about our role in the salvation of others? Scripture is clear that God is the Author of salvation, the only One who grants forgiveness of sins and restores those who once were enemies of God to a right relationship with Him. Jesus is the only way of salvation (John 14:6). There is no other name under heaven given to people by which we must be saved (Acts 4:12).

At the same time, God has entrusted the gospel to us - an awesome privilege, and a weighty responsibility that not even holy angels possess. Christians are the secondary means by which people are reconciled to our offended Creator. On the Day of Pentecost, after Peter preaches an inspired message of Christ crucified to his Jewish brothers, they are pierced to the heart and ask the apostles, "Brothers, what must we do?" Peter replies, "Repent, and be baptized, each of you, in the name of Jesus the Messiah for the forgiveness of your sins, and you will receive the gift of the Holy Spirit" (Acts 2:37b-38). About 3,000 surrender their lives to Christ, are baptized, and added to the church (v. 41). It is a message repeated throughout the Book of Acts, resulting in salvation (see Acts 4:1-4; 8:26-38; 13:46-48; 16:13-15).

Our role, then, as Paul later writes, is simply to preach Christ crucified (1 Cor. 1:23). As for those who profess Jesus, and then find themselves drifting into the vortex of false doctrine, we must humbly and firmly seek to bring them back to the solid ground of biblical truth, careful not to be swept away with them.

Thomas Schreiner writes, "Probably Jude spoke of those who had fallen into the libertinism of the false teachers. Even in this case mercy should still be extended. But the readers should be extremely careful, avoiding the danger of being stained by the sin of these opponents."[14]

The departed

The third group under the influence of false teachers consists of those we may call the departed. They are fully under the power of apostates who have infiltrated the church. Even so, we are to regard them with "mercy in fear, hating even the garment defiled by the flesh" (v. 23). They are objects of mercy because the riptides of false doctrine have swept them into the miry deep, and they are beyond the view of any landmark that would bring them safely to shore. They are so convinced of their newfound beliefs that they cannot be swayed by Scripture, reason, or passionate persuasion.

But we are not to give up on the departed. We are to have mercy on them - in fear. This means being gracious to them, taking every opportunity to share a word of biblical truth, but not allowing our compassion to morph into complacency about the truth, lest we find ourselves embracing the same false teachings we warn against.

So, how should we approach, warily, those who once professed faith in Jesus (and still might), but now have departed the core doctrines of Christianity? To begin, we should acknowledge the dangers that come with engaging in spiritual warfare. Here are a few:

1.   The danger of doing nothing. This may be rooted in an overestimation of Satan's power to deceive. No doubt, the evil one prowls the earth like a lion, seeking whom he may devour (1 Peter 5:8). And he masquerades as an angel of light, as do his false apostles (2 Cor. 11:14-15). He is, without question, a formidable foe. But he also is a defeated foe, whom Christ conquered in His finished work on the cross. As the apostle

John writes, "The Son of God was revealed for this purpose: to destroy the Devil's works" (1 John 3:8b).

Even so, we may fear an encounter with deceived persons. We tell ourselves that it's too late. Or we know too little about the organization to which they belong. Or we claim 2 John 10-11 to rebuff conversations with deceived persons, failing to understand the proper context of John's warning not to feed and house itinerant false teachers. None of this does the objects of our mercy - the departed - any good. In fact, it may embolden them to think their newfound faith is indisputably true.

2. The danger of doing too much. While it's important to invest time and attention in those we are trying to bring back to sound teaching, we must not allow our departed friends to write an open-ended ticket against our own spiritual health. Allowing them to argue their points *ad nauseam*, place more and more of their organization's literature into our hands, or start a "Bible study" in our home goes beyond the bounds of earnestly contending for the faith.

When there is no give-and-take discussion, no willingness on the part of the departed to consider other points of view, no acknowledgement that their newfound views could be wrong, it's probably time to put an end to engagement - for now. Our own spiritual lives need daily care and feeding. Others who doubt, or are deceived, may be much more open to our attention.

It's difficult to know when enough is enough. But keep in mind that even Jesus sets limits for Himself and His followers. He doesn't endlessly engage the religious leaders of His day; in fact, He ultimately declares their damnation and leaves them to their own devices (Matthew 23, particularly vv. 37-39). In the Sermon on the Mount, He cautions His listeners against hypocritical judgment (Matt. 7:1-5). Immediately thereafter, however, He says, "Don't give what is holy to dogs or toss your pearls before pigs, or they will trample them with their feet, turn, and tear you to pieces" (v. 6). Jesus uses dogs and pigs as symbols of those who ridicule, reject, and blaspheme the gospel presented to them.

As a writer for the Christian website gotquestions.org makes clear, "We are not to expose the gospel of Jesus Christ to those who have no other purpose than to trample on it and return to their own evil ways. Repeatedly sharing the gospel with someone who continually scoffs and ridicules Christ is like casting pearls before swine. We can identify such people through discernment, which is given in some measure to all Christians (1 Corinthians 2:15-16)."[15]

3. Finally, the danger of going along to get along. This means compromising on the non-negotiables of the Christian faith - the very doctrines that define biblical Christianity. As we noted earlier in this study, these doctrines include, but are not limited to, the Trinity; the deity of Christ; the sacrificial and substitutionary death of Jesus on the cross; His physical resurrection from the dead; salvation by grace alone, through faith alone, in Christ alone; and the imminent personal, bodily, glorious return of Jesus to earth to set things right.

    Evangelical Christians may respectfully disagree on secondary and tertiary doctrinal issues such church polity, the doctrine of election, and eschatology. But we vigorously embrace the primary doctrines for which the apostles died, when compromising may well have saved their skins.

    For example, a Christian denomination that requires speaking in tongues as proof of baptism in the Holy Spirit may be out of the mainstream of evangelical Christianity, but it does not embrace heresy. However, a self-proclaimed Christian organization that denies the deity and personhood of the Holy Spirit has advanced a dangerous false teaching to the front lines of the doctrinal debate. One group may be playing with fire; the other is consumed by it.

Defiled garments

Before closing this section, we should consider Jude's admonition to have mercy in fear, "hating even the garment defiled by the flesh." It is a sobering task to reach out to people being drawn to the warm glow of false doctrine. While the rewards of "snatching them from the fire" are deeply satisfying, the risk of being scorched ourselves is great. Moving too close to the fire, for too long, has the potential to melt away our confidence in the fidelity of Scripture.

Jesus warns His followers to beware of the "yeast" of the Pharisees and Sadducees - that is, their teaching (Matt. 16:6). Paul quotes the poet Menander to urge the Corinthians to be right-minded: "Do not be deceived: 'Bad company corrupts good morals'" (1 Cor. 15:33). Paul further challenges the Galatians: "You were running well. Who prevented you from obeying the truth? This persuasion did not come from Him who called you. A little yeast leavens the whole lump of dough" (Gal. 5:7-9).

And a few verses later, the apostle reminds his readers of the spirit with which they should seek to restore a sinning brother or sister: "Brothers, if someone is caught in any wrongdoing, you who are spiritual should restore such a person with a gentle spirit, watching out for yourselves so you won't be tempted also" (Gal. 6:1).

It's clear that Christians are to engage others in defense of the gospel, and to urge those who profess faith in Christ to remain true to His Word. At the same time, we should be mindful of our own fleshly desires, which alluring false doctrines may ignite. In fact, the danger of close association with those who have departed the faith is so severe, Jude uses graphic imagery to warn us. The English word "garment" translates the Greek word *chiton* and refers to the clothing that people of Jude's day wear under their outer tunics. Simply put, it is their underwear. Jude depicts these garments as "defiled," which means stained or spotted, most likely by bodily functions.

Jude may be drawing from Zech. 3:3-4, where the high priest Joshua stands in "filthy clothes" before the Angel of the Lord. The Hebrew word for "filthy" is the word for excrement (see, for example, Deut. 23:14; 2 Kings 18:27; Ezek. 4:12), and in the case of Joshua signifies sin. In a similar manner, the sin of those engaged in libertarian practices in Jude's day are so vile that they threaten to pollute anyone who comes near. "Such a picture shocks the readers with how polluting and corrupting sin is. Believers are to beware lest their mercy is transposed into acceptance, and they themselves become defiled by the sin of those they are trying to help."[16]

Jesus commends a few people in the dead church at Sardis "who have not defiled their clothes, and they will walk with Me in white, because they are worthy" (Rev. 3:4). The rest have embraced apostasy and effectively killed the church. They, like other dead churches, have rejected the warning of the apostle Paul, "Now I implore you, brothers, watch out for those who cause dissensions and pitfalls contrary to the doctrine you have learned. Avoid them; for such people do not serve our Lord Christ but their own appetites, and by smooth talk and flattering words they deceive the hearts of the unsuspecting" (Rom. 16:17-18).

Key words

In this chapter, we learned several key terms. Fill in the blanks to test your knowledge.

Propitiation. This word is *hilasmos* in the Greek and conveys the idea of _____. That is, while God's _____ demands satisfaction for our sins, His _____ provided that satisfaction in the sacrificial and substitutionary death of His Son on the cross, thus restoring a peaceful _____ between holy God and sinful humans.

Comparing English translations of *hilasmos* (from 1 John 4:10):

HCSB	KJV	NIV	NASB	ESV
propitiation	propitiation	atoning sacrifice	propitiation	propitiation

Judaizers. Paul battled these false teachers in _____. They promoted a mixture of _____, through Christ, and _____, through the keeping of the law.

Snatching. The Greek verb *harpazo* means to _____, carry off, or take something or someone by force. It's the same Greek word Paul uses to describe what happens to Christians on earth on the day of _____. These living believers are "_____ _____" with the resurrected saints to meet the Lord in the air (1 Thess. 4:17).

Comparing English translations of *harpazo* (a reference in Jude 23 to "snatching" people from the fire of false doctrine):

HCSB	KJV	NIV	NASB	ESV
snatching	pulling	snatching	snatching	snatching

Garment. When Jude writes, "hating even the garment defiled by the flesh," he uses the Greek word *chiton*, which refers to the _____ that people of Jude's day wear under their outer _____. Simply put, it's their _____, which Jude depicts as "defiled," or stained.

Application
Questions for personal or group study

1. Jude urges us to construct a defensive perimeter around our spiritual lives, using Scripture, prayer, discipline, and an eternal perspective. What do the following verses say about the day when our construction efforts come under divine inspection?
   - Rom. 14:10-12
   - 1 Cor. 3:10 - 4:5
   - 2 Cor. 5:1-10

2. Jude instructs us to pray in the Holy Spirit (Jude 20). Consider Rom. 8:26-27; Gal. 4:6-7; and Eph. 2:18-22, 6:18. What role does the Spirit play in our prayers?

3. As Christians, we are to "keep [ourselves] in the love of God" (Jude 21). If God always loves us, unconditionally, what can Jude possibly mean by this exhortation?

4. How do the following passages address the issue of divine discipline?
   - Acts 5:1-11
   - 1 Cor. 5:1-5
   - 1 Cor. 11:27-32
   - Gal. 2:11-14
   - Heb. 12:3-12

5. Jude tells his readers to "have mercy on some who doubt" (v. 22). Consider the following:

    • Is it possible for a true follower of Jesus to have doubts about the Christian faith? Why or why not?

    • In what ways can doubts be healthy - either in terms of strengthening a Christian's faith, or in cementing an unbeliever's realization that he or she needs Christ?

    • How might you distinguish between sincere doubts and defiant expressions of unbelief?

    • If some doubts prove healthy to our faith, when do they cross the line and become spiritually dangerous?

    • What are some common doubts you hear today about Christianity? How might you respond?

6. Jude further urges Christians to "save others by snatching them from the fire" (v. 23). Think through these questions:

    • What evidence in this verse, and in other New Testament texts, supports the notion that Jude is describing people who have become disciples of false teachers and thus are in danger of hell fire?

    • What do the following passages say about hell?
      » Matt. 3:7-12
      » Matt. 13:49-50
      » Mark 9:47-48
      » Rev. 20:15

    • What does it mean to "snatch" those who are deceived from the fire? And what are some ways to accomplish this?

    • How might we reconcile our "saving" actions with the sovereign work of God in the salvation of sinners?

7. Jude concludes verse 23 with these words: "on others have mercy in fear, hating even the garment defiled by the flesh." Consider:

    • What should Christians fear when dealing with people who have embraced false teachings?

- What does Jude mean by "hating the garment defiled by the flesh?"

- What are the subtle dangers in the following statements:

  » "There is one God who reveals Himself either as Father, Son, or Holy Spirit."

  » "The Holy Spirit is a powerful force God uses to accomplish His will."

  » "Salvation is by grace, but not by grace alone."

  » "A loving God would never send anyone to hell for all eternity."

  » "Jesus is the Son of God, the first being created by Jehovah."

  » "As recipients of God's grace, we are free to live as we please. If we go too far, we just claim 1 John 1:9."

  » "For the sake of unity in the Body of Christ, we should stop arguing over the doctrines that divide us into denominations."

  » "The Bible is inspired in the way that all religious works are inspired."

  » "The alleged virgin birth of Jesus has no bearing on who He really is and what He accomplished during His time on earth. Likely, it's a myth added later to His biography."

  » "At the end of the day, we all worship the same God."

8. Jude warns Christians to be careful when seeking to bring back those who have departed from the faith. How do you know when to stop pursuing someone trapped in a false belief system?

16

Doxology:
To the Only God Our Savior

*Now to Him who is able to protect you from stumbling
and to make you stand in the presence of His glory,
blameless and with great joy, to the only God our Savior,
through Jesus Christ our Lord, be glory, majesty, power,
and authority before all time, now, and forever. Amen.*

(Jude 24-25 HCSB)

The epistle of Jude is rich with graphic imagery and stark warnings. It is an urgent message, a wake-up call to the saints, imploring them to wrestle vigorously in defense of the core doctrines that define the Christian faith.

False teachers have crept into the church. They are ungodly, promiscuous, arrogant, immoral, disrespectful, blasphemous, beastly, selfish, fearless, grumbling, flattering, scoffing, and devoid of the Spirit. Their judgment has been marked out long ago. They have passed the point of no return. Their goal is to take as many people as possible to hell with them in a stretch limousine.

Israel's history shows that their ilk goes down for the count beneath the judgment of God, yet they persist in their wickedness. They are dangerous reefs, waterless clouds, fruitless trees, wild waves of the sea, and wandering stars.

It seems overwhelming to contend with such foes. Equally frightening is the nagging fear that no doubt runs through the minds of Jude's readers, including us: If the apostates were immersed in Christianity and still walked away, could the same thing happen to us? And then, the unthinkable: Did they lose their salvation - and could we?

But Jude's warning comes with an ironclad guarantee. Yes, God judges the wicked, but He also remains faithful to His own. And, in the end, He keeps them secure. No one is able to pry them from His loving arms.

If true followers of Jesus are elect, they are eternally secure. These are inseparable guarantees - forming an unbroken chain from eternity past to eternity future. Everything in between - regeneration, justification, sanctification, adoption, glorification, and much more - is anchored in the bedrock of election and perseverance of the saints. This is not due to any intrinsic goodness in the redeemed; rather, it rests totally in the sovereign hands of the triune God.

The closing verses of Jude, then, offer up a marvelous doxology to the glory of God, who does all the work:

- He is able to protect you (v. 24).

- He is able to keep you from stumbling (v. 24).

- He is able to make you stand in the presence of His glory, blameless and with great joy (v. 24).

- He is the only God our Savior, and Jesus Christ is our Lord (v. 25).

- To Him belongs glory, majesty, power, and authority before all time, now, and forever (v. 25).

Though the days grow dark in the long shadows of deception, we may rest assured that the Bright Morning Star shines with eternal light (Rev. 22:16). In the end, we are simply ... safe.

How does God protect us from stumbling?

A question arises, unexpressed, in the minds of Jude's readers as they near the end of this short epistle. The author anticipates it -

and answers it. The question is: Who will deliver us from these false teachers and protect us from the apostasy that has swept them away? Jude's response assures them that God is able to preserve His people, and to present them in good standing before the Father.

Specifically, Jude writes, "Now to Him who is able to protect you from stumbling and to make you stand in the presence of His glory, blameless and with great joy, to the only God our Savior, through Jesus Christ our Lord, be glory, majesty, power, and authority before all time, now, and forever" (24-25).

We know that God is *willing* to save. The Hebrew Scriptures reveal God's desire for people everywhere to repent and receive Him. "Turn to Me and be saved, all the ends of the earth," He declares. "For I am God, and there is no other" (Isa. 45:22). The Lord's invitation to enjoy fellowship with Him is extended again a few chapters later: "Come, everyone who is thirsty, come to the waters; and you without money, come, buy, and eat! Come, buy wine and milk without money and without cost!" (Isa. 55:1).

Further, God's reluctance to punish the wicked is made clear through the prophet Ezekiel: "'Do I take pleasure in the death of the wicked?' This is the declaration of the Lord God. 'Instead, don't I take pleasure when he turns from his ways and lives?'" (Ezek. 18:23). He continues, "For I take no pleasure in anyone's death.... So repent and live!" (Ezek. 18:32). Later, He says again, "'Tell them: As I live' - the declaration of the Lord God - 'I take no pleasure in the death of the wicked, but rather that the wicked person should turn from his way and live. Repent, repent of your evil ways! Why will you die, house of Israel?'" (Ezek. 33:11).

New Testament passages repeat the willingness of God to save. Jesus concludes the parable of the wedding banquet for the king's son with these words, "For many are invited, but few are chosen" (Matt. 22:14). The invited guest who appears without proper attire - a simple linen robe offered to and required of all attendees - has just been bound hand and foot, and thrown into outer darkness. Jesus' summarizing statement maintains a tension, seen elsewhere in Scripture, between the sovereignty of God and the ability of people to make choices for which they are held accountable. Every person is invited, and the King has ample white linens in which to clothe them (the righteousness of

Christ). But their refusal to honor the King, and to accept the garment of righteousness freely offered them, exposes their self-righteousness, as well as their rejection of the Son.

The apostle Paul echoes God's willingness to save. In 1 Tim. 2:1-4, he encourages believers to offer "petitions, prayers, intercessions, and thanksgivings" for everyone, "for kings and all those who are in authority, so that we may lead a tranquil and quiet life in all godliness and dignity. This is good, and it pleases God our Savior, who wants everyone to be saved and to come to the knowledge of the truth."

Peter offers a similar message, although this one is in the context of judgment and is meant to assure Christians that God's delay in coming is to make sure that all the elect are brought in: "The Lord does not delay His promise, as some understand delay, but is patient with you, not wanting any to perish, but all to come to repentance" (2 Peter 3:9).

Regardless of your view on the doctrine of election, it is biblically faithful to say that only God knows the full list of names on the kingdom's registry. He commands His followers to cast the net of evangelism broadly, until all of the elect are gathered safely to shore. Truly, "The Lord knows those who are His" (2 Tim. 2:19a; cf. Num. 16:5).

No doubt, Jude's readers know that God is *willing* to save. But, is He *able*? Can He truly prevent His fragile people from falling away from the faith, especially in light of the onslaught of demonic doctrines permeating the church? Jude offers gentle, and confident, assurance that the Lord indeed is "able to protect you from stumbling ..."

Consider just a few places in Scripture where the Holy Spirit, speaking through divinely selected writers, establishes God's sovereign ability. God is able to:

- Deliver three Hebrew men from Nebuchadnezzar's furnace of blazing fire, and from the king's power (Dan. 3:17)

- Raise up children for Abraham from mere stones (Matt. 3:9)

- Build us up in grace and give us an inheritance (Acts 20:32)

250

- Fulfill His promises (Rom. 4:21)

- Provide us with an avenue of escape from temptation (1 Cor. 10:13)

- Comfort the afflicted (2 Cor. 1:4)

- Supply all our needs (Phil. 4:19)

- Guard the gospel entrusted to us (2 Tim. 1:12-14)

- Help us when we are tested (Heb. 2:18)

- Save to the uttermost those who come to Him through Christ (Heb. 7:25)

There is nothing too difficult for God (Jer. 32:17b). There is nothing impossible for Him (Gen. 18:14; Mark 10:27; Luke 1:37). He sustains all things by His powerful word (Heb. 1:3). And He keeps our inheritance secure by His power (1 Peter 1:5).

Each of these assurances about God's sovereign power is another brick in the protective wall God places around His own. If He is able to do all these marvelous deeds, surely He is able to protect us from stumbling. Jude uses the Greek word *aptaistos*, translated "from stumbling" in the HCSB. It is the only time this Greek word appears in the New Testament, and Jude means for it to make a lasting impression.[1] God is both willing and able to keep His own from falling into apostasy, where the false teachers have landed.

While Jude's false teachers approach the threshold of God's kingdom, they never enter, and they never will. John captures the essence of the apostate's heart in his first epistle, referring to them as "antichrists." The Amplified Bible renders John's description this way: "They went out from us [seeming at first to be Christians], but they were not *really* of us [because they were not truly born again and spiritually transformed]; for if they had been of us, they would have remained with us; but *they went out* [teaching false doctrine], so that it would be clearly shown that none of them were of us" (1 John 2:19 - emphasis in translation).

In contrast, the elect, who are in the kingdom, are kept there securely. They may be enticed to venture toward the kingdom's gates by those who beckon from without, but our Savior ensures that they remain safely in the fold. He employs all of His resources to ensure the perseverance of the saints, including: the sealing of the Holy Spirit; the promises of Scripture; the entry of our names into the Lamb's book of life; the bridal chamber Christ prepares for us in heaven; the encouragement of fellow believers; even divine discipline that may include physical (but not spiritual) death. All of this, and more, serves as a guarantee that "He who started a good work in you will carry it on to completion until the day of Christ Jesus" (Phil. 1:6).

Edward Pentecost writes, "Victory over apostasy is found in Jesus Christ! He is the One who will 'keep' believers. Christ will present believers to His Father without fault and with great joy - joy both for Himself and for them (Heb. 12:2; 1 Peter 1:8). Here is the greatest theme of victory to be sounded, the highest note of praise and adoration possible, and the greatest assurance for the redeemed."[2]

Jude never entertains the thought that genuine believers may lose their salvation. The opening words of his epistle make this clear as he refers to Christians as "called [elect, chosen], loved by God the Father, and kept by Jesus Christ" (v. 1). At the same time, Jude exhorts followers of Jesus to faithfully walk the path of good works God prepared for them in eternity past (Eph. 2:10). He is able to ensure that our daily walk is one in which we do not stumble or fall. "God does not promise that true believers will never sin," writes Thomas Schreiner. "He promises that he will preserve us from committing apostasy, from abandoning the faith once and for all."[3]

Think about this sobering reality: If it's possible to lose our salvation, we all would. Adam is created innocent and lives in a perfect environment, yet he falls, plunging himself and the human race into sin, and bringing a curse upon the cosmos. Moses talks face-to-face with God (Ex. 33:11) and must veil himself so as to keep from frightening the Israelites with the radiance of his countenance (Ex. 34:29-35). Then, in a rebellious outburst, he disqualifies himself from entering the Promised Land (Num. 20:10-12). David is a man after God's own heart (Acts 13:22 KJV), but he commits adultery and murder. Peter is one of the Twelve, walking with Jesus every day for three years, but he promptly denies his Lord on the night of His betrayal. Even Paul laments over his "body of death," in which the "law of God" wages war with the "law of sin" (see Rom. 7:13-25). Only God keeps him from falling.

Redemption is a completed act in the eternal mind of God, and it plays out over time in our lives. While we may, at times, wander far from the warm glow of the Father's hearth, He remains faithful to finish the good work He began in us (Phil. 1:6). It may help us to think of salvation as a golden strand, stretching unbroken from eternity past into eternity future, tying together the great elements of God's redemptive work. This golden strand includes, but is not limited to:

- Election - God's gracious choosing of the redeemed, which ensures our everlasting life (John 10:27-29; 1 Cor. 1:8-9; Eph. 1:4-6; Phil. 1:6; 1 Thess. 5:23-24; 1 Peter 1:4-5; Jude 1)

- Regeneration - the work of the Holy Spirit making us spiritually alive and bringing us into an unbreakable relationship with God (John 1:12-13; 3:3-8; Titus 3:5; 1 Peter 1:3)

- Justification - God's declaration that we are in right standing before Him based on the finished work of Christ (Rom. 5:1, 9; 8:30)

- Sanctification - God's work of setting us apart (positionally) and conforming us to His image (practically) (Rom. 6:22; 2 Cor. 1:21-22; Eph. 1:13-14; 1 Thess. 4:3-8; 2 Thess. 2:13; 1 Peter 1:2)

- Glorification - God's future call to us from our graves, completing the work of redemption by giving us incorruptible bodies that are like His resurrected body (John 5:28-29; 11:24-25; Acts 24:14-15; 1 Cor. 15:12-58; Heb. 11:35; Rev. 20:6)

If it's possible to lose our salvation, which of these divine knots in the golden strand comes unraveled? Can genuine believers become unelected, with the Father changing His mind about us if we cross some invisible line? Can we become unregenerate, passing into spiritual death for a second, or third, time? Is it conceivable that we could become unjustified, and thus subject to double jeopardy, having at one time been acquitted of all sins before God's throne in heaven? Can we become unsanctified, with the Spirit unsealing us, departing His dwelling place in our hearts, and rescinding the down payment on our home in heaven? Finally, could we become unglorified, with God revoking His promise to redeem our mortal bodies? The very thought of such possibilities shakes our assurance to its core and calls into question the ability of the Righteous One to save us forever (Heb. 7:25).

Thankfully, salvation is the gift of God, which Christ paid in full through His work on the cross. As Peter writes, God has given us "a new birth into a living hope through the resurrection of Jesus Christ from the dead, and into an inheritance that is imperishable, uncorrupted, and unfading, kept in heaven for you, who are being protected by God's power through faith for a salvation that is ready to be revealed in the last time" (1 Peter 1:3b-5). John MacArthur writes, "Because God is perfectly faithful, supremely powerful, and infinitely loving, He will not allow His children to fall away from saving faith or defect from the gospel so as to be lost again in their sins."[4]

And there's more. Not only is God able to protect us from stumbling; He is able to make us stand in the presence of His glory, blameless and with great joy. Today, we stand in the grace of God (Rom. 5:1-5), and one day we will stand in His glorious presence (Col. 3:4; 1 Peter 5:10). The very thought of being in that glory should inspire fear and trembling while we are in our mortal state. It certainly did for Isaiah (Isa. 6:5); Ezekiel (Ezek. 1:28); Peter, James, and John (Matt. 17:5-7); and again the apostle John, who falls as a dead man when coming face-to-face with Jesus in a vision (Rev. 1:17). Elsewhere in the New Testament, the term "stand" refers to eschatological vindication at God's throne on the last day (Rom. 14:4; 1 Cor. 10:12).

To stand in the presence of God's glory requires blamelessness, provided only when the righteousness of Christ is imputed to us. The Greek word *amomos* (rendered "blameless" in Jude 24 HCSB) means "faultless" and describes the sinless state in which one day we will stand. Followers of Jesus today are justified, or declared in right standing with God. The Holy Spirit is sanctifying us, or making us more like Christ. But the ultimate act of divine redemption comes on a future, unknown day when we are glorified, or bodily resurrected and fully conformed to the image of Christ. Put another way, we stand *declared* righteous today; one day, we actually *become* righteous, seeing Jesus as He is and being made like Him.

254

This future reality should erupt within us, producing great joy that overflows in our words and deeds - even when our circumstances invite us into the abyss of despair. James encourages us to "consider it a great joy" when we experience various trials, knowing that the testing of our faith produces endurance, which results in spiritual maturity (James 1:2-4). Paul writes a message of encouragement to Philippian believers from his prison cell, exhorting them to "Rejoice in the Lord always. I will say it again: Rejoice!" (Phil. 4:4). And Jesus, who comes into this world to die, endures the cross and despises the shame "for the joy that lay before Him" (Heb. 12:2).

Ultimately for the Christian, joy comes, not just in moments or in seasons, but in unbroken streams throughout eternity. We watch with great anticipation for that midnight when the Bright Morning Star splits the skies, calls us to Himself, and fulfills His promise to make us just like Him. On that glorious day, God dwells with us, wipes the tears from our eyes, and abolishes the former things that have characterized the sinful and fallen world He died to redeem (Rev. 21:4).

Jude's doxology

Jude ends his epistle with a wonderful four-part doxology, or word of praise. To "the only God our Savior, through Jesus Christ our Lord," Jude offers:

Glory – the sum total of all that God is and does. The word "glory" captures all the divine attributes in their radiance. The Greek word *doxa*, from which we get "glory," means honor; renown; an especially divine quality; the unspoken manifestation of God; splendor. We see this in Yahweh in the Old Testament. In the desert, the Lord provides a place in the crevice of a rock for Moses, and covers His servant with His hand to protect him from the certain death that results when sinful humans see God's glorious face (Ex. 33:20-23).

Such glory belongs only to God (Isa. 42:8; 48:11). However, in the New Testament, we see divine glory as an attribute of Jesus - an attribute He shared with the Father before the creation of the world (John 17:5). On the Mount of Transfiguration, Jesus shows Peter, James, and John his glory. His face shines like the sun, and even His clothes become as white as light (Matt. 17:1-8). The writer of

Hebrews notes this about Jesus, "He is the radiance of His [God's] glory, the exact expression of His nature ..." (Heb. 1:3a).

Majesty – God's greatness or magnificence. He is not simply King; He is King of kings. He is not merely Lord; He is Lord of lords. "Majesty" is *megalosune* in the Greek, and it appears three other times in the New Testament (HCSB). In Heb. 1:3, after Jesus makes purification for sins, He sits down at "the right hand of the Majesty on high." The writer of Hebrews goes on to emphasize, "[W]e have this kind of high priest [Jesus], who sat down at the right hand of the throne of the Majesty in the heavens" (Heb. 8:1). Peter writes, "For we did not follow cleverly contrived myths when we made known to you the power and coming of our Lord Jesus Christ; instead, we were eyewitnesses of His majesty" - a reference to the Transfiguration (2 Peter 1:16).

Jesus, who possessed this divine magnificence in eternity past as a member of the Godhead, temporarily set aside His majesty - but not His deity - to become a man and offer Himself in our place on the cross. For this reason, God highly exalts Him, bestowing on Him the name above every name, so that at the name of Jesus every knee will bow, and every tongue will confess that Jesus Christ is Lord (Phil. 2:6-10).

Power – dominion, might, strength. The Greek word *kratos* carries the idea of complete control. God is sovereign over all He has made and over all that plays out in the universe: the course of the stars, human history, angelic destiny, and the ultimate regeneration of a fallen creation that groans beneath the weight of sin (see Rom. 8:18-23). *Kratos* appears in a number of New Testament doxologies, including:

- 1 Tim. 6:16 - God is "the only One who has immortality, dwelling in unapproachable light, whom none of mankind has seen or can see, to whom be honor and eternal *might*."

- Heb. 2:14 - "Now since the children have flesh and blood in common, He [Jesus] also shared in these, so that through His death He might destroy the one holding the *power* of death - that is, the Devil ..."

- 1 Peter 4:11 - "If anyone speaks, his speech should be like the oracles of God; if anyone serves, his service should be from the strength God provides, so that in everything God may be glorified through Jesus Christ. To Him belong the glory and the *power* forever and ever. Amen."

- 1 Peter 5:11 - "To Him be the *dominion* forever. Amen."

- Rev. 1:6 - To Him who "made us a kingdom, priests to His God and Father - to Him be the glory and *dominion* forever. Amen." (emphasis added in all quotations)

Authority – the right to exercise power. The Greek word used here is *exousia*. While the word *dunamis* means physical power - which the New Testament depicts God, angels, persons, and even things manifesting - *exousia*, when used of God, denotes absolute and unrestricted authority. All authority is properly God's, who may delegate it to others (see, for example, John 19:11; Rom. 13:1-7).

Jesus possesses the same intrinsic authority as God the Father because He is co-equal with the Father (John 1:1; 10:30; Phil. 2:6; Col. 1:16; 2:9-10). At the same time, because of the unique pattern of relationships within the Trinity, especially during Jesus' incarnation, there is a sense in which the Father gives Jesus His authority (Matt. 9:8; 28:18; John 5:22; Eph. 1:20-23; Phil. 2:9-11; Rev. 2:27).

As Steve Lemke points out, "Jesus' authority was manifested in His incarnation by His authority to forgive sin, provide salvation, heal sickness, cast out demons, and judge humanity.... As Jesus carried out His teaching ministry, He spoke with authority which was immediately recognized by His hearers as being absent in the teachings of the scribes and Pharisees."[5] This authority, as Jude makes clear, is God's "before all time, now, and forever" (v. 25).

Last word

Jude concludes this short epistle with a powerful reminder that God is in control. We are slaves of Christ. But more than that, we are precious friends sovereignly called, graciously loved, and securely kept. We are the recipients of His mercy, peace, and love. He has granted us a "common salvation" that is detailed in a body of doctrinal truths known simply as "the faith," which we are to vigorously defend against false teachers who have infiltrated the church.

God has equipped us to build a defensive perimeter around our spiritual lives, by which we keep ourselves in the love of God, and from which we launch rescue missions to buoy the doubters, wake up the deceived, and grieve over the departed.

Defending the Christian faith is not a spiritual gift, nor is it an office of the church. It is the command of God to everyone who claims Jesus as Lord. As all followers of Jesus enjoy a "common salvation," we also share a common call to contend for the faith that defines our standing in Christ.

The apostle Peter implores every Christian to "set apart the Messiah as Lord in your hearts, and always be ready to give a defense to anyone who asks you for a reason for the hope that is in you." Equally important, we must do this "with gentleness and respect" (1 Peter 3:15-16).

Our fundamental goal in defending the Christian faith should never be to win an argument, stalk a debate, or own the last word. Rather, it should be to share biblical truth gently with our drifting friends as we acknowledge the sovereign roles of the Triune God: The Father, who draws (John 6:44); the Spirit, who convicts (John 14:7-11); and the Son, who alone can save (Acts 4:11-12).

The closing verses of a Puritan prayer express the vanity of life apart from God, and the end for which He created us:

O may I never fall into the tempers and vanities,
the sensuality and folly of the present world!
It is a place of inexpressible sorrow,
a vast empty nothingness;
Time is a moment, a vapour, and all its enjoyments are
empty bubbles, fleeting blasts of wind,
from which nothing satisfactory can be derived;
Give me grace always to keep in covenant with thee,
and to reject as delusion a great name here or hereafter,
together with all sinful pleasures or profits.
Help me to know continually that there can be no true
happiness, no fulfilling of thy purpose for me, apart from
a life lived in and for the Son of thy love.[6]

Key words

In this chapter, we learned several key terms. Fill in the blanks to test your knowledge.

Blameless. This word is *amomos* in the Greek and describes the _____ state in which one day we stand. Today, as believers whom God has justified, we are declared righteous; one day, we actually _____ righteous.

Comparing English translations of *amomos*:

HCSB	KJV	NIV	NASB	ESV
blameless	faultless	without fault	blameless	blameless

Glory. The Greek *doxa* means honor; renown; an especially divine quality; the unspoken _____ of God. Glory is the sum total of all that _____ is and does.

Majesty. This is God's _____ or magnificence. "Majesty" is *megalosune* in the Greek. Jesus, who possessed this divine magnificence in eternity past as a member of the _____, temporarily set aside His majesty - but not His deity - to become a _____ and offer Himself in our place on the cross.

Power. The Greek word *kratos* carries the idea of complete _____. God is _____ over all He has made and over all that plays out in the universe, including the course of the _____, human history, angelic destiny, and the ultimate _____ of our fallen creation.

Comparing English translations of *kratos*:

HCSB	KJV	NIV	NASB	ESV
power	dominion	power	dominion	dominion

Authority. This is the right to exercise power. The Greek word used here is *exousia*, which denotes God's _____ and unrestricted authority. All authority is properly God's, who may _____ it to others.

Application

Questions for personal or group study

1. In Jude 24, why do you think Jude emphasizes God's *ability* to protect us from stumbling rather than His *willingness* to do so? ("Now to Him who is *able* to protect you ...")

2. Jude uses *aptaistos*, translated "from stumbling," in verse 24. It is the only time this Greek word appears in the New Testament. Jude means to make it clear that God is able to keep His own from falling into apostasy, where false teachers have landed. Consider:

   • How do we know that apostates are not Christians, according to Jude?

   • What does God do to ensure that genuine believers do not become apostates?

   • How does knowing we are secure in Christ impact our engagement with false teachers?

3. How do Phil. 1:6 and 1 John 2:19 contrast genuine believers with false teachers? What other Scriptures shed further light on this divergence?

4. Review the "golden strand" of God's redemptive work, which includes, but is not limited to, election, regeneration, justification, sanctification, and glorification. Reflect:

   • For followers of Jesus today, which of these saving works already have occurred? Which are ongoing? And which take place in the future?

- In what ways do these redemptive acts connect eternity past to eternity future?

- Why do you think the apostle Paul refers to our glorification in the past tense in Rom. 8:30?

- If it were possible for genuine believers to become apostates, which of God's redemptive works would be negated?

- In what ways does the New Testament speak about sanctification both as a completed act and an ongoing work?

- Why doesn't glorification take place at death?

- In what ways is it comforting to see salvation from God's perspective as expressed in His Word?

5. What is the difference between being "declared righteous" (justified) and "becoming righteous" (glorified)?

6. Jude offers praise to "the only God our Savior, through Jesus Christ our Lord" (v. 25). How do the Father, Son, and Holy Spirit work together to secure our salvation? What specific acts of redemption - such as election, regeneration, and justification - are most often associated with individual members of the Godhead?

7. How is Jude's closing doxology similar to words of praise expressed by other New Testament writers? Consider, for example:

- Rom. 8:38-39; 15:5-6

- Eph. 3:14-21

- 1 Thess. 5:23-24

- 1 Tim. 1:17; 6:15b-16

- Heb. 13:20-21

- Rev. 1:5b-6; 5:12-13

Notes

Introduction
1. D.J. Rowston, "The Most Neglected Book in the New Testament," *New Testament Studies 21* (1974-75), 554-563, cited in Thomas R. Schreiner, *The New American Commentary: 1, 2 Peter, Jude*, Vol. 37 (Nashville, TN: B&H Publishing Group, 2003), 403.

Chapter 1. Jude, a Slave: The Attitude of Apologetics
1. "This Chinese Millionaire Has The Most Ridiculous Business Card," found at https://www.buzzfeed.com/tanyachen/this-chinese-millionaire-has-the-most-ridiculous-business-ca?utm_term=.tymoWI3B2#.ba85IamDe, viewed May 7, 2016.

2. Gregory Koukl, *Tactics: A Game Plan for Discussing Your Christian Convictions* (Grand Rapids, MI: Zondervan, 2009), 38.

3. Dallas Willard, *The Allure of Gentleness: Defending the Faith in the Manner of Jesus* (New York: HarperCollins Publishers, 2015), 3.

4. *Ibid.*, 4-5.

Chapter 2. Jude, Slave, Brother: The Identity of Apologists
1. Found at http://www.cracked.com/article_19307_6-famous-people-whose-identities-we-still-dont-know.html, viewed May 7, 2016.

2. George E. Meisinger, "Judas," found at https://bible.org/article/judas, viewed April 6, 2016.

3. Thomas R. Schreiner, *The New American Commentary: An Exegetical and Theological Exposition of Holy Scripture, 1, 2 Peter, Jude, Vol. 37* (Nashville, TN: B&H Publishing Group, 2003), 407.

4. John MacArthur, *The MacArthur New Testament Commentary, 2 Peter & Jude* (Chicago: Moody Publishers, 2005), 142.

5. E.A. Judge, "Slavery," *New Bible Dictionary, 3rd Ed.*, (Leicestera, England; Downers Grove, IL: InterVarsity Press, 1996), 1113-1114.

6. *Ibid.*

7. James A. Brooks, "Slave, Servant," in C. Brand, C. Draper, A.England, S. Bone, E.R. Clendenen, and T.C. Butler (editors), *Holman Illustrated Bible Dictionary* (Nashville, TN: Holman Bible Publishers, 2003), 1511-1512.

8. There also is James, the father of Judas Iscariot (Luke 6:16; Acts 1:13). Nothing further is known about him, and obviously he is not the James we seek in connection with Jude.

9. MacArthur, 142.

Chapter 3. I Reckon So: The Apologist's Standing in Christ

1. An excellent resource is *Chosen But Free: A Balanced View of Divine Election* by Norman Geisler. Another is *Perspectives on Election: Five Views*, edited by Chad Owen Brand. You also may visit oncedelivered.net/election to view my feeble attempt to explore this remarkable doctrine.

2. Frederick L. Godet, *Commentary on St. Paul's Epistle to the Romans* (Grand Rapids, MI: Zondervan, n.d.), 324.

3. The ESV Study Bible (Wheaton, IL: Crossway Bibles, 2008), 2172.

4. MacArthur, 151.

5. *Expository Dictionary of Bible Words*, edited by Stephen D. Renn (Peabody, MA: Hendrickson Publishers Marketing, LLC, 2005), 547.

6. Ralph Earle, *Word Meanings in the New Testament* (Peabody, MA: Hendrickson Publishers, Inc., 2002), 183.

7. *A Critical and Exegetical Commentary on the Epistle to the Romans*, International Critical Commentary (Edinburgh: T&T Clark, 1895), 215-216.

8. It should be noted that some translations like the KJV render the word "sanctified" rather than "loved." They rely on the Majority text, but the textual tradition "overwhelmingly supports 'loved' rather than 'sanctified,'" according to Schreiner, 430.

9. ESV Study Bible, 2449.

10. Also known as Calvinism, which typically embraces five doctrines: total depravity; unconditional election; limited atonement; irresistible grace; and perseverance of the saints.

Chapter 4. Copycats? The Apologist's Challenge Concerning Jude and 2 Peter 2

1. "5 Insanely Blatant Acts of Plagiarism by Famous People," found at http://www.cracked.com/article_20889_5-insanely-blatant-acts-plagiarism-by-famous-people.html, viewed May 13, 2016.

2. Thomas R. Schreiner notes that scholars have proposed dates between A.D. 50 and 160. See Schreiner, 409, footnote 29.

3. Schreiner, 417-418.

4. D.B. Wallace, *Jude: Introduction, Argument, and Outline*, at http://www.bible.org/studies/soapbox/jude.htm, cited in Schreiner, 418.

5. Arno Gaebelein, *Commentary on Jude*, Titus Books, Kindle Edition (2013-12-02), Kindle locations 44-46.

6. Daniel B. Wallace, "The Synoptic Problem," found at http://www.bible.org/article/synoptic-problem, viewed May 13, 2016.

7. Chicago Statement on Biblical Inerrancy with Exposition, found at http://www.bible-researcher.com/chicago1.html, viewed Feb. 23, 2016.

8. Wayne Grudem, *Systematic Theology: An Introduction to Biblical Doctrine* (Leicester, England: Inter-Varsity Press, 1994), 127.

Chapter 5. I Found It Necessary: Going from Good to Better in Defense of the Faith

1. Brad King, executive director of Battleship Cove naval ship museum in Fall River, Mass., quoted in Linton Weeks, "5 Other Surprise Attacks That Changed History," Sept. 6, 2011, found at http://www.npr.org/2011/09/06/140156564/5-other-surprise-attacks-that-changed-history, viewed May 8, 2016.

2. Mary Fairchild, "Christianity Statistics," http://christianity.about.com/od/denominations/p/christiantoday.htm, viewed May 14, 2016.

3. A cult may be defined as a religious organization whose members claim to be Christians, and who use the Bible and Christian terms, yet who deny the central beliefs of historical Christianity. Simply put, a cult is counterfeit Christianity. Examples include the Jehovah's Witnesses and the Church of Jesus Christ of Latter-day Saints.

4. "A Call for Theological Triage and Christian Maturity," May 20, 2004, http://www.albertmohler.com/2004/05/20/a-call-for-theological-triage-and-christian-maturity-2/, viewed May 14, 2016.

5. *The Baptist Faith and Message*, Article I, The Scriptures (Nashville, TN: LifeWay Christian Resources, 2001), 7.

6. "The Nicene Creed, also called the Nicaeno-Constantinopolitan Creed, is a statement of the orthodox faith of the early Christian church in opposition to certain heresies, especially Arianism. These heresies, which disturbed the church during the fourth century, concerned the doctrine of the trinity and of the person of Christ." From "Nicene Creed: Background," https://www.crcna.org/welcome/beliefs/creeds/nicene-creed.

7. Nicene Creed (Grand Rapids, MI: CRC Publications: 1987), found at https://www.crcna.org/welcome/beliefs/creeds/nicene-creed.

8. Mohler.

9. *Ibid.*

10. E.C. Pentecost, "Jude," in J. F. Walvoord & R. B. Zuck (Eds.), *The Bible Knowledge Commentary: An Exposition of the Scriptures*, Vol. 2 (Wheaton, IL: Victor Books, 1985), 919.

11. W.W. Wiersbe, *The Bible Exposition Commentary*, Vol. 2 (Wheaton, IL: Victor Books, 1996), 549.

12. Ralph Earle, *Word Meanings in the New Testament* (Peabody, MA: Hendrickson Publishers, Inc., 2002), 455.

13. MacArthur, 156.

Chapter 6. Who Are Those Guys? How Apologists Identify False Teachers

1. http://www.imdb.com/character/ch0008493/quotes.

2. MacArthur, 158.

3. Bill Warner, *The Life of Muhammad: The Sira* (USA: SCPI, LLC, 2010), 58-59.

4. MacArthur, 159.

5. *Ibid.*

6. J.N.D. Kelly, *A Commentary on the Epistles of Peter and Jude*, Thornapple Commentaries (Grand Rapids, MI: Baker, 1981), 230-231.

7. "What is Christian Gnosticism?" found at http://gotquestions.org/Christian-gnosticism.html, viewed May 5, 2016.

8. Biblestudytools.com/dictionaries/bakers-evangelical-dictionary/judaizers.html.

9. Rick Renner, "Who Were the Nicolaitans, and What Was Their Doctrine and Deeds?" found at http://lightsource.com, viewed May 5, 2016.

10. *Ibid.*

11. Schreiner, 436.

12. Robert M. Bowman Jr., J. Ed Komoszewski, *Putting Jesus in His Place: The Case for the Deity of Christ* (Grand Rapids, MI: Kregel Publications, 2007), 98-99.

13. Kenneth S. Wuest, "In These Last Days: The Exegesis of Jude," *Wuest's Word Studies From the Greek New Testament*, Vol. 2 (Grand Rapids, MI: Wm. B. Eerdman's Publishing Company, 1973), 238.

14. Wuest, 236.

15. Richard C. Trench, quoted in Wuest, 237.

16. MacArthur, 161.

17. MacArthur, 162.

Chapter 7. The Lessons of History: Remembering the Past to Defend the Faith

1. Cited in "George Santayana," https://en.wikiquote.org/wiki/George_ Santayana, viewed Sept. 3, 2016.

2. "Quotes about doomed to repeat it," found at http://www.goodreads.com/ quotes/tag/doomed-to-repeat-it, viewed May 15, 2016.

3. Wuest, 239.

4. Wiersbe, 551.

5. The surrounding cities to which Jude refers are Admah, Zeboiim, and Zoar, though Zoar is spared the disaster (see Gen. 19:19-22; Deut. 29:23; Hosea 11:8).

6. MacArthur, 88-89.

7. Schreiner, 453.

8. James R. White and Jeffrey D. Niell, *The Same Sex Controversy: Defending and Clarifying the Bible's Message About Homosexuality* (Minneapolis: Bethany House, 2002), 46.

9. *Ibid.*, 51.

10. For a more thorough treatment of this issue, see *What Every Christian Should Know about Same-sex Attraction* by Rob Phillips.

11. "Why so many Christians won't back down on gay marriage," *The Week*, online edition, Sept. 3, 2014.

12. Denny Burk, *What Is the Meaning of Sex?* (Wheaton, IL: Crossway, 2013), 88-106.

13. For a fuller discussion of the scientific evidence, see Joe Dallas, "Speaking of Homosexuality," *Christian Research Journal*, Vol. 29, No. 06, 2006; and Robert A.J. Gagnon, *The Bible and Homosexual Practice: Text and Hermeneutics* (Nashville: Abington Press, 2001), 395-432.

14. Schreiner, 454.

Chapter 8. Kept, with Eternal Chains: When Angels Desert

1. Found at https://www.youtube.com/watch?v=bWGtjqv19ZA, viewed May 21, 2016.

2. The title Book of Enoch often is used interchangeably with 1 Enoch.

That's because there are two other books named Enoch: 2 Enoch, surviving only in Old Slavonic (Eng. trans. by R. H. Charles 1896), and 3 Enoch (surviving in Hebrew, c. fifth to sixth century A.D.). See "Book of Enoch," https://en.wikipedia.org/wiki/Book_of_Enoch.

3. For further details, see Schreiner, 447-450.

4. 1 Enoch 10:4-6, cited in Schreiner, 449, footnote 21.

5. Wiersbe, 551-552.

6. Satan and demons may possess human beings - and even animals - and Satan disguises himself as an angel of light, but neither the evil one nor his demonic minions has the authority to create earthly bodies for themselves. If they did have such power, imagine the field day they would have with "resurrections" and "incarnations" - counterfeit Saviors traveling the globe, displaying the marks of crucifixion, and deceiving shallow and gullible legions to embrace "another Jesus" (2 Cor. 11:4).

7. Allen P. Ross, "Genesis," in *The Bible Knowledge Commentary: An Exposition of the Scriptures*, ed. J.F. Walvoord and R.B. Zuck, Vol. 1 (Wheaton, IL: Victor Books, 1985), 36-37.

8. *Ibid.*

9. *Ibid.*

10. Wayne McDill, "7 Principles of Biblical Interpretation," found at http://www.lifeway.com/pastors/2014/03/12/7-principles-of-biblical-interpretation/, viewed Sept. 14, 2016.

11. *Ibid.*

12. *Ibid.*

13. The Apologetics Study Bible (Nashville TN: Holman Bible Publishers, 2007), 1859.

14. Wuest, 240.

Chapter 9. The Lord Rebuke You: Michael and the Devil

1. "Garter snake," found at https://en.wikipedia.org/wiki/Garter_snake, viewed June 12, 2016.

2. MacArthur, 171.

3. Schreiner, 456.

4. *Ibid.*, 457.

5. "Who Is Michael the Archangel?" jw.org/en/publications/books/bible-teach/who-is-michael-the-archangel-jesus/, viewed June 7, 2016.

6. "St. Michael the Archangel," catholic.org/saints/saint.php?saint_id=308, viewed June 7, 2016.

7. A.C. Gaebelein, *What the Bible Says about Angels* (Grand Rapids, MI: Baker Book House, 1987), 20.

8. Gary Kinnaman, *Angels Dark and Light* (Ann Arbor, MI: Servant Publications, 1994), 123.

9. John Calvin, *Calvin's Institutes* (Grand Rapids, MI: Associated Publishers, n.d.), 76.

10. Kinnaman, 123.

11. C. Fred Dickason, *Angels Elect & Evil* (Chicago: Moody Press, 1975), 68.

12. Schreiner, 460.

13. *Ibid.*, 459.

Chapter 10. Woe to Them! Cain, Balaam, and Korah

1. "15 of the Worst Role Models," http://www.therichest.com/rich-list/most-influential/15-of-the-worst-role-models/, viewed June 20, 2016.

2. *That the Worse Attacks the Better,* 32,78, cited in Schreiner, 462.

3. Or Targumim: spoken paraphrases, explanations, and expansions of the Jewish scriptures that rabbis give in the common language of the listeners, which in the first century is Aramaic.

4. *Pseudo-Jonathan and Neofiti,* cited in Schreiner, 462, specifically, "The Targumic Versions of Genesis 4:3-16" in *Post-Biblical Jewish Studies,* SJLA 8 (Leiden: Brill, 1975), 97-99, translated by G. Vermes.

5. M. G. Easton, *Easton's Bible Dictionary* (New York: Harper & Brothers, 1893), Logos Research Systems.

6. Wiersbe, 554-555.

7. MacArthur, 102.

8. *Ibid.*, 103.

9. Quoted in Wuest, 248.

10. Biblical Antiquities 18.13, *Old Testament Pseudepigrapha,* J.H. Charlesworth, ed., 2:326; referenced in Schreiner, 463.

11. Wiersbe, 554-555.

12. For more on the Word of Faith movement, see Rob Phillips, *The Apologist's Tool Kit*, 3rd Edition (Jefferson City, MO: MBC, 2016), 243-277.

13. Gordon D. Fee, *The Disease of the Health and Wealth Gospels* (Vancouver, British Columbia: Regent College Publishing, 1985, 2006), 28.

Chapter 11. Crossing the Line: Can Apostates Be Christians?

1. Eugene E. Carpenter and Philip W. Comfort, *Holman Treasury of Key Bible Words* (Nashville, TN: Broadman & Holman Publishers, 2002), 227.

2. *Ibid.*

3. John MacArthur, *The MacArthur New Testament Commentary: Hebrews* (Chicago, IL: Moody Publishers, 1983), 270-271.

4. Earle, 375.

5. Grudem, 509.

6. *Ibid.*

Chapter 12. Wild Waves and Wandering Stars: The Doom of False Teachers

1. "What is a meteorite?" http://www.meteorite.com, viewed June 28, 2016.

2. "5 Most Destructive Meteor Strikes in History," http://history-facts.top5.com/5-most-destructive-meteor-strikes-in-history/, viewed June 28, 2016.

3. "Chelyabinsk meteor," https://en.wikipedia.org/wiki/Chelyabinsk_meteor, viewed June 28, 2016.

4. Some English translations use "blemishes" or "spots" rather than "dangerous reefs." The parallel text in 2 Peter 2:13 clearly refers to the apostates as "stains" or "blemishes," but Jude uses a slightly different Greek word: *spilades* instead of *spiloi*, and this word is commonly used in Greek literature for rocks, according to Robert Jamieson, A. R. Fausset, and David Brown, *Commentary Critical and Explanatory on the Whole Bible*, Vol. 2 (Oak Harbor, WA: Logos Research Systems, Inc., 1997), 544.

5. MacArthur, *The MacArthur New Testament Commentary, 2 Peter & Jude*, 180.

6. Wuest, 249.

7. Schreiner, 466.

8. Wiersbe, 555.

9. MacArthur, 180.

10. Alfred Edersheim, *The Life & Times of Jesus the Messiah*, Vol. II (Grand Rapids, MI: Eerdmans, 1947), 374.

11. Edward C. Pentecost, "Jude," in *The Bible Knowledge Commentary: An Exposition of the Scriptures*, ed. J. F. Walvoord and R. B. Zuck, Vol. 2 (Wheaton, IL: Victor Books, 1985), 921.

12. Schreiner, 467.

13. N.T. Wright, *Evil and the Justice of God* (Downers Grove, IL: InterVarsity Press, 2006), 14-15.

14. Charles R. Swindoll, *Insights on Revelation* (Grand Rapids, MI: Zondervan, 2011), 272.

15. Pentecost, 922.

16. MacArthur, 182.

17. Paul Sumner, "'Elohim' in Biblical Context," http://www.hebrew-streams.org/works/monotheism/context-elohim.html, viewed Oct. 10, 2016.

18. "What Do Jehovah's Witnesses Believe?" https://www.jw.org/en/jehovahs-witnesses/faq/jehovah-witness-beliefs/, viewed Oct. 10, 2016.

Chapter 13. Look! The Lord Comes: The Prophecy of Enoch

1. "The Second Coming: Questions and Answers about the Second Coming of Christ which are held by orthodox Muslims," http://www.message4muslims.org.uk/muslim-doctrines/qa-the-last-things-eschatology/qa-second-coming-of-christ-1/, and "The Return (Second Coming) of Jesus Christ," http://www.discoveringislam.org/return_of_jesus.htm, both viewed Oct. 11, 2016.

2. Robert M. Bowman, Jr., *Jehovah's Witnesses* (Grand Rapids, MI: Zondervan Publishing House, 1995), 60.

3. "What is the Baha'i faith?" http://www.gotquestions.org/Bahai-faith.html, viewed July 8, 2016.

4. *The Second Coming of Christ: The Resurrection of the Christ Within You*, cited in https://en.wikipedia.org/wiki/Second_Coming#Other_views_and_commentaries, viewed July 8, 2016.

5. The title Book of Enoch often is used interchangeably with Book of 1 Enoch. See note 2 in Chapter 8 for more information. As for the term "pseudepigraphcal," these are falsely attributed works, texts whose claim to authorship is unfounded.

6. Schreiner, 468.

7. Pentecost, 922.

8. Robert Jamieson, A. R. Fausset, and David Brown, *Commentary Critical and Explanatory on the Whole Bible*, Vol. 2 (Oak Harbor, WA: Logos Research Systems, Inc., 1997), 541–542.

9. MacArthur, 188.

10. Wuest, 251.

11. Book of Enoch, from *The Apocrypha and Pseudepigrapha of the Old Testament*,H.R. Charles (Oxford: The Clarendon Press0, found at http://www.ccel.org/c/charles/otpseudepig/enoch/ENOCH_1.HTM, viewed July 9, 2016.

12. Pentecost, 922.

13. James VanderKam, "The Theophany of Enoch 1:3b-7, 9," *Vetus Testamentum* 23.2 (1973): 148-50, cited in "1 Enoch 1:9," Triablogue, http://triablogue.blogspot.com/2010/06/1-enoch-19.html, viewed July 9, 2016.

14. George W.E. Nickelsburg, 1 Enoch 1 (Fortress Press, 2001), 149, cited in "1 Enoch 1:9," Triablogue, http://triablogue.blogspot.com/2010/06/1-enoch-19.html, viewed July 9, 2016.

15. W.M. Dunnett, "The Hermeneutics of Jude and 2 Peter: The Use of Ancient Jewish Traditions," JETS 31 [1988]: 289, quoted in Schreiner, 469.

16. MacArthur, 188.

17. Jamieson, Fausset, and Brown, 541-542.

18. The HCSB uses "ungodly" three times. The word "ungodly" appears four times in other translations such as the KJV, NIV, and ESV, which take what the HCSB translates as "to convict them" and render it "to convince all that are ungodly" (KJV); or "to convict all the ungodly" (NIV and ESV).

19. Craig L. Blomberg, *Can We Still Believe the Bible?: An Evangelical Engagement with Contemporary Questions* (Grand Rapids, MI: Brazos Press, 2014).

Chapter 14. Merely Natural: Scoffers without the Spirit
1. William MacLeod Raine, "Dodge - Old Hell-Raising Trail's End," found in *Legends of America*, http://www.legendsofamerica.com/ks-hellraisingdodge5.html, viewed July 19, 2016.

2. *Dictionary of Biblical Prophecy and End Times*, J. Daniel Hays, J. Scott Duvall, C. Marvin Pate, editors (Grand Rapids, MI: Zondervan, 2007), 254.

3. "What is the day of the Lord?" found at http://www.gotquestions.org/day-of-the-Lord.html, viewed July 25, 2016.

4. J.S. Wright, "Day of the Lord," ed. D.R.W. Wood et al., *New Bible Dictionary* (Leicester, England; Downers Grove, IL: InterVarsity Press, 1996), 261.

5. In his sermon in Antioch of Pisidia, Paul uses a different Greek word, translated "scoffers" in the HCSB, in quoting from Hab. 1:5; see Acts 13:41.

6. W.E. Vine, *Vine's Expository Dictionary of Old and New Testament Words*, Vol. 3: Lo-Ser (Old Tappen, NJ: Fleming H. Revell Company, 1981), 78.

7. Marvin Vincent, quoted in Wuest, 253.

8. Pentecost, 922-923.

9. While nearly all English translations render the Greek word *pneuma* as "Spirit" (meaning Holy Spirit) in Jude 19, a few commentators believe it should be "spirit," the part of man that gives him God-consciousness and enables him, when in possession of salvation, to worship and serve God. Greek scholar Kenneth Wuest holds this view, but adds, "Of course, since these false teachers are devoid of the higher spiritual life and its accompaning (sic) sensibilities, it is clear that they do not have the Holy Spirit." From Wuest, 254.

10. MacArthur, 199.

11. I do not wish to be dogmatic about the so-called "trichotomous" view of humanity. There are good arguments in favor of the "dichotomous" view, which understands the Bible to describe people as physical (body) and non-physical (soul/spirit). I simply prefer the trichotomous view because I believe it better fits the biblical narrative of creation, fall, and redemption.

12. "What does the Bible mean that we are not to judge others?" found in http://www.gotquestions.org/do-not-judge.html, viewed July 23, 2016.

Chapter 15. But You, Dear Friends: Hating the Garment Defiled by the Flesh

1. "The Smelly Car," found in https://en.wikipedia.org/wiki/The_Smelly_Car, viewed July 27, 2016.

2. Schreiner, 481.

3. Rather than four key elements of building a defensive perimeter, Schreiner argues that Jude offers one imperative - "keep yourselves in the love of God" with three participles: building yourselves up in the faith, praying in the Spirit, and waiting eagerly for the return of Christ (481).

4. Wuest, 255.

5. Wiersbe, 559-565.

6. Quoted in "Praying In The Spirit," *Knowing & Doing: A Teaching Quarterly for Discipleship of Heart and Mind*, excerpted from J. Oswald Sanders, *Prayer Power Unlimited*, found at http://www.cslewisinstitute. org/webfm_send/650, viewed July 30, 2016.

7. Excerpted from J. Oswald Sanders, *Prayer Power Unlimited*, found at http://www.cslewisinstitute.org/webfm_send/650, viewed July 30, 2016.

8. *Ibid.*

9. Schreiner, 484.

10. MacArthur, 201.

11. Schreiner, 487.

12. Wiersbe, 559-565.

13. Schreiner notes that the context of Zechariah 3 clarifies that Joshua is destined for the fire because of his sin, illustrated by his filthy garments (Zech. 3:3-5). The removal of his filthy clothes, and the endowment of clean ones, symbolize the forgiveness of his sins (488).

14. Schreiner, 487.

15. "What did Jesus mean when He said not to cast your pearls before swine (Matthew 7:6)?" found at https://gotquestions.org/pearls-before-swine. html, viewed Oct. 30, 2016.

16. Schreiner, 489.

Chapter 16. Doxology: To the Only God Our Savior

1. Similar Greek words are used in Acts 21:21 (*apostasian*, "abandon," "fall away," "forsake"), and in 2 Thess. 2:3 (*apostasia*, "apostasy," "rebellion," "a falling away").

2. Pentecost, 922-923.

3. Schreiner, 491.

4. MacArthur, 204.

5. Steve W. Lemke, "Authority, Divine Authority," ed. Chad Brand et al., *Holman Illustrated Bible Dictionary* (Nashville, TN: Holman Bible Publishers, 2003) 145-146.

6. "Man's Great End," *The Valley of Vision: A Collection of Puritan Prayers & Devotions* (Edinburgh, UK: The Banner of Truth Trust, 1975), 23.

Additional Resources

Other apologetics resources available from the MBC:

The Apologist's Tool Kit: Resources to Help You Defend the Christian Faith

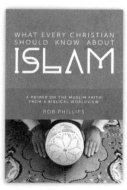

What Every Christian Should Know about Islam: A Primer on the Muslim Faith from a Biblical Perspective

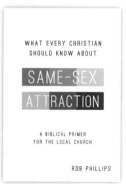

What Every Christian Should Know about Same-sex Attraction: A Biblical Primer for the Local Church

Order printed copies at **mobaptist.org/apologetics**

Print and Kindle editions available from Amazon